HISTORY, THEOLOGY, and FAITH

HISTORY, THEOLOGY, and FAITH

*Dissolving
the Modern Problematic*

TERRENCE W. TILLEY

ORBIS BOOKS
Maryknoll, New York

Founded in 1970, Orbis Books endeavors to publish works that enlighten the mind, nourish the spirit, and challenge the conscience. The publishing arm of the Maryknoll Fathers and Brothers, Orbis seeks to explore the global dimensions of the Christian faith and mission, to invite dialogue with diverse cultures and religious traditions, and to serve the cause of reconciliation and peace. The books published reflect the views of their authors and do not represent the official position of the Maryknoll Society. To learn more about Maryknoll and Orbis Books, please visit our website at www.maryknoll.org.

Published by Orbis Books, Maryknoll, New York 10545-0308.
Manufactured in the United States of America.

Library of Congress Cataloging-in-Publication Data

Tilley, Terrence W.
    History, theology, and faith : dissolving the modern problematic / Terrence W. Tilley.
       p. cm.
    Includes bibliographical references (p.   ) and index.
    ISBN 1-57075-568-X (pbk.)
    1. History–Religious aspects–Christianity. 2. Modernism (Christian theology) I. Title.
BR115.H5.T55 2004
231.7'6–dc22
                                                          2004008973

To Maureen

Historian, Teacher, Friend, Lover

Contents

Preface

Some problems should not be resolved, but dissolved. The problem of faith and history is one of the latter. Or so this book argues. The unexamined assumption that the problematic ("faith and history") has two terms, a presumption that has dominated the discourse for some two hundred years, creates the problem. Hence, the title of this book uses a three-term problematic. It argues that whatever solutions there are to the problems of relating the investigations of historians to the analyses and syntheses of theologians, and to believers living in and living out their faith, those solutions, resolutions, or dissolutions are *ad hoc*, not systematic.

The research for and writing of this book was supported by a Fellowship for University Professors awarded by the National Endowment for the Humanities (FA-37529) and by a sabbatical leave from the University of Dayton for the academic year 2003-04. I thank you for your support ("your tax dollars at work" through the Endowment), and Dean Paul Morman, Associate Provost Deborah Bickford, and Provost Fred Pestello for their support.

I am most appreciative of the many who have helped with this work. I am sure I shall forget to thank someone, but that is an occupational hazard. Will the unthanked please forgive me? Undergraduate assistant Paige Eppenstein and graduate assistants Jonathan Malone, Gary Agee, Brian Peterson, and Aaron James helped with the research. Colleagues Dennis Doyle, Bill Portier, Sandra Yocum Mize, Una Cadegan, Therese Lysaught (Dayton), Bill Hasker (Huntington College), Bill Wainwright (University of Wisconsin-Milwaukee), Bill Shea (College of the Holy Cross), and Dermot Lane (Mater Dei Institute, Dublin) read and commented on substantial parts of the manuscript. Some even recommended further reading! Which I did! The argument is far better and surely clearer for their (sometimes rather pointed) help. Pat Johnson, Brad Kallenberg, Bill Trollinger, James L. Heft, S.M., and Janet Bednarek (Dayton) discussed some of the issues in this text with me and pointed me in the right direction when I was occasionally confused. Maureen Tilley read the whole manuscript (parts of it more than once). My debts to her as we complete our thirty-fifth year of marriage are academic—and much more! The willingness of all these good people to help a colleague develop his work does not imply that they agree with the shape of the argument or its conclusions. The problems that remain, of course, are likely due to my not relying sufficiently on the advice of all these careful and thoughtful people.

Prof. Elizabeth Clark (Duke) allowed me to read the manuscript of her important book, *History — Theory — Text* as I prepared this book. Our purposes and intended audiences are quite different, but I commend her book strongly to anyone doing theology or religious studies in a contextualized or historicized manner (see p. 112 below). For those interested in "influences" I can also identify Van Harvey, Paula Fredriksen, J. D. G. Dunn, Richard Rubenstein, Elizabeth A. Johnson, and, especially, the late Jim McClendon as influencing my thinking—sometimes by having to make clear why I disagreed with them. This list could go on and on, and others may spot equally important influences lurking in the background, but I am most conscious of very different debts to these scholars.

Three papers read to the College Theology Society and two to the Society for Philosophy of Religion have contributed especially to chapters four, six, and seven. Some of these were published as articles (Tilley 1999, 2001, 2003). The audiences at the academic meetings raised helpful questions and made me clarify my work. My primary respondents at the S.P.R, Rickey J. Ray (Northeast State Technical Community College) and Jim Keller (Wofford College), made insightful comments that improved the work. Thanks also to William M. Shea of the College of the Holy Cross, who invited me to give a Deitchman Family Lecture in Religion and Modernity in 2004. Much of that lecture appears in chapter six.

Finally, many thanks to my patient, witty, and insightful editor, Susan Perry, Catherine Costello, and all the folks at Orbis Books who have made this book possible.

Terrence W. Tilley
Pentecost, 2004

Introduction

The methods and results of critical historical investigations have undermined religious, theological, and ecclesiastical claims since Nicholas of Cusa and Lorenzo Valla independently showed in the fifteenth century that the "Donation of Constantine" was a fraud. The document, purportedly from Emperor Constantine to Pope Sylvester I (314-335), granted the pope the Lateran Palace and sovereignty over Italy and the West. It had been used as major support for papal claims to superiority over other primates of the ancient church and for the legal system that rendered clergy subject only to church law and thus immune from civil law. Other historical investigations over the centuries challenged particular Christian claims. However, until the end of the eighteenth century, the overarching story told in the Christian tradition remained largely unscathed by historical attacks.

The modern "problem of history" emerged in the late eighteenth and early nineteenth century when the authority of the biblical narrative of the world broke down. The great story—of God's creating the world that was then corrupted by human sin, of God's redeeming the world when the Word of God became incarnate, a story not yet over, a story celebrated and remembered in the communities that kept the tradition alive hoping for God's final consummation of the world by establishing God's reign—collapsed. It was shattered from the inside by disagreements and was eclipsed by the critical reasoning practices emerging in the Enlightenment.

Christian theologians (including religious authorities) had accepted this story as given. They had appealed to acts of God and God's church in the past to authorize contemporary beliefs and practices. The emergence of critical history made such appeals far more problematic, not only with regard to documents like the "Donation of Constantine," but to the Christian traditions, scriptural and otherwise, as a whole. The modern problem of history rocked central beliefs of Protestant theologians from the beginning of the nineteenth century and Catholic theologians especially in the "modernist" controversy (1891-1908).

The problem of history is not a single problem but is a set of problems of credibility. These problems are the result of both the practice of critical historical investigations and the results achieved in historical investigations. In general, historical investigations are seen as undermining the warrants traditional religious believers and theologians of the Western monotheistic traditions use to support current practices and beliefs as normative. Historical investigations are seen as undercutting the appeal to God's or humans' past acts which warrant present practices. A key aspect of the problems is that, with the collapse of the biblical narrative, the burden of proof has shifted from the critic to the defender of the tradition. The tradition is no longer presumed to be true, but has, in some way, to show its truth despite the onslaughts of historical investigations.

One indicator of this is the shift in the status of miracles as evidence. As late as the end of the seventeenth century, miracles were taken as evidence for one's claims. Miracles were "proofs." By the mid-eighteenth century the problem was one of "the evidence *for* miracles, as opposed to the evidence *of* miracles" (Datson 1994, 270). Miracles were no longer evidence *for* one's claims; rather, claiming that an event was a miracle required a practically unbearable burden of proof. Similarly, in the nineteenth century, the problem was that appeals to the Bible could no longer provide evidence for one's position. The biblical narrative itself was no longer taken for granted as the narrative of the world, but was in competition with other worldviews. The biblical narrative needed evidence and argument to show that it was true narrative. It could no longer be presumed. The burden of proof shifted—a point explored more fully in chapter six.

The modern problem of history is, in general, a problem of authorization. For over two centuries, appeals to Scripture and tradition as authorities have been often undermined by historical investigations. Some theologians have often finessed this problem by appeals to the normativity of classic texts, persons, and practices for a religious tradition (for example, see Tracy 1975, 49-52; 1981, 99-173; for a different approach, see Lindbeck 1984). Such theological moves are of real value, yet have profound weaknesses when the issue is not the evidence *of* or *in* the tradition, but the evidence *for* the tradition. Chapter six also addresses the claim that many contemporary Christian theologians are engaging in practices analogous to those of the premodern phase of the tradition, when miracles were taken as evidence for truth claims. David Tracy, for example, endorsed the notion that there must be some control on the range of interpretations by historical methods (1981, 107), but the recognition of a classic that gives rise to a tradition is a matter of its power over us to disclose "a reality we cannot but name truth" (1981, 108). Chapter six argues that such "classics" alone cannot finally bear the burden that Tracy and others place on them, but that the contemporary appropriation of these classics is different from the premodern understanding of the status of the biblical narrative.

Some theologians address the modern problem of historical authorization more directly. Much of twentieth-century theological discourse has been dominated in this area by responses to a naturalistic solution to the problem derived from the work of German historian and theologian Ernst Troeltsch over a century ago. Bluntly, these theological uses of Troeltsch have tended to give all the trumps to history. Faith and theology have been in fact, if not in rhetoric, consigned to the purely personal, individualistic, and/or non-rational realms of human discourse.

The thesis of this book is that theoreticians of religion, including theologians, should not try to solve the "problem of history." I argue that the problem should be dissolved and multiple patterns of the relationships between the practices of history, theology, and faith be recognized. I also argue, however, that theologians cannot properly "retreat" to commitment, to an unconditional acceptance of a text as classic unless the theologian is willing to take the classic texts as providing meaning, but not as a warrant that can help support claims to truth.

Theologians bear responsibilities beyond those of the ordinary believer. In terms we shall explore in chapter ten, theologians are charged to discover (including using the tools of historians and other social scientists), understand (including using the tools of philosophers and cultural critics), argue for transforming when necessary and proclaim when appropriate (adding rhetoricians' tools) the convictions (embodied in narratives and practices) that express the faith of the community. "Believers" have to live in and live out the faith tradition and in doing so to manifest and to proclaim the faith. Believers are not called to investigate, analyze, or transform the tradition—unless they take the role of theologian, for example, in response to existential challenges to their faith. I have previously discussed the "role-specific responsibilities" of theologians and other practitioners with regard to the wisdom of making and sustaining commitments to and in a religious tradition (Tilley 1995, 121-54). I shall not, for the most part, repeat that material here, but refer the reader to the text of my earlier work for further elaboration of the issues touched on, especially in chapters ten and eleven.

The term "convictions" is used here with a specific meaning. A conviction is "a persistent belief such that if X (a person or a community) has a conviction, it will not be easily relinquished and it cannot be relinquished without making X a significantly different person or community than before" (McClendon and Smith 1975, 7, 91-94). Religious traditions are carried through time by religious institutions and handed on by convictional communities. Some of these communities have extensive sets of convictions, others more modest sets. Among those convictions are some which articulate principles that give the tradition its enduring identity; the significance of such principles is discussed in chapter six. Convictional formulae which articulate such principles may change, but the principles articulated in those convictions cannot change without the community becoming a different community.

Some of a tradition's convictions can and do change while the tradition lives on. The introduction into Christian discourse, for example, of the novel term *homoousios* to articulate the relationship of Jesus Christ as son of God to his Father was a novelty in the early fourth century. It emerged as the orthodox expression of Christology in contrast to a subordinationist view common in earlier centuries and then held by the Arian party (Thiel 2000, 134-39). Of course, the battles over christological claims in that century illustrate that convictional change is neither easy nor trivial. The tradition was significantly different, but it was still identifiably Christian.

Individuals who belong to religious traditions have sets of convictions that are influenced by, but are typically not identical to, the convictions of their religious communities. Participants in religious traditions are also citizens of their nation or subjects of their queen; they may be members of strongly identified ethnic and/or political groups, have specific socio-economic locations, and personal commitments to spouses, families, friends, employers, colleagues, customers, and sports teams. As members of each of these groups, individuals may come to share with members of those various communities convictions that are not part of their religious community's set of convictions.

The modern dualistic problematic of faith and history, the modern problem of history for theology/faith has become an inadequate way to understand the issues that arise around history, theology, and faith. Any account of the relationships of history, theology, and faith must be more than "two-valued." A viable understanding of the "problem of history" must avoid the classic dual or polar dichotomous formula such as "faith and history." There are no simple or general solutions to the problem of history. Rather, there are numerous particular problems that historical investigations create for religious believing and theological construction. These need to be solved individually, not *en masse*.

Both history and theology have changed in profound ways in the final third of the twentieth century. Many events and movements have made theology in the twenty-first century quite different from theology in 1966: the fallout from Vatican II; the development of revisionist, liberationist, practice-oriented, postmodern, and postliberal forms of theology (sketched in Tilley et al. 1995); the changes in patterns of religious practice and belief (especially the rapid evolution of religious institutions from culturally mandatory to personally voluntary communities); the assimilation, especially in the United States, of some ethnic groups defined by specific religious traditions into more homogenized and even secularized polities, and the resistance of other ethnic groups that develop religious practices and theological methods in distinction from or opposition to the perceived Euro-American hegemony; the increasing cognizance of the significance of religious pluralism; the movement in many areas of the social location of theology from the clerical domains of seminaries and divinity schools to laic domains of universities; the emergence of a strong minority of women's voices in what had been a thoroughly male discourse; and the rise of fundamentalist, renascent, and neoconservative movements—to name just a few.

History has also become a set of disciplines and fields quite different from the historical practices and judgments that gave shape to the "problem of history": the debates of intellectual and political historians with social historians, microhistorians, intellectual historians, psychohistorians, institutional historians, cliometricians, and others in the fields of history about what historians can creditably warrant and even should attempt to say about the past; the ongoing disputes about the purposes of doing history; the disagreements about whether historians can or should use narrative forms and, if so, which forms those should be; the questioning of whether there are such things as historical "facts"; the arguments about whether historical writing is fundamentally rhetorical or representative of the past; the questions of how historians' narratives can succeed, if at all, in presenting events or patterns of the past for a present readership; and the waxing and waning of institutional and intellectual histories.

To survey all the changes and the arguments among historians and theologians would make this book unreadable. In effect, I would simply be summarizing and rehearsing the arguments of others *ad infinitum*. There are books that do this sort of work well. In the field of historiography, Breisach (1994) and Clark (2004) provide excellent surveys and analyses; in the field of modern theology, Livingston (1997; 2000) provides a standard text. But these rather comprehensive texts, while making arguments about the shapes of their disciplines, function more as orientations for beginning graduate students and as reference works.

The present book is selective. It highlights representative figures and disputes to illustrate and analyze key issues. I have chosen figures and disputes that strike me as very important and that have one key component: they lay out clearly the issues in dispute. I have not sought out figures who are easy foils, straw persons, or whose arguments or style lend themselves to easy dismissal. Nor have I chosen figures with whom I simply agree. I have chosen figures I have learned from, even when I disagreed with them. Indeed, more than once as I wrote this book, I found myself changing my assessment of their views. Nonetheless, I sometimes may seem to handle the positions in these disputes roughly. It is *not* to be assumed that I do not respect the authors discussed or their work. Quite the contrary. Their work has taken us far—but not far enough. If my arguments are sharply drawn, it is simply because we have much to learn from the arguments I criticize; but for some points at issue, I argue that we need to take paths other than the ones they mapped out.

This book has four goals. The first is to dissolve the modern problem of history in its "history and faith" or "history and theology" versions. The first three chapters of this book are devoted to delineating how the problem of history has been shaped in its modern formulations. Chapter one portrays the shape of the modern problem of history and some attempted resolutions. The modern problematic tended, at least in the Christian and Jewish context, to focus on scriptural texts. Chapter two shows that the literary forms and historic functions of the Hebrew Bible, the Christian Bible and the Qur'an give rise to *different* problems of history. The most important reflection on the problem of history was Van Harvey's book *The Historian and the Believer*, first published in 1966. I discuss this text at length in chapter three. In effect, Harvey fomented a revolution against the classic form of the problem. He argued against the abstract construal of the problem as a general or universal one of faith in tension with history or historical method. He argued for a new focus on the differing particular ways that historians and believers properly formed and warranted their beliefs. Harvey sought to turn theologians away from sterile debates about historical methods and to consider the ways in which historians warranted their judgments concerning historical claims and in which believers formed their beliefs. The key tensions were not between history and faith but between historians and believers.

Unfortunately, too few theologians recognized the importance of this intellectual achievement. Many continue to attempt to solve or resolve "the" problem as defined by Troeltsch and his followers as if Harvey had never written. Some reformulate the issues (Tracy 1981; Schillebeeckx 1979; Fiorenza 1984, 31-33) but do so without extensive consideration of what historians actually do. They also tend to be more concerned with the use of historical evidence and argument *in* the tradition rather than *for* the tradition, an issue addressed directly in chapter ten. Perhaps Harvey's challenges to business as usual and insights about the problem of history were lost in the glare of the "death of God" movement in the era in which he wrote. Perhaps the weaknesses in Harvey's sketch of a solution to the problem of the differing intellectual "moralities" of historians and believers overshadowed his accomplishments.

An implication of this book is that Harvey's transformation of the argument from the dualist classic problematic of "faith and history" to the dualist problematic of "historians and believers" was not radical enough. Nonetheless, some have learned much from Harvey's work, including the present writer. I read and reread *The Historian and the Believer* early in my career as graduate student and scholar, and returned to it and read it closely as I began work on the present book and after I had written articles (Tilley 1999; 2001), some of whose arguments have been adapted for use in the present text. I recognize and acknowledge how much his work has influenced my thinking, sometimes without my knowing it—at least insofar as attempting to dissolve the "problem of history" goes.

Some of Harvey's later writings also helped me break down the dualistic or polar pattern of the earlier "problem of history" problematic and of Harvey's own dualistic contrast of the moralities of "the modern historian's principles of judgment and the Christian's will to believe" (Harvey 1968, front cover).

Chapters four and five argue that the modern problematic of faith and history can and should be dissolved. Chapter four unpacks the unwarranted assumptions that theologians have often made in discussing the relationship of history and theology. Chapter five argues that unpacking claims of Jewish theologian Richard Rubenstein and Christian theologian Marcus Borg shows that historical investigations, often thought to undermine faith, do not do so unless one makes additional philosophical claims not necessitated either by religious convictions or by the practices of historical investigation. The first five chapters are the argument leading to the first goal.

The second goal is to understand how history is related to religious traditions beyond the dualistic problematic. Chapters six and seven turn to specific theological issues beyond the modern problematic. Chapter six argues that there are specific religious principles that are immune to undermining by the evidence of history. These principles go far to give religious traditions their identity. The convictions that express those principles are not invulnerable, however, to historical evidence. Additionally, some persons may be in situations that render the convictions that shape their own faith incredible, in part due to the marshaling of historical evidence; that issue is explored more fully in chapter ten. Chapter seven shows the problems that arise when one neglects to distinguish between such identity-giving principles and the historically conditioned convictions that formulate them. A key component of this argument, then, is the distinction between enduring (but rather empty) principles in and of a religious tradition and the particular (and rather robust) articulations of them as operative convictions.

The third goal of the book is to attend to the actual practices of historians rather than to the theories of history distilled by philosophers. I have argued elsewhere (Tilley 1995, 5-13, 53-89) that philosophers' distillations of religious propositions from religious practice in a tradition can be misleading. Similarly, I find that theologians dealing with the problem of history rarely, if ever, look at what historians actually do; theologians tend to use philosophical accounts of history and historiography, rather than to examine the practices of history. Chapters eight and nine show the "history" side of the issue: historians' principles and practices are much more complex and controversial than many theologians seem to recognize. Chapter eight analyzes the extensive disputes over the status of historical claims in light of the collapse of the "noble dream" of historical objectivity in the twentieth century. The argument there shows, in general, that history *qua* history cannot easily function as an "authorizing" discourse, *pace* the approach of many theologians to the problem of history. Chapter nine analyzes a specific dispute over how to approach the issue of the "historical Jesus" to show that religious historians are not immune from the progressive loss of the "authorizing" function of historical investigations.

The final goal of the book is to show that the relationships between historical investigations, theological construction, and religious practice are *ad hoc* rather than systematic. The final two chapters analyze patterns that can be discerned in those relationships, though, since I claim the relationships are *ad hoc*, I cannot claim to have a complete account of those relationships. Chapter ten argues for a nuanced understanding of the relationship of history and theology. Chapter eleven shows how the problems of history—and theologians' attempts to work with those problems—can affect religious practice and belief. Both chapters presume a "practical" approach to the problem. As chapters eight and nine looked at the practices and responsibilities of historians, so chapters ten and eleven look at the practices and responsibilities of theologians and believers in light of the contemporary challenges (not the "modern problem") of historical investigations to theological construction and religious practice and belief. Underlying this work is the fundamental assumption that one's religious commitments have to do not merely with one's belief but with one's life and the practices which give that life structure and which give one's convictions their distinctive meaning (cf. Tilley 1995, 5-57, which argues against the construal, especially in philosophy of religion, of religion as constituted by "beliefs" or "propositions," and argues for an understanding of religion as a set of practices; also see Tilley 2000, 50-87). A final chapter rehearses the argument and claims that it was and is necessary to make this journey.

Both history and theology are quite different from what they were seen to be in the mid- to late twentieth century. Hence, it is time to dissolve the problem of history as we have construed it and to reconfigure our understanding of the relationships of historical investigations, theological constructions, and religious convictions. In sum, that is the task of this book.

CHAPTER 1

The Problem of History

History always seems to lead to doubt rather than to faith.
                                              —H. Richard Niebuhr

If three million Israelites (600,000 men, "not to mention" their wives and children; see Exod. 12:37) walked ten abreast as they crossed the Red Sea with Moses in the Exodus from Egypt, the line of marchers would have stretched out about 180 miles long. Their passage through the sea would have required at least nine days! The one-day miracle portrayed in the Bible physically could not be true. Moreover, given the contradictions in the narratives of the resurrection of Jesus, the reasonable inference is that the resurrection is a fiction, at best. Or so argued Hermann Samuel Reimarus (1694-1768) in his *Apology for or Defense of the Rational Worshiper of God*, left unpublished at his death. Gotthold Ephraim Lessing (1729-1781) published sections of this immense manuscript in the *Beiträge zur Geschichte und Literatur* from 1774 to 1777 as the "Wolfenbüttel Fragmente eines Ungenannten." The author's daughter insisted that they be published without attribution to her father, probably, in part, because he found the narratives of Jesus' miracles and his resurrection historical forgeries (cf. Livingston 1997, 30-31; Tonnelli 1967), Thus began in earnest the "problem of history" for Christian faith and Christian theology. If this were a news story, the headline would read: "Historical Investigations Debunk Faith: Theologians Shattered by Historians' Discoveries."

Constructing the Problem of History

The problem of history in its most general terms is that modern historical investigations create serious difficulties for the credibility of traditional religious belief. Of course, critical history poses no problem for non-believers. Some even delight in exposing religion as "irrational"—for only the irrational would dwell in the house of faith after its foundations had been demolished. Religious believers and theologians of various sorts have spent centuries trying to resolve the problem of history. Bluntly, the problem has not been solved. A solution requires attending to, without succumbing to, the challenges. All too often, theologians solve the problem by sidestepping it. Or they "solve" it by construing religious claims as non-rational.

Christian theologians and believers since Reimarus have construed the problem in a variety of ways. One particular and enduring problem is that of the "historical Jesus." Historian James C. Livingston recognized another of Reimarus's *Fragments* as raising "a fundamental issue for any doctrine of Christology, namely, the tension between the historical reality and message of Jesus and the Church's memory and portrayal of him in the New Testament" (Livingston 1997, 30). Later, in the nineteenth and twentieth centuries, this tension became crystallized in the formula "the Jesus of history and the Christ of faith." From Reimarus to the present, historians and theologians of Christianity have explored who we can say "the Jesus of history" really was or is, what is essential to expressing one's faith in Jesus of Nazareth as the Christ, the Son of the Living God, and the relationship between the "assured results" of historical investigation and the "essential doctrines" of the Christian tradition. More generally, this problem has been construed as the problem of "history and faith," "history and belief," or, more recently, of "the historian and the believer" (Harvey 1968). However configured, the problem of history identifies the key issue as the tensions, contrasts, or conflicts between historical claims and religious beliefs.

Legions of theologians and philosophers have sought to solve the problem of history. Their solutions can be grouped into four patterns or types of solution (compare Dulles 1996; also see pp. 87-96 below).

First is the "history against belief" type. This is a pattern usually associated with the undermining of religious claims by rationalists. Historical investigations and arguments are used to show that religious beliefs are unwarranted. When the support for religious claims fails to measure up to the rational standards of historians, the rational thing to do, then, is to drop those religious beliefs. Rational persons proportion their beliefs to the evidence and arguments that support those beliefs. Since religious belief has little or no evidence to support it in the wake of historical challenges, the rational thing to do is to stop assenting to traditional beliefs. This is especially so if traditional beliefs support and are supported by a theological or ecclesial establishment. Rationalists of various kinds suspect ecclesial elites of imposing religious beliefs on the masses in order to maintain their own power. That traditional religious beliefs seem often supported by authorities, but unsupported by reason and evidence, renders both the beliefs and the authorities' motives even more suspect. The pattern of "solving" the problem of history by rejecting or radically revising traditional patterns of belief can be seen in the work of scholars from the eighteenth century (Reimarus) through contemporary scholars as different as Richard Rubenstein and Marcus Borg (discussed in chapter five). When belief collides with history, history undermines belief.

Some philosophers and theologians, working out of fundamentalist, evangelical, and reformed traditions, however, offer a curious inversion of the rationalist pattern. This is a fideist pattern. Rather than measure religious belief by the standard of "pure" historical warrants, these thinkers reverse the rationalists' standards and measure the methods, procedures, and results of historians' work by the received faith. Some historical methods and results support belief and may be useful for clarification, but those methods and results which debunk faith or tend to dismantle the traditional web of belief are ruled out. Proponents of this approach typically claim that rationalists, who use reason, including historical reason, to measure faith claims (and find them wanting, of course), cannot warrant their procedures or their preference for the standard of reason over the standard of faith. Why assume reason is a surer way to truth—especially Big Truths—than faith in divine revelation? What evidence and argument support that view? Isn't commitment to reason as the ultimate arbiter of truth really faith in the constructs of human reason rather than in God? Philosopher Alvin Plantinga displays this pattern in a number of his works (see especially Plantinga 2000); it is a characteristic also of fundamentalism. For the fideist, when history and faith collide, faith trumps history. In both rationalist and fideist approaches, history is "against" faith.

Second, there is a "history irrelevant to faith" pattern. In this pattern, the results of historical investigations are construed as unrelated to faith. This pattern began with G. E. Lessing. While scholars debate what his own views were and exactly what his argument was, one way of understanding it is this: Lessing could find no way to leap over the "ugly broad ditch" between historical claims and metaphysical claims. Some orthodox theologians have tried to use proof of the resurrection of Jesus (a historical claim) to warrant theological claims about Christ. But Lessing found this completely unwarranted because historical claims are contingently true or false, and the theological claims about Christ are not contingent, but necessary: not only can they not be false, but they must be necessarily true. Lessing put it this way:

> To jump with that historical truth to a quite different class of truths, and to demand of me that I should form all my metaphysical and moral ideas accordingly . . . if that is not a "transformation to another kind," then I do not know what Aristotle meant by this phrase. . . . *That, then, is the ugly broad ditch which I cannot get across, however often and however earnestly I have tried to make the leap.* If anyone can help me over it, let him do it. I beg him. (Livingston 1997, 35)

Lessing's point is that these claims are of profoundly different "classes" or "kinds." It is confused, Lessing argues, to "jump" from one to the other.

Historical claims are contingently true; any given claim may be, and be assessed as, true or false, adequate or inadequate, accurate or inaccurate. Claims are supported or refuted by empirical investigation, by examining the evidence and the arguments supporting them. Claims about the actual man Jesus who lived in Nazareth and was executed near Jerusalem fall into this group. The events or states of affairs represented by historical claims might have been otherwise. Jesus' crucifixion, for example, might have been somewhere other than Golgotha. The claim that he was crucified, even if true, is "contingent." We could even discover that he was crucified elsewhere, but that would not make it false that Jesus was crucified. Contingently true claims are true based on *relevant* contingencies. The event would still be Jesus' crucifixion, even if we realized that the tradition had "misplaced" the event.

Metaphysical claims are necessarily true; they cannot be false. Claims about what God has revealed must fall into this category, for if God is all-good and all-knowing, then God cannot lie or be mistaken. What God reveals, then, literally cannot be false; such revelations are necessarily true. That Jesus Christ is a unified person with not merely a human nature but also a divine nature cannot be established by historical investigation but must be a divine revelation, and thus necessarily true. One does not check necessary truths by examining evidence or argument. Rather, one comes to see such claims are false if one finds them self-contradictory. Some have alleged that being one person with two natures is a self-contradictory claim, but a defense against this allegation shows it not sustained (Morris). One might also figure out that a set of claims entailed contradictory claims, in which case at least one of the members of the set cannot be true. One example of this is the modern problem of evil, which alleges a contradiction between the existence of God as all-knowing, all-good, and all-powerful, and the reality of evil in the world because an all-good God would want to do something about it, an all-knowing God knows about it, and an all-powerful God can do something about it; the believer must either deny one or more of God's attributes or the reality of evil. A defense against this allegation also shows it not to be sustained (Plantinga 1971; 1974; 1979).

It is Lessing's point that these two sorts of claims are profoundly different: they have a different logical status. We check them differently if we have difficulties with them. We defend them differently if others challenge them. If we collapse them into one type of belief, we inevitably develop serious confusions.

Contemporary theologians like Van Harvey and George Lindbeck fit this type. Their terminologies and analyses, as we shall see, are different from and clearer than Lessing's ironic (or confused) arguments (see Livingston 1997, 33-35). But they nonetheless assert that there is a difference in type between claims that are amenable to verification or falsification by historical argument and claims that are in some way essential to faith and immune to historical investigation or irrelevant to established historical claims.

A third type is the "history shaping theology" type. Unlike rationalists and fideists, these thinkers do not allow history to be the defining standard for theology or vice-versa. Unlike the second type, they do find that historical work is relevant to faith claims and vice-versa. Many scholars have wanted to use historical investigations to reform traditional expressions of faith, to pare ancient formulations of belief, no longer plausible or tenable in a contemporary setting, away from the core of faith. Perhaps the most famous twentieth-century project of this type was Rudolf Bultmann's *Entmythologisierung* ("demythologizing" is our unhappily negative English rendition of this term). In the space age, we can no longer in any literal or serious way accept the biblical notion of heaven above us in the clouds or hell under the plane of the earth. The "three-decker universe" is enshrined in the Bible and creeds. But it is not "of the essence" of the faith. Rather, it is simply an incorrect (by our standards) cosmology assumed by almost all writers of biblical times and untenable now. Similarly, feminists have argued convincingly that the patriarchal household codes embedded in epistles attributed to Paul (but not written by him) are not of the essence of the faith but simply part of the cultural milieu that New Testament writers took for granted. To treat them as of the essence of the faith is to take historically conditioned sexist patterns as permanently normative. In both cases, historical work gives us grounds for reworking our theological expressions in ways that are not intellectually untenable or socially demeaning.

Bultmann seemed very close to the "irrelevancy" type: he argued that what was truly important for faith was not *what* Jesus had done, but the fact *that* God acted in history. Some feminists strike traditional believers as rationalist critics trying to undermine their faith. But Bultmann, his followers, and many feminists do not give historical work a "veto" over faith, but seek to allow historical investigations to play a role in reshaping the *expression* of faith and in reforming the life of faith today. Even many of those involved in the repeated "quests" for the "historical Jesus" (a very confused and confusing term, as we shall see) have sought to use history to aid in defining and reforming theological claims. The results of historical investigation are used, then, to shape and reshape the expression of religious convictions.

A fourth type can be labeled a "theology shaping history" type. Theologians placed in this group typically analyze the presuppositions of the work of historians and offer an alternative perspective. This alternative perspective may simply incorporate the work of historians but shows that the historian does not have the final word, even on historical matters!

One example of this type can be found in *The Meaning of Revelation* by American theologian H. Richard Niebuhr. He argued that we have construed "history" as if history is always "objective," written from the perspective of external narrators who present the facts and nothing but the facts in their constructions of the past. Without rejecting such an approach, which Niebuhr dubs "external history," he finds another way of telling the story, which he calls "internal history." Here history is written from the perspective of a participant who stands within a tradition. The participant observes the tradition as one who owns—and is owned by— the tradition. External history is "their story"; internal history tells "our story." External history uses a third-person framework ("When they wandered . . ."). Internal history uses a first-person plural framework ("When God led us . . ."). Using the same methods, procedures, standards, and rigor, the internal historian seeks to get "the facts" just as straight as the external historian does. But whereas the external historian invests those facts about a people with significance in proportion to that community's effect on other communities, the internal historian focuses on the significance of the past for us in the present. The external historian recognizes the Roman Empire as "great" in its ability to impose its rule on a world that extended out from the Mediterranean to Syria, England, Portugal, and Egypt. But because there is no "we" who carry on the empire, there can be no "internal" history of the Roman Empire today.

The internal historian has a different perspective and finds the significance of those facts not in their effects on the world but in their effects on and significance for the ongoing community. External historians have detailed the origins and outcome of the modernist movement in the Catholic Church, which lasted from about 1891 up until its condemnation in 1908. Alec Vidler, an Anglican, won the Norrisian Prize Essay in 1933 with a work, *The Modernist Movement in the Roman Church*, so even-handed and "objective" that the examiners could not tell if Vidler was a Catholic or not. Nonetheless, it was presented as though it were an external history. However, many internal historians of Roman Catholicism have recognized the repression of modernism in the Roman Catholic Church as a disastrous turning point because it stultified intellectual and spiritual growth in a community and finalized the Catholic Church's rejection of the modern world. In both types of history, the constellation of occurrences and the possible ways of stating the facts about those acts and events are roughly similar; but which occurrences are highlighted and which obscured, which facts given prominence and which facts are dust-binned, will depend on the perspective of the historian—and the audience for which the historian writes.

The audience for which one writes is correlated with the purposes for which one writes. This means that an author's intended audience determines, in part, the shape or slant of the work. Niebuhr unsurpassably illustrated this point by quoting two short segments not from religious history but from secular history. "The Gettysburg Address" and the *Cam-*

bridge Modern History both told about the founding of the United States. Here is his brilliant apposition of them:

> Four-score and seven years ago our fathers brought forth upon this continent a new nation, conceived in liberty and dedicated to the proposition that all men are created equal.

> On July 4, 1776, Congress passed the resolution which made the colonies independent communities, issuing at the same time the well-known Declaration of Independence. If we regard the Declaration as the assertion of an abstract political theory, criticism and condemnation are easy. It sets out with a general proposition so vague as to be practically useless. The doctrine of the equality of men, unless it be qualified and conditioned by reference to special circumstance, is either a barren truism or a delusion. (Niebuhr 1960, 44-45)

Lincoln's "Gettysburg Address" is inner history; the *Cambridge Modern History,* outer history. They are written for different audiences. Both tell a true story about the same events. But the purposes of the authors, the shapes of the narratives, and the style of their rhetoric are shaped in large part by the audiences and occasions for which they were written.

Niebuhr began, and others like John Milbank (in some strands of his work) today continue to contribute, an "ideology critique" of the practices of external historians. Theologians like Niebuhr have something to say to historians: "Your rendering is not the only historically true one, but a useful perspective, not the final 'objective' truth about times past." Indeed, historians themselves have been arguing these points extensively, especially over the last forty years, as chapter eight shows. Retelling tales of the past from different perspectives does change our perceptions of the past. Different perspectives may surface different historical claims. All historians write from a perspective and for an (intended) audience. That all historians' work is perspectival does not imply that anything goes. It does imply that even those historians most rigorous in investigation and committed to uncovering what is true cannot write absolute truth or final truth. As Lessing might remind us, all our historical claims are contingent and thus, in principle, open to revision. In short, the differences between writing internal or external history are not properly historical but have to do with differing ideological and/or historiographical commitments that inform the stance of the author doing the writing, differing purposes the author has in writing, and differing audiences addressed by the writing. Chapter seven argues that versions of this approach can be found in the works of a number of Catholic theologians. Many versions of this approach, however, sidestep the problem of history. I will argue that such tactics are not always appropriate.

Dissolving the Problem of History

While I obviously have been significantly influenced especially by the insights of the second, third, and fourth types of solution, and appreciate the work and insights of writers who fall under each of the types, I cannot subscribe to any of these systemic ways of attempting to solve the problem of history. My view is that the "problem of history" is not a problem to be sidestepped or ignored or solved or resolved, but *dissolved*. The problem itself has been constructed in a dialectical or polarized or dualist way. The problem always contains two terms, history and X, where X may be faith, theology, belief, tradition, Scripture, and so on. This dualistic construction is contingent, yet theologians have tended to treat the construct as if the dualistic pattern of tension or opposition was necessary. H. Richard Niebuhr, who began deconstructing the problem of history by analyzing two very different problems, purposes, and narrative structures in historical work, kept the dichotomizing approach; and, as we shall see, this is one of the signal problems with his work. Van Harvey came closest to providing a fresh approach to the problem by recognizing that it is not the abstractions "history" and "theology" (or whatever) that pose the problems, but the fact that historians and believers warrant their claims and shape their beliefs in different practices. Yet he leaves the dualist or polar problematic fundamentally intact. Since the dualizing approach leads consistently to intractable problems, isn't it time to explore a solution that deconstructs the dualized pattern and thus dissolves *the* problem of history into different problems?

In general, those who accept the dualist problematic have particular ideological commitments that point them to a particular "solution" of the problem. Often they elevate one of the disciplinary practices of history or theology as the standing norm or method for judging or relating historical or theological claims. In the next three chapters, I will lay out three key areas in which ideological commitments have shaped the problem of history and argue that these patterns are at best not necessary and at worst confusing.

The first area concerns key differences between the Hebrew Bible, the Christian Bible, and the Qur'an. These sacred texts of monotheisms have different literary forms, different authoritative status, and narrate very different kinds of acts of God in history. Hence, the ways in which each of these texts and the traditions that hold them sacred are in tension with critical historical work differ. The dualist approach obscures these differences. I will argue that once we examine the "geography" of the differing realms of discourse and kinds of texts, we will see that there are multiple problems of history, not a single formal problem of belief and history or faith and history.

The second area involves epistemic issues. In 1966 Harvey found two contrasting ethics of belief. The historian was the empirical investigator shaped by suspicion, questioning everything, and investigating the past. The believer was shaped in trust, taught in some instances that even to doubt a religious belief was immoral or sinful, and was not encouraged to investigate the warrants for religious, theological, or ecclesiastical claims. I will adapt arguments made elsewhere (Tilley 1995) to show that this picture is also oversimplified. Harvey himself (1986 [1979]) opened up this possibility by his introduction of the concept of "role specific epistemic responsibilities," but he did not treat in any significant way the dichotomy he had introduced in his earlier work.

The third area involves the presumptions of doing history. I argue that philosophers and theologians have written as though the *presumptions* that are claimed to render historical investigations possible are also *assumptions* that the historian has to believe to be generally, if not universally, true. I argue that distinguishing procedural presumptions from substantive assumptions unmasks the pretensions of historians to have "the last word" (in a way somewhat different from H. Richard Niebuhr's argument) and allows historical work an appropriate place, but not as the final arbiter of truth.

One of the ideological commitments that gave rise to the problem of history was a dualistic view of faith and history. One of the ideological commitments of the present dissolution of the problem is a pluralistic ideology captured in the following motto: "Whenever confronted with a dualism, pluralize." The great nineteenth-century German thinkers G. W. F. Hegel and Karl Marx approached dualisms differently: they caught up the thesis and its antithesis into a new synthesis (which then became the "thesis" of a new triad *ad infinitum*). They sought to conquer by synthesis. By contrast, the present approach seeks to free up tangles by analysis. My own philosophical background is influenced more by American pragmatism and British analysis than continental approaches. Feminist philosophers and theologians, among others, have taught us that no perspective is without its blind spots; no social location from which we write is innocent; no one of us can ever achieve a God's-eye view. But we do what we can to try to gain some advance over previous perspectives. Even as we attempt to surpass them in some way, we rely on them (a point which may be construed as an Anglo-American's nod to Hegel and company). We use the tools in our rhetorical chest to persuade others (who are interested in the problems that interest us) that we have moved the problem forward. Specifically, I argue that dissolving the "problem of history" and constructing a more pluralistic and particular account of the problems eliminates the conundra endemic in the dualistic problematic, overcomes some oversights, and suggests some insights.

We cannot offer G. E. Lessing and his present-day followers a boost to leap over that ditch to get from this historical side to the side of the Absolute. But we can discern a number of steppingstones to help us ford the river and to reach an island from which we may take new bearings as we continue our journey in later chapters. The first steppingstones are the arguments of the next chapters. Once we have seen that the modern problem of history and its dualistic problematic both can and should be dissolved, we will be in position to reformulate the issues in more useful ways.

CHAPTER 2

A Geography of Textual Forms

Historicizing is not identical to relativizing, much less debunking.
—Lorraine Datson

The problem of history afflicts all the monotheistic traditions. Judaism, Christianity, and Islam each claim that God has acted in and through historical events, has constituted a religious tradition by that action, and also affected other events by that action. While other religious traditions have gods and goddesses acting in the world, the claim that the Unoriginate One, who solely created and sustains the universe, acted at specific times and places to redeem people and even to right the universe, distinguishes the monotheistic traditions. Given the presumptions of modern historical work that exclude any reference to the actions of non-natural entities, the clash between critical historical investigation and traditional religious claims seems inevitable. However the problems of history are construed, there are similarities among the traditions both in the problems and the responses.

Because they affirm that God acts in and through particular events, the monotheisms share in the general problem of history. Historians are by their discipline skeptical, at best, about claims that some events are the result of acts of God. However, because their sacred texts tell of the acts of God differently, the monotheisms have distinctive versions of the problem. The purpose of the present chapter is to highlight those similarities and differences in order to show that the shape of the problem of history is irreducibly different for each tradition, however much there are also similarities.

Judaism

First, Judaic traditions are fundamentally shaped by the intertwined literary forms of saga and law code in the Bible to portray divine action. Whether one finds God's giving the Law or the saga of the people that shapes their history to be more fundamental, the acts of God they lift up are fundamentally covenantal. God is and pledges to be the God of Israel. Israel is and pledges to be the people of God. It was God who led the people of Israel out of Egypt, God who gave the law to the people through Moses, God who allowed the establishment and eventual destruction of a kingdom in the land that God had given them, and God who rescued the people from captivity in Babylon. It was the people who prayed for deliverance from slavery, received the Law, sought a king, strayed from covenantal obligations and were punished, especially by God's distance or absence, and were finally rescued when God used Cyrus, king of the Persians and the Medes, to free God's people.

One may suspend belief about the accuracy of the narrative of any of these events or movements. One may question whether God was the responsible agent. But one cannot reasonably deny that the saga so briefly sketched here and the law code merely mentioned both articulate in their specific literary forms God's acts according to Jewish tradition. This is not to deny that other literary forms, from myth and countermyth to legend and fairytale, genealogy and jeremiad, sharp-edged prophecy and dull recording of didactic expositions, are also found in the biblical text and important for the tradition. But the fundamental form narrating God's covenantal acts are saga and law code. As we shall see in working with the thought of Richard Rubenstein in chapter five and Michael Goldberg in chapter eleven, the covenant and its code narrated in the saga of Judaism are central principles in the tradition.

Christianity

Second, Jesus of Nazareth is born into the people who continue to live in and to live out this saga. God's acts are specifically associated with this one individual. Yet the religion that originated with his life, work, death, and resurrection at least requires writing a new episode in the saga. More importantly, it uses literary forms of gospel, letter, and later, creedal formulae as central to its story. It also records and sometimes interprets some of the parables of Jesus. This is not to say that these literary forms were invented out of whole cloth. They were not. Letters and creedal formulae were not unique literary forms. The literary form of the gospel may be a variation on popular forms, including Greco-Roman "novels," historical narratives, and hero stories. And Jesus was not the first person to tell parables. But without the good news, the *euangelion*, presented in gospels, codified in letters, and clarified in creeds, there would be no Christianity.

Considered literarily, Christianity does not succeed or supersede or reject Judaism. There is harsh rhetoric in the New Testament, authored by Jews (and Gentiles in some cases) who followed Jesus, against their fellow Jews who did not follow Jesus. However one interprets this rhetoric,

Christianity turned a new page in Jewish history by using new literary forms to proclaim a new and distinctive act of God. That these forms took much from Jewish law, prophets, and writings is clear. But the literary form that comes to express God's action is fundamentally not saga but a new literary form called "gospel."

The crucial act of God is the incarnation, the enfleshment of God in a specific individual, Jesus of Nazareth. Through him God redeems and sanctifies the world. This act of God in and through this specific person is narrated in the stylized stories of his life, death, and vindication, clarified through didactic letters, and rendered into short creedal formulae. Which came first—formulae, letter, gospel—is not for our purposes relevant at this point. These literary pieces tell of a specific act of God or set of God's acts. Here the divine agency is not seen as the producer of a code or as the guiding light of a people on a journey or settled in the land, but as incarnate in and exercised by a specific individual.

Crucial Differences

The contrast between these central Christian literary forms and central Jewish forms cannot be more stark. In the Jewish narratives, God acts for a people, shaping and using events in ways to benefit them and strengthen or rebuild the covenantal relationship. In the Christian narratives, God still acts for people—both Jews and Gentiles. But God does so in a way so outrageous that some Jews found Jesus' followers' claims about God's fundamental act blasphemous. Moreover, how Jesus' followers could even articulate that act of God was hotly debated in antiquity—and is difficult to imagine at any time: God actually became human and acted in and through a specific individual. Jesus was no mere servant or inspired human being or messenger or agent sent by God; Jesus was God exercising divine agency as a human person. Once such Christology becomes full-blown and the gospel narratives become far more important to Jesus' followers than the saga of Israel, separation seems to have been inevitable, however tragic.

The crucial thing to note, then, is the profoundly different ways in which God is construed to act—and the need for different literary forms for the action. For the gospel of Jesus is not a saga, and the saga of Israel is not a gospel. God's acts for Israel require something like a saga in order to be told; God's acts in and through Jesus cannot be told as a saga. The differing kinds of divine acts require differing literary forms if we are to speak of them at all. The issues that occupy Marcus Borg and N. T. Wright, as discussed in chapter nine below, are distinctive of Christianity. The kinds of disputes about methods and purposes of analyzing the New Testament to seek the historical Jesus simply would be irrelevant in a Jewish context.

These differing kinds of narratives also create different versions of the problem of history. Theologians like Niebuhr have sometimes failed to notice that critical historical investigations have to be shaped differently when approaching a history-narrated-as-saga and a very different type of history-narrated-as-gospel. Niebuhr's examples and insights are drawn from analysis of the former. Indeed, his "external vs. internal history" distinction, mentioned in the last chapter, fits historical work on sagas quite nicely. However, just as the investigative and narrative techniques of a national historian are different from those of a biographer, so the critical historian of saga differs from the historian of gospel. This difference is crucial.

For example, consider the Exodus. Critical historians have argued that to make some historical sense of the Exodus, given what we know from the saga and other ancient sources, we have to recognize that the Bible exaggerates the number of people involved in the Exodus and the effect on the Egyptians' life and economy, and probably misplaces the location of the crossing (perhaps the Sea of Reeds rather than the Red Sea). The story also incorporates many legendary accretions and the dire warnings so well conveyed even in imaginative tales. It is not only the rationalist Reimarus, but even a Catholic priest, who could find the Exodus story exaggerated. As Fr. John L. McKenzie put it, the exodus of 600,000 Jewish men ("not to mention" women and children) from Egypt would not merely have devastated the Egyptian economy, but would have had to have been the exodus of the Egyptians, since a few centuries earlier Thutmose III had conquered "all of Canaan, and a good deal besides . . . with an army of 18,000 men" (McKenzie 1979, 90). And there is no record of a collapse in the Egyptian economy, either!

But however the critical historian retells the tale, the event of the Exodus in some shape can stand fast. A historian can tell a truly revisionist tale, claiming that most tribes and extended families who would come to form Israel and Judah were not participants in the event and did not even have ancestors that participated in the event (see Gottwald). Hence, our understanding of the Exodus undergoes revision. But our belief that the event occurred in some sense and can still be seen as religiously significant—a narrative of God's act—is not irrational. Even if the most warrantable story (as narrated from an "external" stance) is one of a rag-tag bunch of slaves running away, escaping pursuit, getting lost, settling in an already-settled land, and forming alliances with some of the indigenous people in Canaan, it can still be the Exodus (told from an "internal" perspective). However much believers may have to reshape their understanding of God's act, they have no reason to think that God could not have acted in the Exodus.

In contrast, consider the resurrection of Jesus. So many monumental tomes have been written on this "event" from so many differing historical perspectives that it sometimes seems that the historically serious believer is left in a state of bewildered agnosticism about whether this was or even could be God's act. The skeptical attacks on the empty-tomb stories, the dismissal of the appearance narratives as exaggerated tall tales based on deceptions, hallucinations, or powerful imaginations, and the incredibility of an utterly unique event of God directly raising a person from the dead to a new, but physically real, form of life, all seem to count against it. The empty-tomb stories are generally acknowledged to be written rather late in the composition history of the gospels. The appearance stories either are so obviously literary constructs with an apologetic or catechetical point (e.g., Luke's story of Jesus' appearance to two of his followers on the road to Emmaus), are so vague, or are told as hearsay, that critical historians can easily completely discount their value as evidence. The resurrection of Jesus by God could easily be the expression of a wish for the end-times to be here when God would raise all from the dead, a wish transformed into a miracle story. Moreover, this act of God is unique. It is not the same as a healer raising someone from the dead. The story of Lazarus being raised by Jesus and other ancient stories of raisings by healers may look similar in some ways to the stories of Jesus being raised by God, but in the case of the resurrection of Jesus, God does it "alone": no human agency or co-agency is to be found in these stories.

What is at issue here, however, is not the "size" or "external historical" significance of this alleged act of God, as someone using Niebuhr's distinctions might be inclined to say. The problem is not one of "historical revisionism." The occurrence of the event itself is at issue. Critical historical research on the Exodus can reshape the story, but some of the events remain; religiously committed people may attribute them to God. But critical historical research on the resurrection seems to undermine any claim that such an event occurred; hence, there is nothing to attribute to an act of God! One can keep the core of one's uncritical belief in the Exodus even after the winds of criticism have blown away the incredible. But Christian theologians who can no longer affirm the historical fact of the resurrection are forced to abandon the resurrection narratives as in any way reliable indicators of what happened. The event cannot be minimized or reformed but must be abandoned as an actual event.

The problem with abandoning a bodily (in some sense) resurrection of Jesus was first identified by St. Paul: "If Christ has not been raised, your faith is futile and you are still in your sins" (1 Cor. 15:17, RSV). If one abandons the reality of the resurrection, then how can one not also abandon the incarnation? If one cannot believe that an omnipotent deity could raise a man from the dead, then how can one believe that the Unoriginated One, who created and sustains the universe, was truly present in that universe in the person of Jesus of Nazareth and in some way acted to redeem the universe? Considered logically, the miracle of the Infinite One becoming finite is far more difficult to account for than is the raising of a dead man to new life.

Some theologians, however, have utilized a revisionist approach. If the physical resurrection narrated in the empty-tomb stories must be abandoned, they then propose to treat these stories as symbolic expressions of God's exaltation of Jesus. They go on to tell a new story, a story of Jesus as the Christ without the bodily resurrection on Easter Sunday. Roger Haight, for example, has argued that the crucifixion itself is the exaltation of the Son by the Father and that the resurrection was not a "separate event." He wrote that it "is better to say that Jesus' resurrection is not an historical fact, because the idea of an historical fact suggests an empirical event which could have been witnessed and can now be imaginatively construed" (Haight 1999, 124). Although it might seem otherwise to some, Haight is *not* denying the reality of the God's acting in, through, and on Jesus. Nor is he denying the reality of the resurrection, to which the empty-tomb stories point. Rather, he is a revisionist historian and theologian. He interprets resurrection as Jesus' being "exalted and glorified" into the reality of God. "This occurred through and at the moment of Jesus' death, so that there was no time between his death and his resurrection and exaltation" (Haight 1999, 126). So Haight basically throws out the empty-tomb stories as representing actual states of affairs. These narratives indicated the occurrence of (but never narrate) an act of God raising Jesus, an act that occurred at a time different from Good Friday, that is, on Easter Sunday. In response to critical historical attacks on the resurrection narratives, Haight has renarrated the point in the story at which the resurrection/exaltation took place. At least we can be sure that the crucifixion happened! The exaltation/resurrection of Jesus is thus not an incredible event, but a theological claim "piggy-backing" on a clearly actual historical event.

The most reliable fact we have about Jesus of Nazareth is that he was crucified under Pontius Pilate. No external historian has shown that this event did not occur. Hence, even if we cannot accept the passion narratives as fully reliable narrations of actual events, believers have no reason to think that God could not have acted in the crucifixion to exalt Jesus. Christians' justifiable conviction that this event occurred means that it is not irrational also to see this as religiously significant and to construct a narrative of this event as revealing an act of God—which is just what Haight does. The stories of empty tombs and appearances are then taken as imaginative legends or useful fictions expressing the disciples' hope that Jesus was not abandoned on the cross, but they are not representations of a historical event or act of God.

However, such a revisionist approach means that a key element in the story of Jesus has been abandoned. The key to understanding this is to notice that the narrative form of gospel is different from the narrative form of saga. Historians' work on sagas may be revisionist to the point of serious doubt or incredibility. But however revised, the saga remains a narrative that one can live in and live out. To use Niebuhr's terminology, the changes required by "external history" revise, but do not destroy, the significance narrated in the "internal history" of our community if we are Jews. In contrast, the historians' work on narratives centered on individuals—as the gospels are centered on Jesus—typically is not revisionist, but undermining. Elements of the gospel are winnowed out as historically unreliable until the pared-down view of Jesus that remains is one of a wandering cynic-sage or a clever Galilean peasant. Thus, there is no reason to think that God acts in and through him any more than in and through any other person. One may add on to this pared-down narrative that God exalts him in death. But that is not a historical fact. If one cannot swallow the (comparative) gnat of the resurrection, how can one swallow the camel of the incarnation? This problem haunts some of the quests for the historical Jesus, as we shall see in chapter nine.

However well it may work in considering sagas, the Niebuhrian distinction between inner and outer history does not work so well for critical investigations of the gospels. The critical historian does not force us to revise and renarrate the story. Rather, we are forced to tell a very different story, as Haight does. Now, such a revisionist approach may be the best way to represent God's acts in, through, and on Jesus of Nazareth in light of what can stand fast after critical historical examination. This approach may be the best way in our era to express the central and fundamental story of the Christian tradition in a credible and orthodox manner. However, in chapter four, I will show that the presuppositions which lead to this kind of revisionist theology are questionable at best.

Islam

Third, the Qur'an records a set of dictations from God through an angel to Muhammad over a relatively brief period of time. Here we have an entirely different type of literary form from saga or gospel. There is no narrative structure. The suras of the Qur'an are believed by orthodox Muslims to be the revelation of God. Neither gospel nor saga, the Qur'an takes the literary form of a collection of the sayings of God revealed to Muhammad.

Unlike the Hebrew Bible, the Qur'an is not composed over a millennium by different authors using even more ancient oral traditions. It is not a saga of the journey of a people chosen by God. Unlike the New Testament, the Qur'an is not the word of God definitively rendering who the Word of God is and what he did for humanity in narratives written over a period of about half a century by numerous hands utilizing earlier oral (and perhaps some written) traditions. It is not a gospel, and Muhammad is certainly not God incarnate. Most Jews and Christians can accommodate historical criticism—obviously with significant tensions—because they do not take their sacred texts as literally the words of God and they recognize the multiple literary forms, numerous authors' hands, and differing times and places of composition of the books in the text. Many Muslims cannot accommodate critical historical work on the Qur'an. They do not treat their sacred text as a composite, despite the early history of the shaping of the Qur'an (see Madigan 2001, 24-28), and typically do take the book as literally the words of God. Muslims can and do dispute how to interpret certain texts and how to apply them today. Should the *sharia*, the law of the community, be applied literalistically or adapted to new circumstances? Does it make sense to cut the hands off of a thief whose theft is electronic? Muslims also debate whether one group of verses, for example, the sword verses, should control the interpretation of other verses, whether some verses should abrogate others, or whether later verses are to be given more central authority than earlier ones. Muslim philosophers have developed proofs of the existence of God and developed philosophical analyses geared to resolving conceptual problems in the texts, for example, how God can will evil in the world. Nonetheless, it seems that Muslims in general have trouble accepting the unbridled historical criticism characteristic of post-Enlightenment Western scholarship. Such criticism can easily be construed as criticism of God, as blasphemy, since the texts are not of human authorship but of divine authorship, despite the fact that "[c]onsidered as canonical document for recitation, the [Muslim] tradition presents the Qur'ân as completely contained in the [codex/text]; regarded as a source for law, the tradition claims that the Qur'ân is in fact more extensive than the [codex/text]" (Madigan 2001, 33). Whereas the Hebrew Bible and the Christian Scriptures can be read as books produced with human contributions to authorship (or even as humanly authored documents witnessing to God's presence and/or actions), the Qur'an is Allah's document (see Esposito 1988, 20-35); it is not a "book in the ordinary sense" (Madigan 2001, 184). To "attack" it may well be to "attack" God. While critical history may force Jews to renarrate and resize the Exodus saga and may require Christians to revise their stories of Jesus significantly, Muslims seem forced either to reject critical history or to reject the Qur'an as the words of God and to give it a status in their traditions more like the Bible in the Christian and Jewish traditions. But many Muslims reject such theological moves. Madigan (2001) shows how such critical appropriation is both possible and implied by the Muslim traditions; but such "Western" analyses are stoutly resisted in much of Islam.

No Single "Problem of History"

When we consider, then, the differing status these sacred texts have in the realms of Jewish, Christian, and Muslim discourse and the differing literary forms these sacred texts take, we can see that the "problem of history" should not be construed as a single kind of problem for each of these traditions. In one sense, all of the traditions are vulnerable to historical criticism because they recognize that God's acts affect or effect events in the world in which we live. In that sense, all of the traditions have a "problem of history." To treat them all as if they had the *same* problem that critical history brings up with regard to sagas is not tenable. Critical history creates very different sorts of tensions in the different realms of discourse. Attending to the geography of those forms and their very different placement in those realms of discourse makes it clear that we are better off recognizing many problems of history, rather than *the* problem of history, and the need for developing different kinds of responses to the problems, appropriate for each of the monotheistic traditions.

CHAPTER 3

The Responsibilities of Believers and Historians

I am convinced that it is precisely because the logic
of the matter has not been clearly delineated that the so-called
problem of faith and history is as muddled as it is
in the contemporary literature.

—Van A. Harvey

In a book first published in 1966, Van Harvey shifted the discourse about the relationships of historical judgment and religious belief. Although he recognized that the "problem of history" was not one but took many forms, he still construed the problem as a tension between two poles. This chapter shows the contributions that Harvey made and suggests points at which his work can be developed to overcome the dualistic presumption that has structured the modern problematic of faith and history.

Most earlier reflection on this tension between faith and history had occurred in a discourse dominated by continental, rather than Anglo-American, philosophical presuppositions. Most scholars posed the problem in terms of the historical method as being the real source of the problem of history for Christian belief. Harvey offered an alternative standpoint for understanding and assessing the problem. He wrote:

> The standpoint is based on the convictions that it is less helpful to talk about the historical method than it is to explore what I shall call the historian's morality of knowledge, or ethic of assent; that it is more confusing to try to define historical understanding than it is to ask how historians go about justifying their claims; that it is more misleading to ask how one can verify a historical assertion than it is to explore the numerous and diverse kinds of judgments historians make and the kinds of assent they solicit from their colleagues and readers. (Harvey 1968, 33)

Harvey utilized insights from analytical philosophy. He focused not on the abstract concepts of "faith" and "history" but on the people who do history and have faith. His central issue was not historical method, but the work historians do.

Historians' Practices and Religious Belief

Harvey's analysis centered on some of the key elements of the *practice* of doing history. A practice is a shared form of life in which the participants intend and seek an end that only participating in the practice can achieve (in this case, roughly, as accurate and adequate a portrayal as feasible of certain events or sets of events in the past). The practitioners employ determinate procedures which can be roughly guided by rules (to examine sources for their reliability and to use them proportionately using the tools of the historian's craft). Engaging in the practice develops a person's abilities and dispositions appropriate to persons involved in the practice (especially those that support seeking the goal and that incline people who participate to use the appropriate means). A practitioner learns the "grammar" of the practice, a set of inferred rules that show how means (methods, procedures) and ends are connected in the patterns of actions that constitute the practice, typically through schooling or apprenticeship (see Tilley 2000, 53ff.).

Harvey highlighted four key elements in the practice of historical investigation (1968, 39). First, historians are radically autonomous. They are not under the authority of the witnesses of the past. Texts and monuments from the past do not have intrinsic authority. They are not evidence but are data to be evaluated for their evidentiary value. That is, they cannot be read transparently but must be interpreted. So, historians are not under the authority of their sources but confer authority on a witness and evaluate the witness's testimony, whether the witness be text or monument or some other relic of the past. If the historian does not approach the sources critically, the historian is "no longer a seeker of knowledge, but a mediator of past belief; not a thinker but a transmitter of tradition" (Harvey 1968, 42).

Second, historians are responsible for their evidence and arguments. Their claims to historical knowledge must "achieve whatever cogency or well-foundedness can relevantly be asked for in that field" (Harvey 1968, 48). History is not science and not held to the standards of natural science or of philosophy or any other field. Historians must construct arguments well-founded by the standards of the field in which they work and recognized by competent practitioners in the field.

Third, historians need to exercise sound and balanced judgment. When historians make specific claims, they seek to show that their claims are true to a certain level of reliability. Historians make some claims about the past that are possibly true, but supported by little evidence or dubious evidence. Some claims are practically certain. They are the most reliably warranted claims—all the relevant evidence supports them.

Fourth, historians stand critically in the present. They must use their "critically interpreted experience as the background against which sound judgments are made about the past" (Harvey 1968, 39). Harvey elaborates on this point as follows:

> The historian, like his witness, is also the son of his time, and his present standpoint may appear to subsequent generations to be relative. But he cannot "jump out of his skull" or return to the standpoint of a former time, for his explanations and language inevitably reflect this one. Moreover, it is only by taking responsibility for this present standpoint that a better, future one can responsibly emerge. (Harvey 1968, 99)

This last quotation from Harvey is a case in point: the lack of inclusive language marks him as a "son of his times" when he first published the book in 1966. We all must presume the linguistic conventions of our times, even as we work to change some of them.

Harvey then went on to play off religious belief and historical explanation. Fundamentally, the "problem of faith and history is not merely a problem of two logics or two methodologies. It is a problem . . . of two ethics of judgment" (Harvey 1968, 104). The historian warranted her claims on the basis of arguments utilizing field-specific evidence and warrants. The orthodox believer who holds a religious belief about history, but who refuses to allow warranted historical claims to count against his belief, by contrast, "is intellectually irresponsible, not so much because he wants certainty, as because he continually enters objections to our normal warrants for no principled reasons" (Harvey 1968, 118). Given the claims that God acts in history, given what Harvey called the Protestant understanding of faith, and given the different practices of the historian and the believer, he found that the liberal theologians at the end of the nineteenth century, the "New Questers" of the 1950s, and the neo-orthodox theologians popular when he wrote were all trapped by what we can call Harvey's paradox. They wanted both to affirm historical truths about the historical Jesus and simultaneously to affirm that historical investigations proper to forming judgments about historical figures could not undermine theologically significant truth claims about Jesus (Harvey 1968, 196-97). Moreover, he claimed that "orthodox belief corrodes the delicate machinery of historical judgment" (Harvey 1968, 119). That is, participating in religious practices tends to render one unfit for participating in the practice of doing history as much as the practice of regular gourmet drinking and dining tends to render one unfit for running marathons.

Here we see Harvey clearly moving away from abstract discussion to a focus on what people do in the practice.

Much of the rest of Harvey's book was devoted to dissecting previous attempts to overcome the opposition between the morality of sound historical judgment and the morality of faithful religious belief. He uses "morality" in a somewhat uncommon sense. It is the pattern of good practice. The morality of the historian, for example, deals primarily with intellectual virtues like intellectual autonomy, responsibility, intellectual wisdom or prudence, and critical self-awareness or authenticity. One learns the forms of these virtues specific to a practice or discipline by learning how to participate in that practice or discipline. His discussion anticipates the later development of "virtue epistemology" (Zagzebski).

Harvey's analysis of the "morality of historical knowledge" is an exercise in naturalized epistemology. Naturalized epistemology does not ask how someone—anyone—*should* form beliefs. Rather, the naturalized epistemologist asks how, in fact, good practitioners *do* form beliefs that are reliable. Harvey seeks to identify how good practitioners *do* produce historical knowledge. Prescriptive and idealized epistemological theories have consistently failed either to count what we knew as knowledge or to eliminate what we knew as mere opinion from the realm of knowledge. In response, Anglo-American philosophers have changed the terms of the discourse by examining knowledge production and verification as it is actually carried out. Although he did not use this terminology, Harvey contributed an important sketch of a naturalized epistemology of historical work.

Harvey's attempt to defuse the problem of history and to create a place for religious belief, however, is not entirely successful. In the final chapters of his book, Harvey sketched a resolution focusing on the individual believer's faith and how the practice of religious faithfulness can be described in a way both faithful to the Christian tradition and compatible with, but different from, the practice of historical investigation and the results of critical history. His sketch sought to provide a perspective that avoided both having religious faith rely on historical knowledge and having historical knowledge be completely irrelevant to faith.

To some critics, however, his positive contribution seemed unable to overcome the dichotomy between faith and history without evacuating Christian faith of much substance other than private and personal response to Jesus (see Harvey 1968, xv-xvi, 282, 285). Harvey found that a "fact cannot provide the ground or the object of faith when faith is properly understood, although it can awaken faith and provide the symbols that faith uses" (Harvey 1968, 283). But rather than showing the relevance of historical investigations and results to faith, Harvey made history essentially irrelevant to faith, that is, to trusting in and committing oneself to God, and to accepting life and creation as a gift and responsibility (cf. Harvey 1968, 280). Historical facts may provide a stimulus to the development of faith, or learning a historical fact may be the incidental event which occasions the beginning of faith. Historical facts may also provide symbols that the believer can use to symbolize or express her or his faith. So historians may provide facts that affect believers' faith marginally, but in the end, history is irrelevant to faith itself. Indeed, Harvey's individualist, existentialist, privatized solution owes much to existentialist theologian and New Testament scholar Rudolf Bultmann, to whom the book is dedicated. While Harvey's analysis has taken the problem forward, Harvey has not provided a satisfying resolution to the problem of history. As chapter seven argues, there is another way to approach this problem, derivable from the work of George Lindbeck, that seems to achieve some of Harvey's goals and to avoid the problems that made Harvey's resolution less than satisfactory.

Beyond the "Faith and History" Problematic

The key problem with Harvey's solution is that it is rooted in the dualistic form of the problematic, which Harvey did not challenge. Indeed, he worked mightily to overcome the dualisms. He asked whether the dichotomy between the historical event and timeless truth is "another of those false and artificial distinctions? What if symbol and event, timeless truth and history, are not strict alternatives?" (Harvey 1968, 252). Unfortunately, Harvey did not take these issues further (e.g., see Harvey 2000, 91-94). I suggest that if we are to move forward in this area, we must move out of the dualistic mindset.

In effect, Harvey examined two practices, religious believing and critical historical investigating. Religious believing produced values. Historical investigations produced facts. Harvey's work reflects the hard distinction between fact and value that characterized much analytical philosophy. That hard distinction, however, has increasingly become problematized. While few want to eliminate facts or values, the distinction has become recognized as a legacy of positivism. The relations between facts and values are much more complex than the relationships between doing historical investigations and being a participant in a religious tradition—points which will be discussed later in this book.

Harvey neglected the fact that everyone participates in multiple practices with multiple "ethics of belief." We can become confused and can and do sometimes allow our wishes for some claim to be true to trump our critical abilities. Sometimes, for some people "orthodox belief corrodes the delicate machinery of historical judgment" (Harvey 1968, 119). Yet we as human beings participate in many practices in which we have to develop knowledge, understanding, and wisdom—from learning arithmetic to courting to marrying to parenting to paying income tax to shopping to vacationing to voting to historically investigating (even a teenage child's story of the past day) to religiously believing to driving a car—just to mention a few common to many folk. We may be prone to wishful thinking or self-deception. But the variety of such practices suggests that Harvey's dichotomy needs to be expanded to include a comparison of multiple practices, not just two. In short, what Harvey has done is to collapse the very different responsibilities (and "moralities") of theologians and believers and contrast them with those of historians.

Of course, not all practices are equal. Some are more central to our lives than others. Some may be more likely to come in conflict—including doing history and believing religiously. Some of us may be prone to self-deception or wishful thinking in some practices but not in others. Sometimes habits or dispositions learned in one form of life (trusting parents) may be applicable in other forms of life (trusting one's spouse), but not in others (trusting used car salespeople). But Harvey's "either/or" approach leaves too many possibilities unexplored.

Harvey himself, in the preface to the paperback edition (1968), suggested that he was inclined to continue rethinking the issues in a more pluralizing way. He distinguishes the kinds of warrants needed for particular historical investigations, general interpretations of history, and total theological perspectives. As he put it:

> Were I to revise the book, I would develop more fully the point that one cannot legitimately demand the same tight rational justification for a total theological perspective of the logical type I proposed as one can demand for specific historical claims or even for a broader interpretation of history like, say, Marxism. Or to use the jargon of analytic philosophy, the logic of "seeing as" is quite different from the logic of claiming some event to have happened in a specific way or assuming some interpretive standpoint regarding history. Correspondingly, the ethics of belief is quite different in each case. (Harvey 1968, xvii)

Here Harvey differentiated the standards for asserting the actuality of a specific historical event and for accepting a certain understanding of what history is. Indeed, this makes good sense. For the practice of investigating specific historical events and sets of events and warranting claims about them, history proper, is quite different from warranting an assertion delineating the historical forces that move history (as Marxism does) or exposing the shape of a historical epoch as a whole (as Gibbon did in *The Decline and Fall of the Roman Empire*) or uncovering a historical pattern often repeated (as Barbara Tuchman did in *The March of Folly: From Troy to Vietnam* [1984]).

Harvey, however, did not distinguish holding "a total theological perspective" from "believing in the trustworthiness of God." The former is an act of a theologian, for theological perspectives are created in the practice of theology. The latter is an act of a believer, for such beliefs are developed in the context of having or coming to have a religious faith. The ethics of belief in each case are somewhat different (see Tilley 1995, 120-53, and chapter eleven below). Just as the ethics of belief in the fields of history needs to be recognized as more plural than *The Historian and the Believer* recognized, so too do the ethics of theological and religious believing need to be seen as more plural.

Role-Specific Responsibilities

Harvey himself opened a way to recognize this diversity in a later essay (1986 [1979]) in which he introduced the concept of "role-specific" responsibility. Briefly, it makes sense to recognize that believers, critical historians, interpreters of history, theologians, and others all exercise different roles and all have different kinds of responsibilities for forming and checking beliefs. Harvey elucidated the concept of "role-specific" responsibilities by reflecting on the strengths and weaknesses of W. K. Clifford's classic essay, "The Ethics of Belief."

Clifford used the example of a shipowner who sends his old, worn-out ship to sea, despite the fact that he had good reason to doubt its seaworthiness. The shipowner simply stifled those doubts. He continued to believe the ship seaworthy although he had not checked it and questions of its seaworthiness had been raised. Clifford argued that if the ship then sank with all hands, the shipowner would be "guilty of the death of those men . . . because he had no right to believe on such evidence as was before him" (Clifford 1877, 19). He had no right to believe because he fails, Clifford argued, in his duty as a human being to believe only upon adequate evidence. Even if the ship made port and the passengers and crew did not suffer for his choice, he would still be guilty, according to Clifford. His failure had endangered the passengers. Just because there were no bad consequences of his belief in his ship and his act of allowing it to sail does not justify his belief. He would still be guilty (at least of reckless endangerment). Even if he believed, perhaps sincerely by the time the ship weighed anchor, that the ship was seaworthy, he had no entitlement to hold that belief. Sincerity is not evidence, and stifling doubts is not a proper method to develop or justify belief.

Clifford wanted to show that humans *qua* human have a responsibility to proportion their beliefs to the evidence supporting those beliefs. Harvey convincingly argued that such responsibilities are not general human duties, but role-specific, particular duties. They are the dispositions and habits one develops by engaging in "good practice." The *owner* of the ship, but not a passenger in it (or a cabin attendant working it), was obliged to check the assumption that the ship was seaworthy before it sailed loaded with passengers just because the owner has the role of owner. Today the pilot of an airliner has the role-specific responsibility of making a preflight walk-around check. The management has the responsibility of hiring only qualified pilots and ensuring that they know their jobs, but they do not have the responsibility to perform the preflight check. The responsibility of allowing a ship loaded with passengers and cargo to sail or an airliner to leave the gate for takeoff would not apply to "anyone," but is specific to the person who has the role of shipowner or pilot. These role-specific responsibilities tie each of them to their "wider duty to the culture and to the safety of its citizens. One fulfills this wider duty by being responsible for one's narrower station and its duties" (Harvey 1979, 198). While all humans may have some responsibility at some time for checking some beliefs, to demand that all of us always and everywhere proportion all our beliefs to the evidence for them is to make the ethics of belief impossibly rigorous. Everyone would be epistemically immoral by this standard. We may be able to check any one or a few of our beliefs at any time, but while we do so, the others stand fast. Which ones we should check in which circumstances can only be delineated by understanding what a wise or prudent person who understood the form of life in which she or he was participating and had a specific role in that form of life would do in such a situation.

People in other roles or stations do not have the same responsibility as the owner to check the vessel's seaworthiness. Others have other duties which contribute to a successful voyage. A shipowner does not have the responsibility to know whether pirates had just been spotted near the ship's destination across the sea. To protect the vessel from pirates is the navy's duty. The pilot does not have the responsibility for air traffic control; that is the controller's duty. The simple fact of the matter is that we are fated to rely on others, on their fulfilling their duties, if we are to do or believe anything. If I am to believe that my next airplane flight is reasonably safe, I have to accept "the word" of people who work for governments and airlines. If I am to commit my body to their hands for the duration of the flight, I have to trust them.

What is needed, then, is an analysis of the appropriate standards of responsibility for belief formation and justification for persons in the roles of critical historian, interpreter of history, religious believer, theological scholar, and so on. The particular abilities appropriate for each of these practices carried by different (but sometimes overlapping) communities need to be analyzed. Anticipating my own constructive argument, but using Harvey's terminology for the present, the "moralities of knowledge" vary as significantly for religious believers as they do for historians.

I have argued elsewhere that the duties of theologians are somewhat different from those who are not trained to do theology (Tilley 1995, 120-53). Later I will build on those arguments to construct a more positive account of the relations between historians, believers, and theologians. For the present, I simply want to suggest that such an approach is possible and that it has the potential for moving us beyond the faith-and-history or historian-and-believer dichotomies that we have constructed and allowed to determine the shape of the discourse so far. Role-specific responsibilities are much more diverse than the dualistic problematic allows. Moreover, in addition to the variety of problems for the monotheistic traditions discussed in chapter two, this approach gives us a second major reason to think that the dichotomy can be surpassed. The following chapter suggests a third major reason to think that the dualistic approach can be overcome.

CHAPTER 4

The Presumptions of History

The central principle of all history—contingency.
—Stephen Jay Gould

Many philosophers and theologians who work in traditions influenced by continental philosophy have written as though the *presumptions* that render historical investigations possible are also *assumptions* that the historian has to believe to be generally, if not universally, true. In this chapter, I argue that a practitioner can accept procedural presumptions that make practices possible without accepting those presumptions as true assertions.

It is very important to distinguish presumptions from assumptions or beliefs. Failure to do so can lead to serious confusion about what people must or can *believe* and what they need to *presume* if they are to participate in a practice. In some cases for some people, there seems to be no real difference between presumptions and beliefs/assumptions. But in some contexts, the difference is crucial. This difference is exemplified in the practice of the criminal justice court.

A person accused of a crime is presumed innocent until proven guilty. The presumption of innocence governs the practice of trying accused criminals, at least in the common law context of the United States. This presumption places the burden of proof on the prosecution. The defense does not have to demonstrate that the defendant is innocent; the prosecution must prove the defendant guilty "beyond a reasonable doubt." Without the presumption of innocence, the American legal system would be profoundly different. It is a fundamental "rule" without which the system as we know it could not function.

Yet because a prosecutor and defense attorney in a case must accept the presumption of innocence does not imply that either of them has, therefore, to assume or believe the assertion that the defendant is innocent. A lawyer who believed that the presumption of the practice of criminal justice meant that she had to believe that it was true that her client was innocent of the crime would be confused or naive, at best. Of course, one may believe true what the practice presumes. A defense attorney may indeed believe that the client is innocent. But the attorney properly forms that belief on evidence quite different from the presumption of innocence in the practice of criminal trials.

Accepting a presumption that is part of a practice or a discipline does not commit one to believing that presumption to be true in particular cases. A presumption is usually stated as a rule; an assumption or belief is usually stated as a proposition or assertion. A presumption can be useful or defective, easy or difficult to follow, and so on, but not "true or false." A belief is true or false.

My argument is that the same kind of distinction must also apply to the practice of history: the presumptions of history as a practice need not be assumed or asserted to be true by those doing historical investigations or interpreting the data of the past. Those who have conflated the rules that guide historians' practices with assertions that historians must accept as true have crossed an ugly, broad ditch (see above, pp. 11-12). Without argument or demonstration, they have taken the kind of leap that Lessing found profoundly objectionable: they have transformed one kind of belief into another without argument. But instead of taking a leap into faith, their translation of the presumptions of history into assertions of metaphysical principles that apply always and everywhere was a leap into skepticism. This was not what Lessing was begging for.

While the example of criminal law makes it clear that we can distinguish presumptions and assumptions in that case, it requires more analysis and argument to make a similar case for the practice of history. I will show that a set of important and representative theologians, inspired by work of the historian and theologian Ernst Troeltsch, and including Rudolf Bultmann, Jürgen Moltmann, and Roger Haight, works with a specific view of the relationship of history and theology that is unsustainable. In brief, my claim is that these theologians and philosophers have unwarrantedly construed the procedural *presumptions*, the "rules of thumb," proper to history as metaphysical *assertions* (compare Martin 1999, 109-10, 116-18). This intellectual sleight of hand is inappropriate because it treats defeasible *methodological presumptions* of a discipline as if they were indefeasible *substantive claims* of a metaphysics or ontology. When this move is made in the context of the dualistic problematic of faith and history, it has led to theological conundra and confusions that could be avoided.

Troeltsch and His Followers

In an influential 1898 essay, Ernst Troeltsch developed three principles for doing critical history. Jürgen Moltmann (1996, 77-78), who takes his own bearings on history from Troeltsch, presented these principles as axioms of probability, correlation, and analogy. He added a fourth axiom to Troeltsch's three which I shall discuss below. There are serious problems with taking all of these axioms as assertions.

The *axiom of probability* claims that historical knowledge is never "absolute" knowledge. Historical knowledge therefore cannot be the foundation of faith. While the antecedents of this claim (e.g., Lessing's description of the ugly, broad ditch) are clear, the logic of the claim is not. No knowledge, save (possibly) some a priori knowledge such as the axioms of logic and mathematics or tautologies, is absolute. In an era in which we find that the quest for absolute certainty has failed, the naive opposition between the absoluteness of faith and the conditionedness of historical knowledge is no longer an axiom we can accept. As Harvey put it, "The real issue, then, is not whether faith is independent of all historical criticism but whether Christian faith requires certain specific historical assertions that, in the nature of the case, are dubious or not justified. But if this is the issue, one must examine such assertions piecemeal" (1968, 249). All knowledge is conditioned, historical, and local, even if it is knowledge of what is unconditioned, beyond time and beyond space. While there may be distinctions to be drawn between faith and knowledge or between metaphysical and empirical claims, the *axiom of probability* does not capture such a distinction, but postulates a total separation.

Harvey also questioned the hard distinction between the symbols of faith and historical understandings: "But . . . is this another of those false and artificial distinctions? What if symbol and event, timeless truth and history, are not strict alternatives?" (1968, 252). Even faith is not absolute in the sense this axiom requires. However it may be generated, our faith is contingent. Christians believe that faith is a gift of God. There is no "necessity" in that gift. God freely bestows the gift of faith (on some or all—a debate that need not concern us here). Moreover, the convictions in which we express that faith are also at least as contingent because of the language we express them in. This is not to claim that language is an arbitrary system of signifiers, but only that languages are particular and conventional, not universal and necessary. For present purposes, we can simply set aside this axiom not only as dubious but also as no longer germane to the issues, if it ever was. While faith and knowledge (notice how this dichotomy is constructed at a high level of abstraction) may be contingent and/or probable in different ways, the assumption that faith could somehow be expressed in absolutely true or necessarily true propositions which underlies this dichotomy is not tenable. Chapters six and seven explore this issue further.

The second axiom, an *axiom of correlation*, is that there are "interactions between all phenomena in historical life. *They are the ontological foundation* . . . for the connections between cause and effect which apply everywhere" (Moltmann 1996, 78; italics mine). Another way of putting this is that historical events are caused by and only by other historical events. The third axiom, an *axiom of analogy*, is that the way events occurred in the past are analogous to the way they occur in the present. This axiom is based on the "homogeneity of all historical happening"

(Moltmann 1996, 78). That is, an event that does not proceed according to the ordinary, natural laws of cause and effect that we understand to be operative is not one that we can understand or accept as historical.

The axioms of correlation and analogy are two sides of the same coin. The former is presented as an ontological foundation; the latter as an epistemological claim based on that foundation. To accept the axiom of analogy is to accept the axiom of correlation. Ontological correlation makes analogical thinking possible in historical analysis and social science investigations. If the past were not like the present, how could we think about it? Analogical thinking in history makes ontological correlations visible. If we could not think in such analogical terms, how could we see the real connections between events? These axioms allegedly state the conditions that make possible historical investigations. It is only because of correlation and analogy, a thinker in this tradition would say, that we have any possibility of understanding the past or predicting the future. For example, a thinker in this tradition would have to claim that an increase in unemployment and an increase in domestic violence and theft in a geographical region makes it possible to surface an ontological correlation between them, to understand the effects of social policies which increase unemployment, and to make actuarial calculations and set insurance rates—commercialized uses of history and social science.

Rudolf Bultmann accepted the linked Troeltschian principles of analogy and correlation. He wrote that "modern science does not believe that the course of nature can be interrupted or, so to speak, perforated, by supernatural powers" (1958, 15). By analogy, such interruptions could happen neither in the present nor in the past. Bultmann simply rephrases the axiom of correlation; he proceeds in his own work by the axiom of analogy. Roger Haight explicitly accepted the principle of analogy as intertwined with the axiom of correlation: "A positive statement of the principle [of analogy] is that one must understand historical events *within a unified ontological framework*" (1999, 127; italics mine). With specific reference to historical research on Jesus, Haight acknowledged the linkage of correlation and analogy: "The majority of the portraits of the historical Jesus in fact presuppose and are constructed on the basis of naturalist assumptions and the principle of analogy" (1999, 39). Haight explicated this assumption in noting that "one should ordinarily not expect to have happened in the past what is presumed or proven to be impossible today" (1999, 127). Haight thus accepted both the epistemic principle of analogy and its ontological foundation in the principle of correlation. These theologians, two German Lutherans and one North American Catholic, represent the pattern of this Troeltschian tradition in historical theology.

The question, however, is whether this approach to the philosophical foundations of history and history's relationship to theology is sound. This approach is clearly exemplified in the axioms of correlation and analogy common to Troeltsch, Bultmann, Moltmann, and Haight. But I will argue that the approach is not sound. The postmodern suspicion of ontology undermines it; historical methodology does not support it; and analysis shows that it misplaces history as a practice and as a discipline.

First, if postmodern theory has taught us anything, it is that ontological foundations are profoundly suspect. Each of the theologians cited here—Troeltsch, Bultmann, Moltmann, Haight—accepted the "ontological foundation" of the principle of analogy. But on what grounds can we warrant that ontological claim? For as we showed above, accepting a presumption, a rule that guides a practice, does not warrant accepting that presumption as a true assumption. Is this not merely a prejudice, as Wolfhart Pannenberg put it, in favor of one specific metaphysics, a metaphysics based on a mechanistic worldview that is clearly "obsolete" (1996, 64, 65)? This axiom, in fact, gives this "ontological foundation" or the "prejudices" of modernity a veto over any claim about the past. But this veto is suspiciously self-serving, for those who invoke it also accept the "modern worldview" as the only possible or most reasonable one.

Moreover, this assumption begs the question. It assumes that "historical" means three things interchangeably: "actual events in the past," "events produced by natural causes," and "events in principle recoverable by historical investigation." However Mary, the mother of Jesus, became pregnant with Jesus, it was through another's agency. Whatever act brought on her pregnancy was, in some sense, a historical event. Yet no historical investigation can recover the agent who performed the act: whether an angel announced it to her as God's act, Joseph had intercourse with her, a Roman soldier raped, seduced, or paid her, or some other agent was involved. Historians may well presume that the pregnancy was brought about by natural causes, even if they cannot say who the agents were. But some actual events are no longer historically recoverable, and some agents may not be visible to the eyes of historians.

Second, historians have attacked this sort of principle. Gertrude Himmelfarb approvingly cites an article of Carl Degler to make the point that even less grand axioms than those proposed here are hardly indefeasible. Himmelfarb wrote:

> The historian, he [Degler] wrote, is guided less by "covering laws" that are presumed to be true in all times and places than by "participant-sources"—that is, contemporary evidence. Thus the historian might think it plausible that the American Revolution was caused by high taxes or the navigation laws, but if he finds no evidence for that in the contemporary literature he has to abandon the thesis; conversely if he finds other reasons given at the time he has to take them seriously, however strange they may seem to him. "The careful historian," Degler concluded, "tries to think as his subjects did, and within their system of values." (Himmelfarb 1987, 30)

Himmelfarb does not imply that one's sources taken at face value are thus reliable evidence or that one cannot also find in the historical record evidence for causal forces that contemporaries might not have recognized. But far more important for historians than "laws" or "axioms" is the particular evidence that can be gleaned from the texts and monuments from the past.

A similar point regarding religious history was made by William A. Clebsch. That most contemporary historians do not experience encounters with deities does not "alter the . . . fact that deities and salvations have been central to past actuality" (1979, 4). Clebsch went on to note that no "available *historical* method can distinguish the way men and women personally and socially understood their universe from the way their universe actually was then and there" (1979, 4). Whatever people in other times and places experienced and gave witness to—unless they were deluded or lying—is the way things were for them then and there. "[A] license to rule out, as illusion or mere apprehension, everything testified to which lies outside the historians' own experience would collapse [historians'] narratives into little more than autobiography" (1979, 4). Clebsch concludes that "critical history issues no warrant for changing what happened into an apprehension of what happened" (1979, 5).

"Critical history" cannot ordinarily warrant *on historical grounds* the redescription of what the witnesses testify was an act of God as "really" some other event caused by some other agent. While the use of sociological and psychological warrants in historical work is a vexing question (as we shall see in chapter eight), using such warrants to reduce their universe to a purely naturalistic one, like that of "modernity," is unwarranted. The fact that their universe is not our universe does not license us to say that they were deluded and that we have it straight. Himmelfarb, Degler, and Clebsch show that these are not *absolutes* for historical work, but defeasible *presumptions*. Like judges and lawyers who presume innocence of the accused in criminal trials, historians can presume that the past is like the future, that the same physical laws were operative then as now. But that presumption is defeasible. And when it comes to psychological and social patterns, that presumption becomes more fragile—not everyone feels as we do, responds as we do to events, or does things the way we do. To *presume* that the world was for them much like it is for us and that they did feel, respond, and act as we do may be legitimate as a rule for historical inquiry. But one needs further warrants to transform that presumption into an *assumption*, especially if their world is strange to us and if their feelings, responses, and actions seem "odd" to contemporary people. And to do so is not the task of a historian.

Of course, we may make a philosophical *argument* for our ontology over that of our predecessors, for our symbolic approach as intrinsically philosophically superior to theirs, or for our having good reason to think them deluded. We may reasonably prefer a scientific view that is incompatible with a flat earth and a domed sky. Yet those are not properly *historical* arguments or preferences, but metaphysical, theological, or practical ones that go far beyond the discipline of history. Those who reduce, for example, the New Testament narratives of the resurrection to code for something else or to illusions all too often assume modern ontology without argument. One can certainly operate with naturalistic presumptions, and historians normally do so. One can refuse to allow non-natural agents to be construed as agents in historical discourse, and historians properly and normally do so. However, as I shall argue below, such presumptions are certainly not absolutes.

Here we can again highlight the importance of Van Harvey's work. The present criticisms of the Troeltschian tradition are influenced by his own critiques. But as he turns to the "morality of knowledge" of the historian, he shows the problems with this approach to "the" problem of faith and history. He writes:

> The real issue is not whether history can be objective or a science but whether, in particular cases, diverse kinds of claims can achieve an appropriate and relevant justification. Just as we do not ask in a sweeping fashion whether legal judgments can be objective or not but attend to the more productive task of sorting out those that are adjudicable, so, too, we ought to foresake the wholesale questions about history and attend to the retail standards by which we can realistically hope to measure historical claims. (Harvey 1968, 55)

Of course we *can* sometimes question whether our legal system has become so degenerate that it can no longer dispense justice. And we *can* ask whether historians' practices have degenerated into unreliability or whether accounts of them are distorted. But that is a different practice. Such investigations require meticulous analysis and deconstructive work, not building metaphysical foundations to "explain" the conditions of the possibility of doing history.

Third, these axioms misplace history as a practice and a discipline. Historian Carlo Ginzburg points out that history deals with individual "cases, situations, and documents, precisely *because they are individual*" (1989, 106; italics in original). History is not a "Galilean science," because science deals with the repeatable and the quantifiable, while history, specifically as a humanistic social science, deals with unique, unquantifiable acts and events. This is not to deny the possibility of comparisons or generalizations, but only to assert that these are done *ad hoc*, not systematically. Making comparisons does not require analogy or correlation, but only two (or more) items and a property for comparison ("Jill is taller than John"; "Contemporary America has a higher literacy rate than Rome of the Silver Age"; "Gabriel is the same angel for Christians as Jibrîl is for Muslims"). Warranting the comparison requires showing the accuracy and relevance of the comparison, and an argument to support the claim. The Troeltschian axioms of correlation and analogy treat history as if it were a Galilean science or a subsidiary of the hard sciences. But by its nature, history is not such a science.

Ginzburg more generally opposes the hard division between the rational and the irrational. His basis for this is not a neo-Nietzschean denial of connections between historical constructions and what they represent (as some deconstructionists or other postmodern thinkers do). Ginzburg is not against construing history as representing what happened. Rather, he questions the opposition between those who think that historical claims require "proof" and those who think that historical claims are merely one more rhetorical trope. For Ginzburg, what is *in* the text is also *outside* the text, but we need to "discover it, and make it talk" (1999, 23). For Ginzburg, historical work does not presume an ontological foundation; its presumptions may be overturned in specific investigations, as the presumption of innocence is overcome in many criminal trials. These axioms are only rules of thumb necessary for engaging in the practice of doing history, descriptions of the common sense of the discipline of history, not philosophical foundations of the practice or metaphysical necessities.

Moreover, social historians generally do not focus on whether specific events actually happened, just as intellectual historians do not focus on whether the ideas transmitted through time are true ideas. This is not to claim that historians do *not* sometimes try to find out "what really happened," but for crucial events, such as Caesar's crossing the Rubicon, the angel Jibrîl's dictating to Muhammad the eternal written word of God, Truman's understanding of what he was doing when he authorized the use of atomic weapons in 1945, claims about the "facts" of "what actually happened" and what specific agents actually intended to be doing seem nearly impossible to warrant to a degree that can claim broad assent. Qualifying the claims (e.g., "Muhammad *said* he heard . . .") or stating them vaguely enough ("Truman ordered . . .") may lead to general assent to vague assertions, but one doesn't need the work of critical historians for that. The significance of these events is not so much the agents' acts or intentions, but the events, movements, or beliefs that followed the events.

Indeed, attempts to verify historically which particular events or agents triggered other historically significant events, beliefs, or movements may not only be insignificant, but answering entirely the wrong question. In an argument against the hard distinction between "rhetoric" and "proof" in historical work, Carlo Ginzburg notes that some events *that never took place* are of great historical importance. For example, the "Great Fear of 1789" in France of "phantomlike bandits in support of an alleged 'aristocratic conspiracy'" was about non-existent bandits. The belief that the kings of France and England could cure scrofula with a touch was about a power the royalty didn't have. "The historical relevance of such events, which never took place, is based on their symbolic effectiveness: that is, on the way in which they were perceived by a multitude of anonymous individuals" (1994, 293). That the events were believed to happen is far more historically important than whether the events happened at all.

Typically, historians find important and interesting the ways in which practices and ideas have spread and the ways in which social, economic, and political constellations have changed. For example, social historians may not be interested in whether the resurrection of Jesus occurred or whether it can be "validated" by historical work. The fact that people believed in the resurrection, the analysis of the conditions under which that belief flourished among groups in the Greco-Roman world, the ways in which the notion of resurrection was connected with the idea of the immortality of the soul, and the significance of all of these for the early Christian movements are key items in their story.

Given these three points, then, we can say that the problem with this understanding of the philosophical foundations of history and the relationship of history to theology is that it raises the defeasible rules of thumb by which historians operate to the level of indefeasible metaphysical principles. These metaphysical principles turn out to be nothing other than the common sense of modern scientific investigations. This common sense has no place for an act of God. When these practical principles of modern common sense or "the discipline of history" are raised to metaphysical principles, the consequences for faith and for theology are profoundly unsatisfactory.

Pannenberg highlights the results of such philosophical canonizations. He argues that a "negative judgment on the bodily resurrection of Jesus as having occurred in historical fact is *not a result* of the historical critical examination of the Biblical Easter tradition, *but a postulate* that precedes any such examination" (1996, 64). Methodologically, historians presume that supernatural entities do not act in history. However, this does not warrant the reductionist claim that actions attributed to supernatural entities must always and everywhere be reduced to historical claims about natural agents because of an indefeasible principle that supernatural agents cannot be said to act in history. The point is that "the historian, as historian, is never able to claim that a given event is supernaturally caused. For an historian to argue that a given event was a miracle, he would have to have some public grounds for claiming that only a supernatural power could have caused it. But historians cannot know this . . ." (Harvey 2000, 93)." This agnosticism is not the result of historians' "presuppositions," but is the result of the way in which historians warrant historical claims.

Like all presumptions of practices, such as the presumption of innocence in criminal trials in this country, the results of engaging in the practice can bear a burden of proof against the presumption. Despite the presumption of innocence, juries find defendants in criminal cases guilty. In the end, as historians, we may want to say that we have no acceptable natural explanation of some events or that multiple explanations are available but not demonstrable in and of themselves. A person working as a historian might remain agnostic about the causes of those events. That does not mean that that person, when she is not wearing the historian's mantle, must remain agnostic.

If we allow historians' rules of thumbs to be raised to metaphysical principles, then we would have to find that historians would be inconsistent at least or irrational at worst to go beyond what their methodological presumptions allowed. William James wittily illustrated the problems of allowing the principles of one practice to overflow into all of life:

> [J]ust as a man who in a company of gentlemen made no advances, asked a warrant for every concession, and believed no one's word without proof, would cut himself off by such churlishness from all the social rewards that a more trusting spirit would earn,—so here, one who should shut himself up in snarling logicality and try to make the gods extort his recognition willy-nilly, or not get it at all, might cut himself off forever from his only opportunity of making the gods' acquaintance. (James 1956, 28)

Besides having such potentially damning consequences, the naturalistic thesis that all events must have natural and only natural causes requires a metaphysical argument about the fictional status of all supernatural agents or a theological argument for the complete separation of historical from religious "facts." More often, our methodological naturalism is simply unquestioned because it "works," especially in the scientific realm. It "works" in the historical realm: we simply don't believe, on naturalistic grounds, that the king's touch *can* heal scrofula or that witches' spells work even if we do believe that people's beliefs about "king's touches" and "witches" had a profound social impact—and in the latter case, such spells may have indeed come to work because people believed in them.

Even if such arguments for radical naturalism could be sustained, these arguments are not ones that historians can give *qua* historians, and, for the most part, they fail to focus on the sorts of questions that are amenable to answers developed by using historical methodologies. In sum, the theologians considered here assume a connection between the axiom of correlation and the axiom of analogy. I maintain that that assumption is not warranted. Analogy is a procedural presumption of historical method, sometimes nearly certain, sometimes fragile. But analogy does not require an ontological correlation as its basis. Moreover, that procedural presumption of analogy may be defeated; we may, upon investigation, find that the universe of the past is not ours, that it is a place stranger than we know.

The real problem is this: For the Troeltschian tradition, "correlation" and "analogy" are two sides of the same coin. Since the world we live in now is dominated by modern science, so must our account of the past be analogously dominated by modern science. But modern science is, as a discipline, atheistic or agnostic—God can have no role in it. Hence, we are committed to atheism or agnosticism. But since these are principles, not presumptions, we are committed in principle to atheism or agnosticism. Since these are ontological principles, this implies that those in the past who "went against" such principles must be wrong.

But this implication is not necessary. That there is in some cases a profound disanalogy between the historical subjects' universe and the historical investigators' universe does not mean our ontology is correct and theirs wrong. Historically, all we can say is that this is the way the world was for them. The immediate move to reductionism—that they were deluded, lying, mistaken, inaccurate, or inadequate in their reports—is another issue and requires a separate scientific or metaphysical or theological argument. While the axiom of analogy may be a good presumption of historical practice, especially of social and intellectual history, it can be defeated within the practices of history (as all good rules of thumb can be overturned occasionally), and its ontological foundation is at least superfluous, at most a canonized modern prejudice.

Given the problems with the first three axioms, Moltmann's fourth axiom also fails. The fourth axiom is that because of the principles of probability, correlation, and analogy, we cannot talk about the activity of a transcendent God in history. History is made by human beings, not by supernatural beings. Hence, the supernatural is precluded from inclusion in history. Moltmann here makes explicit the transubstantiation of procedural principles into metaphysical claims.

As the previous axioms are undermined, this one is as well. First, Moltmann attributes this axiom to Troeltsch. Troeltsch, however, does not make this fourth axiom explicit in the article Moltmann cites. Given that Troeltsch was *distinguishing* historical from theological methodologies, talk of God's act in history would be a theological claim, not a properly historical claim. For Troeltsch, it was not so much a question of fact or truth but of trying to clean up muddy disciplinary boundaries. Second, Moltmann seems, as does Bultmann, to rule out the possibility of such assertions on any grounds. Historians may presume in their work that divine agents have not acted in history, but it is not proper for them to say that that presumption cannot be overturned in a particular investigation. While as a historian I may be able to say that an event, such as the curing of a withered hand or the remission of an intractable metastatic cancer, may be inexplicable, given what we know presently, as a historian I can finally rule out neither a claim that a medical explanation might be available in the future nor a claim that this was an effect of an act of God. I may be able to warrant on historical grounds a claim that the witness was lying or deluded or that the alleged event did not take place as narrated.

Beyond the Troeltschian Tradition

Today we can see that philosophers' accounts of what historians do is the major source of the problem of history. Philosophers think that history needs a foundation if it is to be a legitimate academic discipline. Hence, they seek to formulate the conditions for the possibility of doing history. But historians' work does not need foundational rules to defend history as a real discipline. Arnold I. Davidson highlights the fact that the best historical work is a matter of disciplined imagination and analysis:

> Evidence is mediated by codes, and an adequate historiography must attend to the heterogeneous procedures by which we encode evidence. . . . We must understand the processes of encoding, of different kinds of evidential distortion, in order to interpret the evidence, to assess its reliability or unreliability, to know what it is evidence *of.* Codes that seemed impenetrable can eventually be deciphered, and new evidence, encoded in new ways can shed light on old evidence, changing our interpretations of codes we had believed were unambiguous. . . . There is no formalizable set of rules that tells us how to decipher historical evidence . . . but there are truly great historical works whose power partly resides in the ability of a historian to read the evidence, to show us how to enter into the codes of evidence in order to see *what* the evidence *is,* what it shows us about the phenomena we are interested in, what the phenomena are. (Davidson 1994, 312, 313).

As with every practice, rules or axioms cannot capture all the ways to engage in the practice.

The modern problem of history has been perpetuated by theologians and others who have accepted the Troeltschian axioms. However, such construal of the problem of history as a single sort of problem is unwarranted. The literary geography of the materials examined and the claims made in those texts prohibit reducing the problems to one, that of the saga. The dualist version of the problem is a historical construct that is certainly not necessary, and, I have argued, not useful. The acceptance of the Troeltschian problematic, very common among theologians, is no longer tenable; indeed, it was not tenable after Harvey's important, but too much neglected, work.

In chapters two through four I have shown that the construct of the dualistic problematic is not necessary. There is good reason to believe that this problematic *can* be overcome. The next chapter argues that each pattern for construing this dualism in modern theology leads to untenable positions. It shows that not only *can* this dualistic problematic be challenged but it *should* be overcome.

CHAPTER 5

History Undermining Belief

Christianity has nothing to fear from scholarship.
Scholars may be a different matter.
—James D. G. Dunn

As the previous chapters have suggested, the results of historical investigation have tended to undermine religious convictions for over two centuries. As H. Richard Niebuhr put it, "History always seems to lead to doubt rather than to faith" (1960, xx). If one takes the naturalistic presumptions of history as atheistic assumptions for one's theology or philosophy of history, one easily accepts this undermining: history leads not only to doubt but to disbelief. As I noted in chapters two and four, however, we need to attend to the differing forms of historical narrative and the differences between presumptions and assumptions or assertions. When we do so, the plot thickens. The relationships between history and doubt or disbelief or belief or theology can be seen differently in light of these analyses.

A careful examination of the works of Richard L. Rubenstein and Marcus Borg reveals insights we can and must learn from them, even though some construe them as undermining traditional religious belief by appeals to history. Examining some moves in their arguments shows that alternative paths may be not only possible but also as plausible as their own approaches. Rubenstein works on the *saga* of Judaism and Borg works on the *gospel* of Jesus preserved by Christians. I need to make two caveats before I begin.

First, I use these authors because they articulate with clarity attitudes that a number of those who have gone beyond traditional belief hold, but do not explore seriously. Rubenstein and Borg have thoughtfully both explored traditional belief and have clearly articulated reasons for moving to new understandings. They have also made significant contributions in their understandings of the relationship of historical understanding to religious faith. Unfortunately, their positions have sometimes been more caricatured than characterized: Rubenstein was facilely dismissed as a radical "death of God" theologian in the mid-1960s, and Borg as the barnstorming entrepreneur who led the publicity-happy Jesus seminar in the late 1990s. Each has much more to offer than those caricatures suggest.

Here I examine only one issue in their works: the problem of history as they each evince it. I am not including a Muslim author simply because the literary form of the Qur'an, the narratives supporting its "deliverance" to Muhammad, and the traditional ways of dealing with evils and reversals to Islam's fortunes have made it difficult for Muslim scholars—unlike Jewish and Christian scholars—to have the sort of problem of history analyzed in this chapter. Madigan has argued that the Qur'an's own self-understanding allows the text of the Qur'an to be a representation (codex) of what God has said, not the very text God dictated. If this is correct, it opens the way for understanding the Qur'an more critically even within Islam. Some Muslin scholars have attempted a rapprochement with modernity in general to help insure the viability of Muslim traditions in the modern world. Nonetheless, it is not clear that Muslim scholars have had to deal with the kinds of challenges raised by believers and scholars in the Christian and Jewish traditions regarding the historicity of the sacred text (see Madigan 2001; Esposito 1988, 127-61).

Examining Rubenstein's and Borg's work shows that their dichotomous understandings of the problem of history lead to further problems. I will argue that there are better approaches to the specific issues they raise. I am not aware of Muslim scholars—though there certainly may be some—for whom similar arguments could be made. In Elizabeth Johnson's felicitous phrase, I believe that their works on the problem of history are best regarded as cul-de-sacs—streets which we can enter, explore, and learn from, but not satisfying termini of our quest to understand and overcome the problem of history.

Second, we must make some distinctions that our authors—again, both influenced by the Troeltschian stream delineated in chapter four—do not make clearly. The key distinction is between "events" and "actions." It is not uncommon to collapse these two very different categories (see Harvey 1968, 229, for example). But they must be clearly distinguished. To surface these distinctions, I use an "ordinary language argument." This sort of argument notes the importance of what people ordinarily say when they are using their native language well. Such an argument is not necessarily decisive, a point recognized by its leading proponent, John L. Austin: "Certainly, then, ordinary language is *not* the last word: in principle it can everywhere be supplemented and improved upon and superseded. Only remember, it *is* the *first* word" (Austin 1961, 133; italics original). Ordinary language analysis can help us make useful distinctions.

In general, events *occur* but agents *perform* actions. For us, the rising of the sun is a daily event. For ancient Romans, the rising of the sun was the act of the sun-god, Phoebus, driving his chariot across the dome of the sky. To say that an event happened is not to say that an agent performed it. Sometimes to speak of events is to ignore, obscure, or find irrelevant any sense of agency. For instance, to read a communique that begins, "It was decided today that . . ." makes one wonder who made the decision communicated. The passive voice of bureaucratic prose often intentionally obscures who was the agent making the decision by making the decision appear to be an event, not an act.

Consider the following fictional dialogue:

Dad: "Jamie, why did you hit your sister?"
Jamie: "I didn't mean to, dad. I was just swinging my arm and she ran into it."

What Jamie is doing here—whether telling the truth or not—is trying to *deflect* the question about an *action* dad presumes she performed. She attempts to get him to think of her behavior as an accident, an *event* for which she cannot be held responsible as an agent—or, possibly, to get him to hold her accountable only for a clumsy act or a careless one, rather a malicious, teasing, or bullying act. If "hitting her sister" is construed as an event, she's off the hook. If it is construed as a careless act, she's in for an admonition. If it is construed as bullying, more severe strictures may well be forthcoming. How Dad construes her behavior, as event or act, makes a difference. And if it is construed as an act, what type of act it is also makes a difference.

Moreover, if we see someone engaging in behavior we don't understand, we ask what they are doing:

Herbert: "Jean, why are you waving your arm like a fool at the traffic?"
Jean: "What? Why, I'm trying to catch Fred's attention; he's supposed to pick me up."

What Jean has done—whether truthfully or not—is to give an account of this behavior to Herbert by telling him the purpose or intention of the behavior. She thus lets him know that the behavior was not a random or incidental *event* caused by a seizure or performed randomly, but was her *act*. She also identifies the act she was performing: trying to get Fred's attention.

The point of these two questions and responses is to show how we ordinarily distinguish events from actions. I do not want to argue here that we ought to limit our understanding of agency to human agency or to intentional agency. Sometimes we take actions for which we are held accountable even if we didn't explicitly intend them, such as some automobile accidents or Jamie's clumsy waving (if that's what it was). However, our ordinary "default" understanding of an action is that an act is intentional. If we don't understand why someone did something, we try to find out "why" or "to what purpose" he or she "did" it. In doing so, we typically *presume* that her or his action was intentional, even if we are not clear on what the intentions were.

This understanding of human action was developed by philosopher G. E. M. Anscombe. She argued there is no real difference between an "intentional action" and an "action." An intentional action is not a special kind of action. Rather, to say that some act is really unintentional is to say that the question "Why did you or she or he or they do that?" is not applicable to a specific action under consideration (Anscombe 1957, 28), for it isn't an *action* at all, but a response or an event or an accident or a mistake.

In sum, if someone tells us what the purpose of her or his action was, the response *ipso facto* validates our presumption that this was an *action* because it acknowledges that the act was intentional or purposeful, even if we doubt the veracity of the report of the intention. If someone responds that she or he really didn't intend anything by the behavior in question, then that person is trying to divert or deflect our questions about motive or purpose and, in so doing, challenges our presumption that the occurrence was an *action*. That person is claiming that what happened was an *accident* or an *event* or an *occurrence*; it was not a fully "human act," as some scholastics might put it; while it was an *actus humani* it was not an *actus humanus*.

Another way of putting this matter is to use an analogy from biology. Often we (not unreasonably) think of "acts" as constituting a species of "events." But if Anscombe and others are right, it is better to construe "acts" and "events" as two species within a genus we could dub "occurrences." Other species in the genus might include "accidents" and "processes." In many contexts, it does no harm to say that acts are events. And some occurrences may seem events in one context or from one perspective, and acts in another context or from a different perspective. But in some contexts, failure to distinguish acts from other occurrences, including events, obscures significant differences.

The significance of this distinction for the present context can be illustrated by considering the resurrection of Jesus. The testimony at the root of the Christian tradition does not claim that an event has occurred, but that God has acted. The resurrection is *not* merely an event. It is fundamentally, and more significantly, an action. The agent is God. The *result* of the action is that Jesus is exalted and glorified. If the occurrence of the resurrection is a fact, that fact does *not* report or represent merely *an event that occurred*, but an *act of God* that brought about a number of events, such as various appearances, a renewed community of disciples, and maybe even an empty tomb. To construe the resurrection as an "event," as theologians all too often do, is to obscure, ignore, or find irrelevant the agent who performed the (alleged) act as much as the passive prose of the bureaucratic announcement does. To talk of the "resurrection event" is imprecise enough to be as problematical as bureaucratic prose or as Jamie might well be in her deflecting of Dad's real question in the sample dialogue above.

One possible way of clarifying the distinction between resurrection-as-event and resurrection-as-God's-act is to use H. Richard Niebuhr's distinction of outer and inner history. In inner history, the history of our life together as a community (which is primary), we call the resurrection an act of God, while from the perspective of outer history, they recognize this event as significant in world history, even if God did not act (see Niebuhr 1960, 44-50). Here there seems to be an example of how the same occurrence can look like an event from one perspective and an act from a different perspective.

The Niebuhrian distinction, however, will not hold up under scrutiny. Inner history is too prone to special pleading, and outer historical narratives are too various for a dichotomous resolution to the problem of history. Moreover, while we can recognize some utterances as inner historical in texture, and others as outer historical, it is not clear either how they can or should be related or, in many instances, distinguished. While the distinction has some initial plausibility, this way of solving the problem of history is, finally, too facile (also see Harvey 1968, 234-42 and Tilley 1985, 148-50). This path is a cul-de-sac.

This event—whether or not the act of God in and through the resurrection actually occurred (and remember the significance of non-occurring events from the last chapter)—clearly had an impact on human history. It was a key factor in the launching of Christianity and its success. The key issue is not whether a specific event occurred. Whatever happened at Easter, Christianity did spread like wildfire and become the dominant tradition in the Roman Empire in less than four hundred years. Whether the risen Lord appeared to this or that person or whether the tomb was empty is irrelevant to the social history of the empire and of Christianity. Historians *qua* historians are finally less interested in uncovering whether that event or act occurred than in explaining the emergence of the Christian tradition as dominant in the West.

But whether God *acted* is clearly a different matter. *That* is of interest, if not to social historians, then to theologians. Historians properly write of human actions and events. They may even attempt to infer what the agents' intentions were in performing specific acts. But while events are within their scope, acts of God are beyond the pale of properly historical research. Acts may trigger events; acts of God, believers claim, may trigger truly important events. Believers construe some events as the result of acts of God. But to reduce an act to an event is to change profoundly its significance, to rule out any inferences about intentions, and even to alter its "logical status," as Anscombe might say. Yet one might continue to believe that God acted even though one no longer accepts some specific events as having occurred—a point we shall explore further in chapter seven, and, in an oddly similar way, in a non-religious historians' dispute noted in chapter eight.

To take what believers find an act of God as an event may be acceptable for social historians of Judaism, Christianity, or Islam. But is it appropriate for theologians who can distinguish events that occur from acts that are performed? I would argue, no. Divine acts may be beyond the pale of history, but not of theology. Theologians who neglect the difference reduce something that God did to something that happened. They obscure the claim to divine agency.

Richard L. Rubenstein:
Undermining the God of History

Richard Rubenstein has been called a "death of God" theologian. This is not strictly accurate. He has consistently adhered to a distinction he made in an early essay: "It is more precise to assert that *we live in the time of the death of God* than to declare 'God is dead.' The death of God is a cultural fact. We shall never know whether it is more than that" (1966, 246). Belief in God has waned in our era. For some Jews and Christians, it was the understanding of the magnitude of the Holocaust or *Shoah* that rendered belief in God incredible. Although survivor narratives circulated and the Nuremberg trials after World War II found many leading Nazis guilty of war crimes, a decade and a half passed before the enormity of the horror of man-made mass death became a real cultural factor, at least in the United States. Raul Hilberg's 1961 book, *The Destruction of the European Jews,* chronicled the enormity of this bureaucratic exercise of mass murder. No longer could the Nazis' final solution be ignored. For others, the acids of Enlightenment rationalism, cultural indifference, or personal traumas have helped dissolve belief. However strong religious belief may be among some certain groups, Europeans and North Americans for the most part no longer live in an age of faith.

Rubenstein introduced the *Shoah,* the destruction of the Jewish people during the Nazi regime in Germany, into theological discourse. Before his essays of the early 1960s—incorporated in the first edition of *After Auschwitz* (1966)—Jewish and Christian theologians had maintained silence about the *Shoah.* Since his work, theologians cannot ignore the *Shoah.* As one younger scholar put it, "Rubenstein was one of the first Jewish theologians to respond to this literature [on the history of the German attempts to exterminate the Jews], practically inventing post-Holocaust theology *de novo* in 1966 with the publication of *After Auschwitz*" (Braiterman 1998, 8).

The challenge of the *Shoah* to the God of history, the God of election and covenant, is obvious. Where was God during the Holocaust? How could the Lord of history allow such an abomination? Does this not destroy faith in any covenant and any God who made a covenant? Or is this part of God's lordship? As Rubenstein put it, "In the aftermath of the *Shoah*, the question whether God, as traditionally understood in biblical and rabbinic Judaism, was the ultimate Actor in the catastrophic events is inescapable for religious Jews" (1992a, 157). In an investigation of the significance of what we shall call in chapter ten the "social experience" of the European (and worldwide) Jewish community, Rubenstein sought to understand God's place in that experience.

On August 17, 1961, Dean Heinrich Grüber affirmed to Rubenstein the position that the German Evangelical Church meeting in Darmstadt had taken in 1948: "that the Holocaust was a divine punishment visited upon the Jews" (Rubenstein 1992a, 169). As Nebuchadnezzar had been God's rod in the sixth century B.C.E., so was Hitler God's rod in the twentieth century C.E. Some Jews (Rubenstein 1992a, 159-63) and some Christians came to see the *Shoah* as God's act of chastisement for Jewish infidelity to the covenant.

Rubenstein was confronted with a dilemma: "*One can either affirm the innocence of Israel or the justice of God at Auschwitz*" (1992a, 171; italics original). If Jews accept the traditional doctrines of election and covenant, then "*we will leave ourselves open to the theology expressed not only by Dean Grüber but also by some of this century's leading Orthodox Jewish thinkers: because the Jews are God's Chosen People, yet failed to keep God's Law, God sent Hitler to punish them*" (Rubenstein 1992a, 13; italics original). Rubenstein could not accept the extermination of six million Jews as the result of an act of divine justice. That experience of the Jewish community would be, bluntly, desecrated by such a claim. He thus was forced to reject the principle that God was a God of history.

Rubenstein sought to contribute to the demythologizing (1992a, 21 *et passim*) of Jewish theology. That God acts in history is a myth unmasked by the course of history. Better to say that "omnipotent Nothingness is Lord of All Creation" (Rubenstein 1966, 225; 1992a, 305). Better to worship a God of nature. Initially Rubenstein advocated a sort of "Jewish paganism" (1992a, xiii; 1966, 123-29) as the way Jews could believe in God. Later, influenced by a Hegelian pantheism and Eastern religious traditions, Rubenstein found the best metaphor to be that "God is the ocean and we the waves" (1992a, 299). But finding that the events of history reveal no "progress" worth the name, however much more gadgetry we have than our ancestors, Rubenstein rejected Hegel's belief that history is progressing to a goal. Rubenstein rather suggested that the creation "may be a vast cosmic detour originating in the Nothingness of God and ultimately returning to God's Nothingness" (1992a, 303). He finds a precursor of this view in the Jewish mystical tradition of Lurianic Kabbalism, in which creation is the exile of part of God from God (1992a, 303-4).

Rubenstein explained his position as a form of an "esoteric" rather than "exoteric" tradition in Judaism. Describing a meeting with the late Swami Muktananda of Ganeshpuri at an American ashram, he wrote:

> The very first thing the guru said to me was: "You mustn't believe in your own religion; I don't believe in mine. Religions are like the fences that hold young saplings erect. Without the fence the sapling could fall over. When it takes firm root and becomes a tree, the fence is no longer needed. However, most people never lose their need for the fence." (Rubenstein 1992a, 293)

The fence is the "exoteric" position. Mature trees develop different traditions. Because of the challenge the historical events of the *Shoah* create and created for belief in the God of history who had elected and made a covenant with the Jewish people and who would redeem the world as proclaimed in the "exoteric" tradition of Judaism, Rubenstein turned to an "esoteric" understanding of the God of the cosmos, immanent in the world, the ground, source and destiny of all there is, and who would reabsorb the diversity of the world as we know it into unity.

Rubenstein has been very forthcoming regarding the reasons for the evolution of his religious thought (1966, 47-58, 209-25; 1974; 1992a, 168-76, 293-306; 1993, 15-24). Indeed, the power in many of his works derives in part from his autobiographical reflections. Many admire and respect his arguments. Yet few seem to have found his positions so compelling as to accept his esoteric view for themselves. While stimulated by his work, his constructing of a "counter-history" or a "counter-tradition" within Jewish thought has not been entirely persuasive (Braiterman 1998, 105). While we should not ignore the questions he raises, should we find his answers more compelling than other ways of reworking the tradition? Although Braiterman, for example, finds that Rubenstein "never possessed the requisite textual familiarity and hermeneutical tools with which to become a truly strong misreader of Jewish tradition" (1998, 111), he recognizes that Rubenstein had an imposing influence and, in a blunt manner, raised the questions appropriate to his context. And *pace* Braiterman, we can see Rubenstein retrieving esoteric strands of the tradition in his later work. Yet, for different reasons, I also do not find Rubenstein's answers compelling.

First, according to Rubenstein, traditional Judaism believes that God is "the infinitely righteous, radically transcendent, and absolutely omnipotent Creator of all things. . . . He is the ultimate Author of all that has happened to the people of Israel, including the Holocaust" (1992a, 157). This understanding is one way of understanding God as all-powerful, omnipotent. It makes God the agent responsible for every event. Every event that occurs—at least as regards Israel and presumably as regards all that happens—is an act of God. Since every act that occurs either proximately or distantly affects the people of Israel, God should be seen as the author of all acts. Whatever events occur are divine acts. Philosophers have dubbed this understanding of omnipotence "omnificence" since God is the maker of all that is and author of all that occurs.

What Rubenstein calls "traditional Judaism" is an amalgam of saga and philosophy. In this amalgam, the saga of the Jewish people is understood to imply or require that certain philosophical elements be reliable. Specifically, God's power, as portrayed in the events that compose the saga, is taken to be, in philosophical terms, a certain sort of omnipotence. Rubenstein is right in noting that this saga, connected to the philosophical concept of omnipotence as "traditional Judaism" connects it, is a "myth," a story that creates a world—and that this world is no longer credible. If Enlightenment rationalism eclipsed the biblical narrative for Christian theologians (Frei), coming to grips with the *Shoah* undermined the myth of traditional Judaism.

Rubenstein's "traditional Judaism" treats God as omnificent. All power is God's, so all agency is God's. All events occur by and only by the power of God. Of course, the proposition "If God is omnipotent, then God is omnificent" is possibly true. It was held by some Muslim theologians, Baruch Spinoza, and possibly Friedrich Schleiermacher, among others (see Urban and Walton 1978, 106-11, 119-27, 192-200). Indeed, if God is "the ocean and we the waves," that proposition may even be tautological, necessarily true—whatever is done is done by God the ocean. But if God is omnificent, then it is very difficult to understand how any other "agent" could be responsible for any action. God has hardened not only the Pharaoh's heart (Exod. 7:3), but every heart! Although we may be called to account for our decisions, we are not in any serious sense responsible for our actions (Urban and Walton 1978, 202). Even Hitler would not be responsible for his actions. For Rubenstein, the myth of traditional Judaism fits with understanding God's omnipotence as omnificence.

Some have chosen to deny God's omnipotence in the face of radical evil (Kushner 1981), rather than deny the God of history. However, other courses are possible. There are other ways of creatively misreading the Jewish traditions (Braiterman 1998, 161-78). One does not have to amalgamate the saga with a specific philosophical conception of omnipotence—one that yields a myth that Rubenstein finds in severe need of demythologization. Indeed, many believers have not taken God's omnipotence to be absolute, that is, taken "omnipotence" to be identical to "omnificence." There are other metaphysical concepts about divine power that are compatible with the saga of Judaism

The most common qualification of God's omnipotence is to say that God's power is limited to the logically possible: Even God cannot make *p* and *not-p* both true. "Jack is bald and he is not bald" cannot be true without equivocating, and even God cannot act in such a way as to make that sentence true. To affirm that God could is not merely to live with a paradox but to affirm to be true a contradiction, a proposition which is necessarily false. Alvin Plantinga, in a series of articles and book-length essays, has shown that it is logically impossible for God to create free humans and bring "it about that they always freely do what is right" (Plantinga 1971, 110). In other words, "God creates all people free and God creates them to do what is right" can no more be true than "He is bald and not bald." God can create people free, but then they are responsible for their choices and deeds. God can create them to do what God wants and only what God wants (which would be "right" since God is all-good), but then they are not free and not responsible for their deeds. To affirm that God could make people freely do what is right is not merely to live with a paradox, but to affirm as true a proposition which is necessarily false. Plantinga has also shown that the amount of evil in the world is compatible with belief in God (see 1974, 7-64; 1979, 1-53). By implication, the real evil of the *Shoah* is not sufficient reason to abandon belief in the God of history.

So here is the dilemma: if humans were not free in a significant sense, then God is responsible for the Holocaust. Humans were not free in the relevant sense to do otherwise than what they did. If humans are free in a significant sense, then God may be responsible for creating them, but they are free and their choices and actions may well have been responsible for the Holocaust. They could have done otherwise. They didn't. It is possible that even an all-powerful God could not have stopped the *Shoah*.

That it is possible that God could not have stopped the *Shoah* does not explain why God did not do so. There are many speculative possibilities about why God did not intervene or did not do more or did not intervene sooner. But these are all speculations. What the (generic) free-will defense to the challenge of evil shows specifically is that we need not take the *Shoah* as authored by God as punishment for the Jewish people or for any other purpose unless we accept a philosophical account of God's power as omnificence. Rubenstein demythologizes one of the ways of understanding God's relationship to the *Shoah*. There are other ways to construe that relationship. Clearly, it is not necessary to take this specific path.

Second, we should not take this route. Rubenstein frequently wrote of the need to "demythologize" Jewish belief. This is partly due to his finding that "until the 1967 war, whenever Israel experienced *radical communal misfortune*, her traditional religious leaders almost always interpreted the event as divine punishment" (1992a, 162). Rubenstein has surveyed other interpretations with fair and balanced representations and insightful criticisms. Yet his critique of the work of Emil Fackenheim revealed a key component in Rubenstein's position:

> While in no sense rejecting the idea that the text of Scripture requires interpretation, *I am convinced that when one is confronted with doctrinal issues as fundamental as God's relation to Israel, the*

"plain meaning of Scripture" must be taken very seriously. If Scripture depicts God as demanding Israel's obedience on pain of dire punishment for disobedience, we cannot soften the intent of the text because we are embarrassed by its modern application, namely, that Hitler is to be seen as a modern Nebuchadnezzar. On the contrary, we are faced with a choice that can neither be evaded nor glossed over: *Either Scripture's account of the covenant is credible, or, however we understand God, Divinity is not the biblical God-who-acts-in-history-and-chooses-Israel* (Rubenstein 1992a, 178-79, italics original; compare Rubenstein and Roth 1987, 318).

But is that dichotomy so unavoidable? I think not.

Rubenstein himself utilized the historical thesis of George Mendenhall that argues on the basis of analyzing ancient Near Eastern texts for a very different account of the origins of the covenant than the one portrayed in the biblical text (1992a, 140-44; 1992b, 166-77). The covenant narratives are not literally true but symbolize the formation of a confederacy of disparate tribes under a new kind of high God, a high God whose worship demands that the tribal gods be abandoned (or seen as local, tribal names for the high God, YHWH). For Rubenstein, covenant and election function as powerful symbols in the social and political life of Christian and Jewish communities (1992a, 326). The idea of covenant was very functionally useful for the conquest or unification of the ancient land of Israel. But this gives us no good reason to accept the belief that there is a God of history who has made a covenant with people.

As Rubenstein acknowledged, many Jews and Christians, whose faith he respects, believe in the covenant. That is what made the concept effective. But people cannot believe what they believe not to be true. For belief in the covenant to remain effective, the people who believe in it must accept as true the fact that there is a covenant with God. But Rubenstein found that it is false (if he is not to accept that Hitler is a modern Nebuchadnezzar).

Yet he proposed a functional concept of covenant for resolving a terrible problem. In his view, the only way to bring peace between Israelis and Palestinians "is an institution similar to that which enabled the Hebrews to unite under God at Sinai, a binding basis for community between men and women who share little but mutual distrust and fear" (Rubenstein 1992a, 152). Yet he found also that there is no God of history under which diverse people could unite now as they did at Sinai in the past. Although he claimed that multiple religious traditions could co-exist and co-operate in the United States because they "bracket ultimate questions" (2001, 161), such bracketing seems an impossibility where the very land is under dispute. Even the originating documents of the United States paid, at minimum, lip service to being "one nation under God." This is hardly "bracketing."

The problem is this: Rubenstein is left with proposing a path to true peace through covenantal relations under what he considers to be a false claim. Rubenstein gets himself into this problematical situation because of his excessive literalism about the events portrayed in the biblical texts, his acceptance of omnificence, and his conflation of believing in the *acts* of God with believing the *events* as reported. It is clear that historical investigations, such as those by Mendenhall, Gottwald, and others, have changed scholarly perceptions of the covenantal events. It is true that Jews and Christians have had to rethink the terms of the covenant. But why would one think that the eternal covenant would be literally unchanging in its laws and not need renewal and revision in every generation? Why would one think that God's commanding voice must be either "a real or a metaphorical event" (Rubenstein 1992a, 181)? Is this not the same problem Harvey identified: "what if symbol and event . . . are not strict alternatives?" (Harvey 1968, 252). By presuming that God's voice had to be real or metaphorical, and finding that it could not be real, Rubenstein had to construe talk of God's voice as literally false.

The root problem is that Rubenstein reduced God's *acts* to the reality of specific *events* having occurred. Because Rubenstein takes all events to be divine acts, and thus collapses the difference between them, any finding that certain events occurred or did not occur means that God acted or did not. As I showed in the beginning of this chapter, reducing acts to events is a confusion.

Moreover, Rubenstein's language betrays this confusion. Events are not metaphorical or real. Reports or interpretations are metaphorical or real; events simply occur. To call events "real or metaphorical" indicates the error. To construe *any* event as an act of God is to use a language that goes beyond event language. Sometimes that language is metaphorical; sometimes it may be another trope; but the event is not metaphorical. We need to understand critically the events that constituted early Judaism. We cannot take the text literally. The covenant is achieved in the confederation of the tribes. This does not imply that we have to deny that God has acted in and through those events. One may still recognize the covenantal events as in some way an act of God for humanity. Indeed, one might argue that it is the responsibility of every faithful generation to learn how to recognize which events can be construed as God's acts in a significant sense, and which events can not. And of the latter group, each generation needs to find out how God is present in and to those events which are not God's own acts in a significant sense, not divine acts.

Rubenstein's religious interpretation of the Holocaust is a formidable, respectable, and authentic response. My analysis here in no way means to suggest that he or others are not entitled to hold it. But it is not a necessary response. Nor does it provide cogent support for his hope for peace in the Middle East. Moreover, if one recognizes the difference between acts and events and abandons biblical literalism, other accounts can be given that provide ways for believers to remain faithful to the God of history even while understanding the terrible events of history.

Marcus Borg: "I Will Introduce You to the Pre-Easter Jesus"

The heading for this section comes from Marcus Borg's popular book *Meeting Jesus Again for the First Time* (1994, 20). Borg's approach seeks to undermine traditional views ("images" in his usage) of Jesus and to present an "alternative image." His work has been subject to trenchant criticism (e.g., L. T. Johnson 1996), but also to important defense (e.g., Wink 1997). His work is one central path followed in the "third quest" for the historical Jesus. Here, I will not attempt to summarize the accomplishments of the third quest, which are significant. Rather I will focus on Borg's use of history. His use of history is not typical of all members of the third quest, but does present one crucial problem that is too often hidden from view: the collapse of the historically reliable into the historically actual.

The problem of history addressed in the quests for the historical Jesus is analogous to the problem of history that confronted Rubenstein. Traditional Christianity as taught by the religious authorities is said to be no longer credible. Here, however, it is not the horror of the memory of the *Shoah* that raises the questions about the saga of Israel, but the critical historical work on the gospels, which can be traced back to Reimarus, that creates the problem of history and faith.

The first quest for the historical Jesus was effectively begun by Lessing's publication of Reimarus's *Fragments*. It was dominated by nineteenth-century German scholars whose images owed more to their philosophical convictions than to their historical investigations. They attempted to remove the husk of the New Testament to get at the kernel of Jesus. The portraits of Jesus they developed were varied. Alfred Loisy and Albert Schweitzer exploded this quest a century ago.

The second quest began after World War II. The emergence of techniques that allowed scholars to trace the development of pericopes in the New Testament made it possible to read backward through the final text to earlier versions. This method allowed them to seek Jesus' existential self-understanding as exemplified especially in his teaching but also in his actions. Numerous scholars (e.g., Harvey 1968, 164-203; Sanders 1985) pointed out the methodological problems with this quest. Finally, the "new quest" could not reliably bridge the gap between the fragmentary reports about Jesus' sayings and doings that they found to be the historically reliable items in the gospel tradition and his own self-understanding of who he is. Not only do the fragments not add up to a clear whole, but even if we had been able to complete a full mosaic of all the significant acts and teachings of his life, we still might not have sufficient warrant to say that we know how he understood his person and work.

E. P. Sanders also effectively initiated the third, current quest (*Jesus and Judaism* [1985]). The present quest starts with what we can know of Second Temple Judaism (Jesus' context) both by analysis and by comparison with other similar societies, utilizes the techniques that the second quest relied upon but not its problematical methods and goals, and centers on those actions of Jesus that historians can affirm he very probably did. Rather than seeking Jesus' self-understanding, the third quest utilizes the social roles available to him to construct a picture of Jesus often rather at odds with the Christologies of the New Testament or of the church's later traditions. Borg is one of the participants in the third quest for the historical Jesus (see Meier, Fredriksen, Crossan, Sanders, Wright for other approaches). Whatever one thinks of the third quest as a whole, it cannot be denied that it truly has made a real contribution; as John Meier put it, "the emphatic reaffirmation of the Jewishness of Jesus will make the whole enterprise worthwhile" (Meier 1999, 486).

There are numerous portraits that can be drawn of Jesus. The images Christians have constructed of him in the past range from Jesus as martyr to Christ the king. The new portraits of Jesus as a wandering cynic-sage, or a revolutionary Galilean peasant, or a Spirit-person, or an eschatological prophet are more additions to the series of images. However, authors of these new portraits or images sometimes claim to be presenting Jesus as he really was. Quite cognizant of the collapse of the "Christ of faith vs. Jesus of history" dichotomy, these authors have adopted more sophisticated conceptual frameworks, such as Borg's "pre-Easter Jesus" and "post-Easter Jesus." But the dichotomies persist: Borg writes that he "introduces both the Jesus of history (the pre-Easter Jesus) and the Jesus of Christian faith (the post-Easter Jesus) . . . " (Borg 1997b, 7; see Borg 1997a, 87). This dichotomy hides a profound confusion. Jesus-as-he-actually-was is sometimes conflated with Jesus-as-the-historians-reconstruct-him.

Edward Schillebeeckx summarized this confusion: "The sum of what systematic historical enquiry may establish about a person is certainly not the same thing as understanding that person in his irreducible individuality" (Schillebeeckx 1979, 87). Terms like "the historical Jesus" and "the pre-Easter Jesus" are often used to refer indiscriminately to "the *actual* Jesus" and to "the Jesus that is *now recoverable by historical means*" (Harvey 1968, 268; italics added). The results of historical investigation cannot introduce us to the actual man Jesus. They can only clarify, verify, or falsify the stories and images we have of him. As Schillebeeckx notes, there is much about the actual Jesus that we cannot recover historically. To equate the actual man with the historical reconstruction is confused. In his work, Borg seems to do so at times.

We have no stories of "the pre-Easter Jesus." All of our images and narratives were composed in and out of faith; the historian investigates them and *constructs her or his own image* based on the results of investigation. When historians attempt to sift out the wheat of the pre-Easter Jesus from the wheat-and-chaff of the post-Easter narratives, they do not "introduce us to Jesus," but to historians' constructs based in or abstracted from the gospel narratives. If the actual Jesus were as diverse as the portraits of the third questers portray him, he would have had a very severe multiple personality disorder.

That the historians' portraits of Jesus are so different is owing to the nature of their sources and the historians' use of them. No sources about Jesus outside of the Christian literature of the New Testament provide any significant historical evidence for Jesus. The gospels themselves are not construed as sources but as amalgamations of earlier sources. Scholars break down the gospels into forms and discern their sources, generally using the (suspect) criterion that the older (in their estimation) the sources behind the gospels are, the more historically reliable they are. But what that procedure yields (at best) is the finding that specific events can be affirmed as having happened with some significant probability. That Jesus was a Galilean, worked wonders, and told parables seems almost as historically certain as his death by crucifixion. Yet if one takes the gospels as fundamentally theological amalgamations of historical memories and fictions, then there is no *historical* evidence for showing how those individual events or types of events and acts are related to each other. The writers of the gospels provide the links through the structures and chronology of their narratives—which the questers have constantly construed as historically suspect because theologically generated. That is, historians of the third quest take the narrative structures of the Gospels that related these events to be theological creations of the gospel writers and not original or historically reliable. Even the connection of the cleansing of the temple to the crucifixion, assumed or accepted by most third questers, has been shown to be uncertain (see Fredriksen 2000, xxi-xxiv). Without a historical narrative structure, the ways in which we put together the narrative of these events and acts are uncontrolled by the meager historical evidence. No wonder the varying portraits!

We, as historians, finally can't say who Jesus was. The evidence that might substantiate one of the pictures over another is simply lacking. Historical questers treat events much like dots on a puzzle page. The various historians choose which dots to accept as worthy of placement on the blank page, arrange those dots in a manner they think appropriate, and then draw various curves and angles to connect them. Which events they focus on as key to the whole and which narrative curves they draw are not entirely independent of each other, of course. Yet even those historians, who (mostly) agree on which events actually occurred and what the actual man Jesus can be reliably said to have done and said, draw different portraits of "the historical Jesus" or "the pre-Easter Jesus." However, they are doing just what the gospel writers did: selecting some events and sewing them into a quilt to form a new narrative or paint a new portrait using the materials they have received or uncovered (see Luke 1:1-4). As Elisabeth Schüssler Fiorenza put it, these scholars "deny the rhetoricity of their research and obfuscate the fact that their reconstructive cultural models and theological interests are not able to *produce* the *real* Jesus but only creative images of him" (2000, 13). Hence, she uses the typological convention "historical-Jesus" to indicate that these reconstructions are modern images created with little historical control, a convention I accept and adopt now. In fact, these "historians" are really "theologians" arguing for changes in convictions about Jesus.

The quests for the historical Jesus in fact parallel traditional Christology. Disciples—and others—sought to create and validate images of Jesus by using the sources they were given. What distinguishes modern questers is that they may work with modern naturalistic presumptions, as discussed in chapter two, and also interrogate their sources more rigorously than did their ancient forebears. But they still seek to make images of Jesus for various purposes, typically theological ones. What often seems to be lacking, however, is a sense that God acted in and through Jesus, a conviction more traditional christologists presume to be true.

While the effect of the quests has been taken to be the undermining of traditional faith, some of the first questers (and possibly some of the second and third) wanted to find a "foundation" in history for Christian faith. Obviously, the wildly varying results of historical investigations are hardly bedrock foundations for Christian faith. Other questers have sought to find a foundation from which they could undermine religious faith. History would reveal the "facts" of the matter and show how faith was really "fantasy." While they have, perhaps, had some success in popular circles, their failure should be as obvious as the failure of other questers. The "historical Jesus" is clearly a historians' construct, an image that they have developed, whether as members of a "Jesus Seminar," as disciples, or as critics. The historians' constructs cannot provide "facts" sufficient either to upset or set up religious belief that God acted in and through Jesus.

Just as the early church used the tools it had to understand who Jesus was and what he did for them, so we must use the tools of our own age, including those of historical investigation. What we can take from the quests is that the properly historical work can provide us with a touchstone for our images of Jesus the Christ. While historical investigations cannot by themselves warrant an image of Jesus, they can provide some insight into what components in our images of Jesus might well be fantasy, exaggeration, or distortion—and what in the evangelists' constructs we might also have to consider fantasy, exaggeration, or distortion. We will look closely at these issues in chapter nine.

In sum, "the historical Jesuses" or "the pre-Easter Jesuses" as constructed by third questers are just more "post-Easter Jesuses," just more Christologies that differ as markedly from the canonical and creedal images as those canonical and creedal images differ from one another (see Dunn or Torjesen for illustrations of the variety of New Testament Christologies). Their images of the historical Jesus are finally no more "historical" in the strict sense than the gospels' images of Jesus.

Conclusion

Rubenstein and Borg both attempt to demythologize traditional faith by utilizing serious historical work as a tool to show that traditional conceptions of faith are incredible in the modern era. Yet Rubenstein's argument is an alternative to a view that requires a rather literalist understanding of the Jewish saga and a conception of omnipotence that is, at best, optional. Borg creates yet another image of Jesus, but Christian theologians have been doing that for centuries. The inability of the third questers to provide enough reliable evidence to make a specific image created in the quest compelling also renders the various images, at best, optional. Such historical work may, but need not, undermine anyone's faith.

The problem with both Rubenstein and Borg is their binary understanding of faith and history. Rubenstein ignores the philosophical component needed to make a historical saga into a myth that he labels "traditional Judaism." This is not to say that he has misidentified traditional Judaism, only that there are approaches to revising it other than direct opposition to such a myth. Borg treats the theological post-Easter Jesus as if there were only one such myth to demythologize (Borg 1997a, 101-4) and one reliable image of the historical pre-Easter Jesus. In another place he finds that the Bible contains history and metaphor, and the two must not be confused lest we slip into confusions (Borg 2001, 47). This binary approach ignores the fact that theological and philosophical constructions in myths mediate between historical investigations and religious convictions. Developing this theme, however, is work for chapter ten.

Beyond the alleged confusion about the historical Jesus, the third quest seeks to portray the acts of Jesus and the events of his life. Yet does the revision of our understanding of the events of Jesus' life require us to abandon the notion that God was present and acting in and through him? The doctrine of the incarnation is surely difficult to understand. Yet no images produced by the third quest have been sufficiently warranted to give one reason to think that God did not act in and through Jesus' life. The findings that Jesus was a wandering cynic-sage or a revolutionary peasant may change our perceptions of how the renderings of Jesus in the

New Testament have to be understood. But none of them can support the claim that would undermine an understanding of the life of Jesus as an act of God in and for humanity.

What these investigations undermine, in effect, is the rigidity of some ways of formulating the central convictions of religious traditions. The myth of traditional Judaism as described by Rubenstein cannot hold in our era; but perhaps the saga of Jewish people in covenant with God can. The dogma that there is only one way to image Jesus cannot hold as divinely given; but practice of discipleship to this one who is/was the sacrament of encounter with God (to quote a title of Schillebeeckx) can.

History can be used to undermine the convictions that express the faith of some people. But an examination of this use of history reveals that the problem of history is akin to the problem of evil. Both offer profound challenges to traditional forms of religious belief. These challenges can overwhelm the faith of some. But other people of faith learn to live with these challenges, even though they may have to revise some of the convictions expressing the faith they live. They recognize that rethinking the shape of events—whether the saga of Israel or the gospels of Christianity—does not entail rejecting the conviction that God has acted in and through what we often identify as events. It may, however, require us to reconceptualize how God acts in and through what we ordinarily see as events and which events we can see not as mere events but distinctively as results of divine action. By showing the contingency of our formulations of faith, historical investigations can also be used to help theologians propose revised expressions of faith. In sum, the common view that history tends to undermine faith is based on an uncritical and unwarranted dichotomy between (rational) historical investigation and (personal or traditional) faith. However, as we have seen in these two key instances, not only is the relationship much more complex than the binary approach allows, but the distinctive work and commitments of history and faith may make room for theologians to creatively adapt, strongly misread, or reinvent their traditions so the old creeds can continue to live in new worlds.

CHAPTER 6

Immunizing Religious Belief from History

Christianity rests on beliefs about God
and Christ that cannot conceivably suffer
at the rough hands of the historians.
— E. P. Sanders

Christianity could not exist without some defining principles. Without such principles, no tradition could exist. These principles are formally—at their most abstract—immune to being undermined by historical investigation. Nonetheless, the identity of these principles, their best formulations, and the ways to revise them (when needed) are matters of some dispute. The present chapter explores what can reasonably be and not be "immunized" from historical investigation into Christianity. To do this properly, though, we must again make some crucial distinctions.

First, a "fact" is not an "event" (or, for that matter, an action or an occurrence). One can *state* a fact; one cannot "state" an event or an act. Events *happen* or *occur*. Facts do not "happen." Generally speaking, facts are linguistic constructs written or spoken in grammatically declarative sentences. Facts are not events, but facts are *about* events, actions, occurrences, persons, or states of affairs. *Stating* a fact is itself an act, a speech act; it is not merely an event. Facts can be accepted, argued for, disputed, and so on, in ways that it would be quite odd to say that events, actions, persons, or states of affairs are. One can make a factual claim about events, persons, actions, or states of affairs, but that does not make events, actions, persons, events, or states of affairs into facts. Facts are linguistic constructions *about* these other items.

Generally speaking, then, a fact is a linguistic representation of something else. Some facts are about a state of affairs: "The sun is shining brightly today." Some facts are about events: "The stock market crashed." Some facts are about actions: "He landed Apollo 13 successfully." Some facts are about the conditions of a social setting or a natural occurrence:

"Thick fog shrouded the town square that night." "The sea shimmered in the heat." Some facts are about things: "That bread is a consecrated communion host." Some facts are about persons: "Winston Churchill served as prime minister of Great Britain during much of the Second World War." A historical fact is a representation of a state of affairs, an event, a thing, a person or persons, or an action that is in the past at the time the representation is made. All of the examples used above in this paragraph could be construed, in proper circumstances, as stating historical facts. While philosophical puzzles abound concerning how any of that past stuff (as a most general term) can be present, how present representations relate to that ongoing or no-longer-present stuff, and how contemporary facts can be distinguished from historical facts, these technical philosophical issues "factor out," for the most part, given our present purposes. We will attend to them only when they are relevant to specific issues under consideration.

In most circumstances, we take a statement as factual if it adequately and accurately represents actions, events, persons, things, or states of affairs, given the context in which the fact is presented and the purposes for which it is presented. We can challenge someone whose statement of "fact" we doubt to be true. We can ask them to warrant the statement or, more loosely, to prove that fact. Note that we cannot ask someone to prove an event or prove an act. We might want someone to prove *that* an event occurred or to warrant a statement *that* an agent performed a given act, but here we are dealing with facts, not directly with what they are supposed to be about. Remember, Sergeant Joe Friday, in "Dragnet," did not say, "Just the events, ma'am, just the events," but "just the facts, ma'am, just the facts." His witnesses could relate facts, not events. We can point at an occurring event, but we cannot *say* an event—we can only state a fact about an event. My point is that linguistically and conceptually, "facts" are not interchangeable with "events" or "acts." They are not the same thing.

We may accept some facts, reject others, be undecided about still others. We may find a statement of facts adequate or inadequate, accurate enough or not, depending on the circumstances. The sentence above about Winston Churchill, for instance, is true and states a fact, but it would not be an adequate statement of fact responding to the question, "Was Churchill prime minister of Great Britain in 1939?" But note we don't (in the same sense) accept or reject, nor are we undecided about, events, actions, things, or states of affairs. We evaluate the *way* events, actions, things, or states of affairs are *represented*. We evaluate *facts* and *statements*. Of course, we also evaluate actions, including the speech acts of stating facts; but to evaluate those actions correctly we have to represent the facts about them rightly. Indeed, the fact (!) that we can morally evaluate agents' actions, but cannot morally evaluate events in the same way (save insofar as those events are the results of actions) reinforces the distinction we made in the last chapter between acts and events; but to evaluate those acts well, we have to have our facts right.

This understanding of facts and events does not imply that "events" or "actions" occur independently of language, that "facts" are linguistic entities while "events" and "acts" are somehow prelinguistic. In a most formal sense, perhaps, one can say events or states of affairs occur whether or not anyone speaks of them as facts. But how one can speak of them and what one can say of them makes them accessible. Odd as it sounds, there are events about which no facts have been uttered or written, and some about which none can be uttered or written. It may be the case that there are some events and states of affairs about which there may be no fact of the matter (such as how many personalities a patient with multiple personality disorder had; see Hacking 1994, 471-72) or facts about "non-existent entities" (such as non-existent wandering bandits who were the subject of a scare of French peasants in 1789; see Ginzburg 1994, 293, 295). My main point, though, is that "facts" and "events" have rather different uses in our language and different conceptual places in our discourses.

Second, facts are also not evidence. Facts *become* evidence "when put in service of a claim" (Meltzer 1994, 47; compare Datson 1994, 243-44). Facts become evidence only if they are used to respond to some particular question raised in a particular situation for a particular purpose. Facts may be adduced as evidence, for example, in legal cases, in scientific work, in historical investigations, or, in general, in those situations in which evidence can help warrant a hypothetical claim or an answer to a question. What facts count as evidence varies from time to time and context to context.

Whether facts are in some way independent of theory is much debated. We have taken it for granted that facts, in science, for example, come to us "theory-laden." Facts are not "given" (save when they are accepted as data in an argument), but "discovered" or "taken." Yet some theories, such as the revisionist accounts that deny the occurrence of the *Shoah*, are said to be incompatible with the facts. Even if, in general, facts are theory-laden, it is possible that some items are to be construed as facts so that a theory that contradicts them cannot be considered true. Similarly, whatever theory one might have about who or what brought about Jesus' death, it must fit the fact that his death was by crucifixion (not stoning or hanging by the neck); a theory that would deny this fact would be hard, at best, to accept. Yet whether "facts" are sufficient to be the "courts of appeal" to decide which theory is better than another in general is another hotly debated item in philosophy of history and science. Perhaps the issue is insoluble at the general level, but only soluble in particular cases. However one comes down on those issues, the fact (!) that in some contexts some facts are irrelevant to the claim being warranted or disputed—they are irrelevant or inadmissible as evidence—and in other contexts facts are undeniable, helps us see that facts are not "evidence" unless they are used and accepted as evidence.

It is not clear that historians' facts are necessarily evidence for or against religious convictions and theological constructs, even if religious beliefs or theological claims are based on historical investigation. Sometimes believers refuse to accept relevant evidence and argument even when it is appropriate. Their response to the problem of history, as Raymond Martin put it, "insulates and isolates to a remarkable degree what a Christian believes religiously from what he or she believes on other grounds" (Martin 1999, 165-66). But sometimes theologians and believers correctly resist evidence against some of the principles that define Christianity. Such principles are often embodied as beliefs, but these "beliefs" have a different place in the discourses of Christianity. In this chapter, we shall differentiate what sort of beliefs might be properly immune from being undermined by the facts turned up by historians' investigations and what beliefs should not be immune to the use of such facts as evidence.

Christian Principles as Rules

Chapter five mentioned the important work of Hans Frei. His work—somewhat emended and supplemented—provides the context for showing how certain principles are candidates for immunity from history. Frei's colleague at Yale, George Lindbeck, charted this approach. While there is controversy about the content and status of these principles, there is reason to believe that they may be immune to suffering from the rough hands of the historians.

Frei argued that a profound "reversal" took place in the seventeenth century with regard to the way people read the Bible (1974, 130). Frei claimed that, prior to the Enlightenment, the Bible was the "real world" in which (Christian) Europeans lived. People read the Bible and understood their lives as shaped by and in the reality rendered in and through the biblical narrative. Frei cites work of German and English thinkers to show that by the eighteenth century, however, these theological savants no longer read the Bible as the narrative of the real world. Rather than limning the world, the biblical text was really about something else, such as universal truths, mythical consciousness, or events (Frei 1974, 307). The Bible was no longer treated as the real story-structured world which contained events, actions, states of affairs, and persons. The sense of an event was no longer given by how it fit into the world constructed by the Bible. The Bible was treated as reporting the facts about the events, actions, states of affairs, and persons in the world. The sense of the biblical text was then given to it by the events, actions, states of affairs, or persons it was about. It became merely a book of facts rather than a narrative inscribing a world. As a book of facts, it no longer gave meaning to the world but derived meaning from the world. Its meaning and truth could then be assessed by methods other than intratextual analysis, especially historical ones.

Intellectually, then, the eclipse of the biblical narrative, according to Frei, was the ground upon which the problem of history grew. Religiously, typological interpretation of the Bible was also eclipsed: people no longer read themselves in or into the real world limned by the Scriptures, but sought to fit the lessons drawn from the stories, laws, and other types of texts in the Bible into the "real world" of their own lives (1974, 124-54). If the sense of the text is no longer the text itself, but given by that to which the text refers, then interpreters sought to understand those reference points in order to explain what the Bible meant and means. Religious meaning, Frei wrote, "was either a truth of revelation embodied in an indispensable historical event or a universal spiritual truth known independently of the texts but exemplified by them, or, finally, a compromise between the two positions . . . " (1974, 124). Theologians had abandoned, then, the practice of doing theology within the world of the text and turned to doing theology on the texts and relating those texts to the "real stuff" these texts were about.

While Frei's analysis rings true with regard to British and German Protestant theologians and their descendants among all branches of Christianity in the twentieth century, his important text almost totally ignores Roman Catholic theologians and any references to popular religion. Since Frei wrote, two other major factors have come to light which require some amendment to his thesis.

First, Michael Buckley has shown that the roots of the deism and atheism of the late seventeenth and early eighteenth century are in the sorts of arguments made by some Catholic theologians of the early seventeenth century, notably Leonard Lessius and Marin Mersenne (Buckley 1987, 42-86). Lessius and Mersenne were working in the context of the bankruptcy of specifically religious arguments. This context is well illustrated by a quotation from an essay of Montaigne written in 1574, "We should meddle soberly with judging divine ordinances." In this essay Montaigne recollects disputes between Protestants and Catholics over the rationality of believing in divine providence. He concludes:

> It is enough for a Christian to believe that all things come from God, to receive them with acknowledgment of his divine and inscrutable wisdom, and therefore to take them in good part, in whatever aspect they may be sent to him. But I think that the practice I see is bad, of trying to strengthen and support our religion by the good fortune and prosperity of our enterprises. Our belief has enough other foundations; it does not need events to authorize it. For when the people are accustomed to these argu-

ments, which are plausible and suited to their taste, there is a danger that when in turn contrary and disadvantageous events come, this will shake their faith. Thus, in the wars we are engaged in for the sake of religion, those [Protestants] who had the advantage in the encounter [i.e., the battle] at La Rochelabeille make much ado about this incident and use their good fortune as sure approbation of their party; but when they come later to excuse their misfortunes at Moncontour and Jarnac as being fatherly scourges and chastisements, unless they have their following completely at their mercy, they make the people sense readily enough that this is getting two grinding fees for one sack, and blowing hot and cold with the same mouth. It would be better to tell them the true foundations of the truth. (Montaigne 1958, 160)

Two warring groups of believers, Huguenot and Catholic, attempt to show that God is on their side. Each can begin by pointing to a military victory as a sign of divine favor for its cause. Yet when each loses a battle this is not a sign of divine displeasure with its cause or favor for the opponents' cause, but a God-given chastisement of the side the divine providence favors (a theme Dean Grüber and others would pick up to rather different ends in the twentieth century). In doing this, the contestants vie for different understandings of how these events fit in the divine plan, perhaps one even limned by the biblical text. They can be seen as working within the world of the biblical narrative—or one much influenced by the biblical narrative.

However, Montaigne rightly mocks the self-serving dissymmetry of such theological polemics. These clever men who can construe all events as evidence in support of their own cause prove far too much. Indeed, it is this insoluble confrontation over the meaning of events in the biblical narrative that forces a new pattern of discourse. These disputants literally could not resolve their dispute on the territory they staked out for disputation. The biblical narrative may give the form of events that make victories into divine support for "us" and correlative divine "withdrawal" from them and defeats into divine chastisements for "us" and divine manipulation of "them" to serve the divine purpose. *But no criteria from the biblical text can tell us which actual, particular contemporary events are abandonments or chastisements, support or manipulation.* This results in no less than a complete theological stalemate. The eclipse of the biblical narrative for structuring European Christendom begins in the wars of religion in the sixteenth century and in the polemical arguments Protestants and Catholics made against the other; it is not merely the result of the intellectual climate of the Enlightenment, as Frei is often understood to imply.

Given the bankruptcy of this pattern of argument, Catholics Lessius and Mersenne began to argue not against Protestants about particular events as divine interventions, but against atheists. Given the stalemate on one intellectual battlefield, they staked out another. Rather than focus on specific events in history, in "the absence of a rich and comprehensive Christology and a Pneumatology of religious experience Christianity entered into the defense of the existence of the Christian God without appeal to anything Christian" (Buckley 1987, 67); these Christian theologians became pure philosophers in their arguments. Theological particularity was caught in the stalemate and abandoned. Buckley shows that this shift in opponents set the stage for Descartes and the ongoing opposition of philosophical rationalism and skepticism that was the battleground for God in the wake of Descartes' work.

In short, the eclipse of the biblical narrative did not emerge full grown from the head of a deistic philosopher. The roots are much deeper. The way was prepared for the undermining of the biblical narrative as a unifying narrative by a generation of theologians who reflected on the favoritism of God in wars of religion of the sixteenth century, and a subsequent generation of theologians in the seventeenth century who abstracted their own views from such inconclusive and unseemly debates and who confronted classical skepticism and atheism as if they were contemporary problems. Whether Epicurus and Cicero articulated problems of the early seventeenth century, those classic problems presented by "unbelievers" were more tractable than the insoluble conflicts between believers. In changing the discourse in this way, Lessius and Mersenne at least participated in, and perhaps even effected, the creation of modern philosophical theism—and its inevitable other, philosophical atheism.

By the end of the seventeenth century, another generation of thinkers had weighed the merits of the earlier arguments and proposed a Christianity completely without mystery, a "theism" with a god so distant from the world of creation as to deserve the new nomenclature of "deism." Deism was in the ascendency among intellectuals, and deism has no place for the acts of God in history on anyone's behalf. The point is this: the eclipse of the biblical narrative began much earlier and in a different context from the one on which Frei focuses. Full eclipse may have been reached only in the eighteenth and nineteenth centuries, but it started much earlier.

The upshot of this is the classic form of the problem of history: historical investigations, in the context of inner-Christian disputes, had shown the authorizing narrative not to be authoritative. The problem of history, as noted in the introduction, in its classic form is a problem of *authorization*. Clearly, the Christian narratives—whether in Protestant or Catholic versions—no longer had cultural authority. Their eclipse meant that they ceased to function as what David Tracy would call a "classic," which disclosed real possibilities of meaning and truth.

Some of the nineteenth-century critical historical investigations of the biblical texts, however, can also be understood as attempts to reclaim some authority for the Bible. If the Bible were no longer "self-authoriz-ing," then perhaps historians could recoup some of the loss by giving the Bible some support from history. Many theologians have found that sort of project a failure for a wide variety of reasons. I must agree, if for no other reason than that it is an instantiation of the dualistic "faith and his-tory" problematic of modernity (compare Harvey 1968, 14-33). Chapter ten addresses this issue more fully.

Second, Lorraine Datson has traced the shifting concepts of "facts" and "evidence" over this same period. The drama begins with the col-lapse of the "preternatural" around 1700. Theology had divided the supernatural from the preternatural for over a millennium: the super-natural was the realm of divine causality, the preternatural the realm of creaturely (angels, demons, possibly occult causes) causality of unusual phenomena. The supernatural could produce miracles, but the preter-natural only marvels. In contrast, the natural order "was a matter of nature's habitual custom rather than of nature's inviolable law, what usu-ally rather than what infallibly happened" (Datson 1994, 249).

In practice, it was difficult to distinguish preternatural from super-natural wonders. They all seemed wonderful. In theory, it was difficult to differentiate natural from preternatural events. They were all of the crea-turely order. Curiosities, portents, prodigal acts were construed as preter-natural wonders through the seventeenth century. But many of these preternatural wonders became identified as the work of demons. Datson describes the collapse of the preternatural as the upshot of fear of and warnings about demonic agency:

> The proximate impact of these warnings was to discredit preter-natural phenomena as true signs from on high; they were rather to be rejected as forgeries from below. The ultimate impact was to naturalize almost all of them. . . . The writings of the demon-ologists show that it was not sufficient simply to posit natural causes for preternatural phenomena in order to naturalize them fully; it was also necessary to rid nature of demonic agency. To simplify the historical sequence somewhat: first, preternatural phenomena were demonized and thereby incidentally natural-ized; then the demons were deleted, leaving only the natural causes. (Datson 1994, 257)

While they began as signs and portents, preternatural phenomena became treated almost as if they were natural, that is, as Baconian, scien-tific, facts.

Baconian facts are queer creatures. By studying all created phenom-ena as natural, Bacon introduced something new. Facts had been partic-ular examples of general tendencies in nature. They were the stuff of history and natural philosophy. But Baconian facts were new, Datson argued. They were "handpicked for their recalcitrance, anomalies that undermined superficial classifications and exceptions that broke glib rules. That is why the first scientific facts retailed in the annals of the Royal Society of London and the Paris Académie des Sciences were often such strange ones" (Datson 1994, 262). But these facts, as recalcitrant, make it much harder for them to be used as evidence. What would they be evidence for? Not for miracles—that was supernatural. Not for natural laws—the factual anomalies upset natural laws. Not for the preternatural—that realm was being naturalized and its denizens rendered impotent. The eclipse of the preternatural involved a concomitant loss of the possibility of attributing "preternatural phenomena" to demonic or other non-natural causes. The upshot was the reduction of preternatural phenomena and their causes to the natural realm since they could not fit properly in the only other alternative, the supernatural realm. Hence, these odd facts, formerly attributed to the preternatural, became Baconian facts, which required some sort of natural explanation despite their oddness. Yet at this point, this evolution in thought leaves the realm of the supernatural, the realm of divine miracles, intact.

The second act's drama can be summarized easily: Whereas the seventeenth-century theologians still construed miracles as evidence of divine providence, once the issue of distinguishing authentic from bogus miracles arose—especially as enthusiasts (the German word for them, *Schwärmerei*, says it all) claimed them as evidence—the problem shifted. All miracle reports were rendered dubitable. As dubitable, they could no longer be accepted as facts. And if not facts, then not evidence. Often the reports seemed to be mere props, tall tales constructed to support deviant doctrines. Many, if not most, were rejected by religious authorities and pronounced fakes. By the middle of the eighteenth century, "the likes of Hume and Voltaire could discuss the problem of miracles as if it were one of the evidence *for* miracles, as opposed to the evidence *of* miracles" (Datson 1994, 270). Rather than miracles' being accepted as evidence, all the evidence was piled up against miracles. Catholics and Protestants alike came to treat the age of miracles as something of the distant past.

The denouement to the drama is clear. As scientific theories developed greater explanatory flexibility, the facts which were important for science became understood less as bizarre singularities and more as regular occurrences. The odd group of Baconian facts, no longer attributable to either preternatural or the supernatural causes, were treated as fictions, anomalies, chance events, or events awaiting explanation as science developed. A few would still pop up as ever ready to upset scientific laws, but they, like miracles, had no real evidentiary value. Christianity became "not mysterious," as philosopher John Toland put it in his title of 1694. "A great deal of the rhapsodizing over law-abiding, commonplace nature that filled the writings of the natural theologians appealed to the desire for a calm religious life, free from nasty surprises and inspired upstarts" (Datson 1994, 273-74). The hubbub over the evidentiary value of miracles contributed, then, to the emergence of deism.

Once again, the roots of the deism that led to the eclipse of the biblical narrative are found in inner-Christian polemics. Miracles had been part of the world, manifestations of God's presence. But their use in polemics, for instance in the controversy over Jansenism in France in the late seventeenth and early eighteenth centuries, rendered them inconclusive signs (Datson 1994, 267, 269, 272). Even if they were pronounced to be authentic, what they signified was unclear. What was God 'saying' in these signs? The attempts to answer this question again led to theological stalemates. The appeal to "the" authority of Scripture or pope or church or miracle is a failure when the issue at stake *just is* the authority of Scripture or pope or church or miracle or history or science.

The full eclipse of the biblical narrative was the work of eighteenth- and nineteenth-century German and British Protestant theologians. But it is too simple a picture to attribute it to the rise of historical criticism (see Frei 1974, 1) and the emergence of new patterns of hermeneutics in the age of Enlightenment. The deeper roots are in the inner-Christian stalemate in fitting the present into the Bible and the shifting standards of evidence. As with miracles so with the Bible: in the light of the instability of the meaning of the biblical narrative "for us," the issue turned to the need of evidence *for* the Bible and its meaning, as opposed to the evidence *of* the Bible for the meaning of the events, actions, states of affairs, and persons in the world. Because the miracles and the Bible were no longer facts that anyone might readily accept, they could no longer be evidence for God's intentions in creating, redeeming, and sustaining the world. What God's intentions were became disputable. Attempts to resolve those disputes stalemated or collapsed into polemics. And eventually any vision of divine intentionality became eclipsed in reaction to those polemics and stalemates among Christians. For when authorities, like the Bible on one hand or history and science on the other, are in dispute, appeals to one of them as authoritative are simply not helpful.

Following Frei, George Lindbeck proposed that we again assume an "intratextual" approach to the Bible. The precritical acceptance of the biblical narrative is transformed into a postcritical, postliberal mode of understanding the text. The Bible could no longer provide a world for European Christendom. It might not be an authority for the entire world, but it can provide the shape of the world in which Christians can and should live together. Even if the biblical narrative can no longer literally display the real world, it can teach Christians how God has ordered the real world and provide principles that can guide Christians as they fit the events, actions, things, and persons they encounter into the world God has made. While Lindbeck would not deny the need for historical criticism of the biblical texts, such critical work should not be the primary way one approaches the narrative. The biblical narrative was recognized as authoritative for Christians, even if it could no longer be the authority for a whole culture.

Lindbeck argued that there are three general rules or principles that give identity to Christianity generated from the biblical narrative itself and embodied especially in classic creeds. He wrote:

> First, there is the monotheistic principle: there is only one God, the God of Abraham, Isaac, Jacob, and Jesus. Second, there is the principle of historical specificity: the stories of Jesus refer to a genuine human being who was born, lived, and died in a particular time and place. Third, there is the principle of what may infelicitously be called Christological maximalism: every possible importance is to be ascribed to Jesus that is not inconsistent with the first rules. This last rule, it may be noted, follows from the central Christian conviction that Jesus Christ is the highest possible clue (though an often dim and ambiguous one to creaturely and sinful eyes) within the space-time world of human experience to God, i.e., to what is of maximal importance. (Lindbeck 1984, 94)

Obviously, these three principles are not themselves doctrines. But Christian doctrines *embody* these principles. Christological and soteriological doctrines, for example, that fail to flesh them out well, such as docetism (which fails to embody the second principle) or Arianism (which sacrifices the third at the expense of the first) fail to be good Christian doctrine. These principles provide the *loci*, the theological "places," in which Christianity comes to have an identity. Indeed, it is hard to imagine a Christian tradition without these principles or something like them. The first principle, independently called "creational and covenantal monotheism" by N. T. Wright (Borg and Wright 1999, 158-60), distinguishes the classic versions of the monotheistic traditions from most Eastern religious traditions and from Western dualistic and pantheistic traditions. As a group, these principles also distinguish Christianity from Judaism and Islam, in both of which a version of the first is operative, but for which the second may be held to be true, but is not a principle, and for which the third cannot be a principle or, possibly, even held to be true. Moreover, discourse concerning the second two principles would not be identity-giving in that these are not the crucial *loci* in which the central claims of those traditions are debated and clarified.

Some caveats are in order. First, further principles besides these could be discovered to distinguish various Christian denominations from one another, but that investigation is beside the point here; more will be said about this in chapter ten (also see Tilley 2000, 125-34). Second, these principles cannot in some simple way be said to "generate" doctrines. Whether these principles are finally to be understood as "rules" guiding Christian faith and life or *loci* that must be traversed in understanding Christian identity, particular doctrines tend to emerge from particular practices in particular, often difficult or challenging, circumstances. The process of discerning which particular doctrines actually embody these principles at any given time can be exceedingly difficult. Some forms of trinitarian doctrine, those that are strongly "social," may violate the first principle (indeed, Muslims' traditional objections to "Christian tri-theism" may indicate a difference in criteria about what does and does not fit this shared principle). A number of forms of trinitarian doctrine, from a non-sequential modalism which finds our authentic and veridical experience of the one God in three personal modes, to a community of three persons coinhering perichoretically in and as one God, may fit with the principles. Whether these principles have been in some sense opera-tive in a doctrinal formulation is not a presumption one makes to discern good doctrines or a criterion one uses to measure candidates for the sta-tus of doctrines, but a conclusion a community draws about some doc-trines expressed in particular ways at particular times. Doctrines do or do not embody these principles well enough to be the useful rules to shape Christian faith. Third, these principles are not all the principles the Chris-tian tradition needs somehow to embody. Arguably, a recognition of the first covenant with Israel, an acceptance of the divine universal salvific will, and a requirement for an ongoing community may be other princi-ples. Some principles may also help distinguish some Christian traditions from others, such as the Catholic analogical imagination as a principle of the identity of the Catholic community. Members of other Christian churches exhibit this principle, but not as an identity principle of those traditions. Fourth, identifying these rules is to make a fundamentally neg-ative claim: that a religious tradition whose doctrines failed to embody these rules or failed to attend to these places in theological discourse would not be the Christian or even a Christian tradition.

I have elsewhere criticized aspects of Lindbeck's thought (Tilley et al. 1995, 101-3) and I also am indebted to it (Tilley 2000). For present pur-poses, I want to show simply that evidence is not clearly relevant to argu-ments about the formation or meaning of the articulations of such principles. Even if they are generated by reflection on the historical course of mainstream Christianity, they are not hypotheses to which evi-dence is relevant.

How might one argue against the first principle? One might examine the texts and monuments of a period of the Christian movement. One might argue then that Christians were indeed not monotheistic, but poly-theistic or henotheistic. One might establish that claim as a set of facts, fair representations of the acts, events, things, persons, and states of affairs of that time and place. But would that be evidence for the non-normativity of the principle? Or for the inadequacy of those Christians' practices and beliefs? One can certainly attempt to argue that allowing patronal saints is insufficiently monotheistic, or that process panentheism portrays a divinity that is hardly monotheistic. But one would be adducing evidence for and arguing about the doctrines that putatively embody the principles, not the principles themselves. For example, even the strongly revisionist work of liberal Presbyterian philosopher and theologian John Hick, *The Metaphor of God Incarnate*, which many Christians would find unacceptable theologically, can be seen to struggle mightily with the significance of historical specificity (summarized in Hick 1993, 150-51), to support monotheism strongly, and to seek to adjust traditional doctrinal formulae to fit better with a form of christological maximalism appropriate to the present age of religious pluralism (Hick 1993, 152-63).

What counts against these principles as principles is not evidence, not even historical evidence. They are immune from evidence because they are principles that are embodied in our day-to-day life as Christians and without which that form of life could not exist. To take a non-religious example of the significance of a principle: David Hume woke Immanuel Kant from his dogmatic slumbers by showing that there was no evidence for the claim "Every event has a cause." His arguments effectively show that what we have as evidence is that there is a "constant conjunction" of events, that *a* constantly follows *b*, for example, but that doesn't mean *b* therefore causes *a*. Some other event might be the cause of both or some unknown event caused by *b* is the real cause of *a*. Such a deconstruction of the principle of causality seems to make the practice of science impossible.

Kant's response was to make causality not a generalization nor an inference nor a law, but a principle of pure understanding. We must accept it as a formula by which we live and work. Whether it is better to treat that principle as a defeasible presumption or to give it some status other than the status Kant gave it, the fact that we cannot find a link other than a constant conjunction between two events might be evidence against a generalization or law, but is not evidence against a principle. Evidence is not sufficient ground to establish a principle, and evidence does not undermine a principle. Evidence may give grounds for accepting or rejecting a hypothesis, but a hypothesis is not a principle. Twentieth-century physics, of course, has played havoc with the formulation of the principle of causality of the eighteenth and nineteenth centuries. Although we have found realms in which the principle seems inapplicable, we still use it in some formulation as a guide to investigations of events "larger" than those that occur at atomic and subatomic levels.

What one does with a principle is to accept and use it or discard it. If one accepts and uses it, one participates in the form of life or practice or community that accepts it. If one discards it, one either is fomenting a revolution within the community in which it is a principle or is removing oneself from the community in which the principle is an identity marker. What Frei describes as the eclipse of the biblical narrative was not brought about merely by adducing historical facts and marshalling them as evidence against the principle that the world we live in is constituted by the biblical narrative. A whole host of intellectual, cultural, political, and social practices shifted. These shifts, especially the stalemates in intra-Christian polemics noted above, reconstructed what constituted facts, what counted as reliable evidence, and thus rendered the biblical narrative incredible as a story of the real world. Given our present situation of religious diversity, the narrative of God's creation, reconciliation, and sustenance of the world to bring it all unto and into the divine life can no longer literally accommodate the miracle of the battle of Jericho or the literal understanding of Nebuchadnezzar as God's rod. What Lindbeck shows, however, is that we can abstract principles from our practice of Christian life and faith and recognize them as constitutive of Christian life and faith, even if we have difficulty in agreeing on what they are or how to understand them.

David Tracy is often presented as a "revisionist" or "correlational" theologian. His work is often construed as Lindbeck's "opponent" in contemporary U.S. Christian theology. There are fundamental similarities between them, however, especially Tracy's strong reliance on the notion of the "classic" in his theology. Tracy wrote:

> We all find ourselves compelled to recognize and on occasion to articulate our reasons for the recognition that certain expressions of the human spirit so disclose a compelling truth about our lives that we cannot deny them some kind of normative status. Thus do we name these expressions, and these alone, "classics." Thus do we recognize, whether we name it so or not, a normative element in our cultural experience, experience as realized truth.
>
> Yet what does it mean to find a normative element in cultural experience? My thesis is that what we mean in naming certain texts, events, images, rituals, symbols and persons "classics" is that we recognize nothing less than the disclosure of a reality we cannot but name truth. (Tracy 1981, 108)

In Tracy's terms, Lindbeck's intratextual theology is the exploration of the Christian classic, construed as a text which carries symbols and manifests the person of Jesus Christ. Whether it becomes a classic for a person or for a culture is not a question within Lindbeck's or Tracy's control.

We can manifest as a community what it means to live within a world created by a classic, and we can proclaim that we find meaning and truth in the classic text. But if someone cannot see it as we do, cannot construe it as a classic, but perhaps as a text of oppression or a cover story for domination by one elite, neither Tracy nor Lindbeck can do more than carry on a conversation with the other about why and how one can discern meaning and truthfulness in and through the classic.

Both Lindbeck and Tracy effectively give the classic text and its classic appropriations a status that gives identity to the tradition. However, neither goes far in answering the question of why one should take this text or that classic as authoritative. In a pluralistic culture, numerous patterns seem to command classic status; many traditions are on offer in the spiritual supermarket. Like it or not, we face a culture not only of external pluralism—that there are multiple religious traditions and communities besides our own—but of internal pluralism—that there are multiple religious traditions and communities that appeal within our context for our acceptance. When Western culture underwent the eclipse of the biblical narrative, Christianity was deeply affected. It was the "culture-religion." Judaism was marginalized. The problem of authority in the past was basically dualist: that of Christianity versus the "Enlightenment mindset."

Now the problem is not dualist, but pluralist. Since the beginning of the nineteenth century the texts of traditions native to India, China, and Japan have gradually become accessible to and a viable option for belief within Western culture. While versions of Christianity may be the most common options available, a small, but slowly growing, minority can now see other spiritual traditions, whether indigenous or imported, as live options. Many spiritual and religious paths are available. Many classics are coming to be well known. They are competing for classic status in an internally pluralistic society. Given the diminishing authority of Christian traditions, even those nurtured in one of the traditions often find themselves choosing among traditions as a way of finding a spiritual path. In this situation, the appeal to tradition cannot work because it is just the status and authority of the traditions that are at stake. To recognize the fundamental status of the classic or the principles of a tradition is important for displaying the identity of the tradition, but cannot alone respond to the issue of authorizing a tradition—the issue that is at the heart of the classic problem of history.

One further crucial distinction implied in the foregoing remains to be made explicit: between principles and formulations of principles. Tracy would find that the classic itself gives rise to multiple formulations. We never fully plumb the classic just as we never can finally articulate a principle. Lindbeck refers to these principles in very abstract ways, as in the quotation on page 77 above. He seems to think that they are in some sense active in the development of doctrinal rules (Lindbeck 1984, 95). The advantage of such abstraction is that it allows principles to be unmoored from any specific formulations of them (see Lindbeck 1984, 92-94). This is not to say that "anything goes," that any formulation might embody a principle or any argument would count as a valid one in one of the central theological *loci*. Some ways of taking classic texts are disputable. It is rather to say that there may be many "right" ways of expressing a principle or responding to a classic. These expressions may rightly differ from time to time and place to place. Multiple versions may all be good expressions of the principles. Sometimes expressions in severe tension with each other, as the example of trinitarian doctrines mentioned above illustrates, may both be good, but not finally exhaustive, expressions of principles. I have argued that changes in these expressions are contextual (Tilley 2000, 81-82, 110-21) rather than progressive. I also accept John Thiel's basic view that we can determine what a tradition is, and a fortiori the principles that shape it or give it identity, only retrospectively (Thiel 2000).

One corollary of this distinction needs also to be surfaced. Embodying a principle well is what *makes* a doctrinal formula right, but embodying a principle is not a *criterion* for determining whether the doctrinal formula is right. I have argued this point at length elsewhere (Tilley 2000, 152-77), so I will simply illustrate it here. What makes the factual claim "There are seventeen books on my desk" true or false is whether there are seventeen books on my desk. If this fact as stated is correct, then it corresponds to the way things are, to the state of affairs that is my desktop. However, there being seventeen books on my desk is not sufficient for us to verify that fact. It alone is not a criterion for the accuracy and adequacy of that claim. We have to count the books, separate them from the article offprints, decide whether a photocopied book counts as a book, and so on. What makes a claim true is not sufficient to be a criterion for the claim being true. Similarly, what makes an economic policy good is whether the economy is thriving. But how we recognize "thriving" is something else. For example, the United States Catholic bishops in their pastoral letter *Economic Justice for All* noted that the criterion of a good economic policy was what it did to the poor, for the poor, and enabled the poor to do for themselves. This criterion was the correct one, they argued, for recognizing whether an economic policy was good. What made an economic policy good might be something else. In formulating this criterion, the bishops implicitly excluded other criteria, such as benefitting "the average person" or "the average family." This was not to suggest that a good economic policy would not benefit the average person as well. Rather, they meant to suggest that the criterion for discerning whether an economic policy was good was how it affected a specific, economically disadvantaged group.

Looking back at Montaigne's comments, then, we can see that everyone knew what made a defeat a punishment: God willed it so. But the disputants had no criterion by which to discern whether this or that defeat was one of God's acts or what kind of act it was. Looking back at the debate about miracles, we can see that, by definition, a miracle is God's act. What makes it a miracle is just that it is an act of God. But the disputants had no criterion to determine whether this specific act is a miracle or a marvel or (sometimes) a fake or what God meant by performing it at a specific time and place, presuming people agreed that God did perform a miracle. Today, the problem is even more difficult: internal pluralism makes the problem plural, not dual.

The conclusion is this: even if principles are understood by reflection on the past, by understanding how a tradition has developed, they are nonetheless not based on properly historical evidence although they are derived from reflection on the past. One may accept them or discard them. One may dwell in or reject a tradition. Some principles may fall out of favor or become inoperative, as the biblical narrative did and any simple principle of causality in modern physics did. If those principles are identity principles, as Lindbeck discussed them, then those traditions die out or are substantially transformed when those principles change or are abandoned.

Another factor is that evidence from historical investigations may persuade individuals or communities to abandon the principles of their tradition. The principles become no longer credible because no formulation of them can be found that squares with the evidence. What is being upset here is not the principles, but their formulations. For example, the claim that the church is of divine institution is a principle characteristic of Catholicism (and some Protestant denominations make similar claims). One formulation of that principle that argued that Jesus of Nazareth founded an organized institution in the time before his death has been found by most scholars to be unreliable; the institution of the church was, they claim, retrojected into the narratives about Jesus by the early church as it solidified its structure. All we can warrant historically, they might say, is that Jesus attracted a band of followers who survived as a group or groups after his death and felt empowered to carry on Jesus' mission and to evangelize even to Gentiles. Assuming for the sake of argument that that position does represent what is historically reliable data, would it be evidence against the principle? Some would say that it would be, that such a historical finding undermines the principle of divine institution because it "shows" Jesus didn't found an organized church. The historians' claim must, therefore, be rejected. This is, in fact, the "integralist" position taken against the "modernist" position articulated by Alfred Loisy a century ago. However, the historical evidence cited would be quite compatible with a claim that Jesus initiated the movement that appropriately evolved into the institutional church under the guidance of the Spirit. Jesus may not have appointed Peter the first pope (*papa* is a term that does not appear for centuries as an appellation for the bishop of Rome) or the apostles to be the first priests (*hieros* is a term that the Letter to the Hebrews reserves for Jesus) or bishops (although we do find *episkopoi* in later New Testament writings). The principle of divine institution could thus stand, but in a more nuanced formula.

Nonetheless, if those are historical facts, they are evidence against specific formulations of the principle, rather than the principle itself. The dispute is not about the episcopal principle, but about the ways in which we understand and formulate it in practice. We must recognize that formulations of the principle may be falsified and require modification or reformulation, while the principle may remain intact (a point made by John Henry Newman; "continuity of principle" is one of his "notes" of authentic development; cf. Tilley 2000, 112-13).

Of course, one may be persuaded that a principle is not to be accepted in any formulation. The principle might die from its formulations being qualified to death. One might leave the church because the teaching authority of the church claimed that it was necessary for one to accept a specific formulation that one could not accept. One might also find that current formulations had indeed broken with the authentic principles that gave identity to the community. Or one might find a classic of another tradition disclosing a reality one cannot but name truth. But in each of these cases, historical evidence *alone* is not sufficient (and may not be necessary) to warrant a rejection of the principles. Other factors are always involved. As we shall see in the next chapter, the issue of the relevance of historical evidence to principles and their formulations remains debated.

If this understanding of principles and their formulation is accurate, then we can usefully revisit Richard Rubenstein's understanding of Judaism after Auschwitz. Rubenstein argued for abandoning belief in the God of history and for accepting belief in the God of nature. But if Judaism has an identity principle that could be termed "the covenantal principle," is Rubenstein's position tenable for a *Jewish* thinker? The *Shoah* surely has been the occasion for rethinking how to construe the covenant. For those who could not imagine the Jewish tradition without a covenant with the God of history, Rubenstein's position must represent a radical or substantial transformation, or an abandonment, of the tradition. There would be no "continuity of principle" in Rubenstein's work. Perhaps such a radical strand in the ongoing tradition that carries and is carried by the Jewish communities is a formulation that provides a stimulus for less radical reconstruction and a hope for those who have trouble with more traditional beliefs. Perhaps there are other strands in the Jewish tradition that could be mined for other ways of understanding the destruction of European Jewry without abandoning the God of history. Jewish theologians continue to debate these issues (cf. Braiterman 1998 and the authors he discusses, for example).

Reflecting on Rubenstein's work reinforces the point that formulations of principles are not immune to historical evidence. How one can understand the covenant may be strongly affected by historical facts and evidence. Historical investigations can turn up facts that can be used as evidence to upset formulations. But if one rejects the principles, one is either rejecting the tradition or engaging in a revolution within the tradition. The reactions to Rubenstein's work within the Jewish community suggest that many Jews could not accept his work because it was a rejection of the covenant or a revolution so radical as to call for a different sort of tradition entirely.

Historical investigations may provide reasons for some people to discard principles. Yet they may indeed recognize that others might give different weight to the evidence the investigations turn up and thus not discard the principles. Even if fundamental principles cannot directly "suffer at the rough hands of historians," as the epigraph to this chapter suggests, formulations that embody them can. In a pluralistic culture, traditions may suffer not at the rough hands of the historians, but from the attractiveness of lovely hands from other traditions. The next chapter explores the relationship of principles to their formulations.

CHAPTER 7

Religious Beliefs and Historical Evidence

The substance of the ancient doctrine
of the deposit of faith is one thing, and the way
in which it is presented is another.
— Pope John XXIII

In the previous chapter, I argued that certain kinds of principles are immune to undermining by evidence turned up by historical investigations. This position is neither fideism nor obscurantism; I am not arguing for immunizing religious belief in general from critical appraisal or justification. Rather, these principles are indefeasible because they are not hypotheses. Nor are they metaphysical claims, true always and everywhere, but principles that give identity to a particular tradition and the community that carries it on. Scholars may debate what those principles are; in the context of debates, the sentences that formulate the principles may function as hypotheses. But the principles as principles central to a religious tradition are not defeasible hypotheses.

The argument of this chapter shows just what can and should be considered immune from historical undermining and what should not be understood as immune. My argument is that the principles are immune, but the formulations that articulate them are not (compare Tilley 2000, 110-12). A particular case study reveals that this is not always a non-controversial task. The distinction between principles and the doctrines that embody them is not always clear. Before we can get to the case itself, however, we need to examine the theological positions of a key participant involved in the dispute.

The position supported here, that principles need to be distinguished from the ways in which they are formulated, embodied, or articulated is one version of the point quoted from Pope John XXIII as the heading for this chapter. John Henry Newman made a similar point when he claimed that the "idea" of Christianity does not develop, even though articulations of Christian doctrine develop (Newman 1846, 56-57; see Tilley 2000, 112-

13), as did Edward Schillebeeckx when he wrote that there needs to be a distinction between "the substance of faith and the model in which the faith is put into words. Theologians often confuse 'the thought' with 'thinking-in-models'" (Schillebeeckx 1991, 309). Such distinctions are essential to avoid identifying a living religious tradition with one culturally conditioned form of that tradition.

Avery Dulles and the Problem of History

Avery Dulles, S.J., identifies as "interpreted history" expressions of some of the identity principles identified by Lindbeck. These expressions are not quite historical reconstructions or analyses, although theologians seem often to surface the principles and their expressions by reflection on the history of a religious tradition. Of course, as the previous chapter noted, a person or a community may debate about how to formulate the principles. They may also argue over whether one formulation or another is the best way to articulate that principle at a given time and place. They may question whether the formulations that the community has accepted articulate all the principles that shape the tradition. But these debates are generally within the theological realm Dulles identified as interpreted history.

A person or a community can simply reject specific identity principles, not merely dispute about their formulation. But if they do reject identity principles, then they either reject or abandon the tradition shaped by such principles—or call for a radical reformation of that tradition with new principles. Historical evidence about the behavior of the community may cause one to reject or abandon a faith community. Such evidence may convince one that the community is structured by unacceptable and unchangeable principles. Some scholars have argued that principles such as misogynism or anti-Semitism are obscured, but real, principles that give identity to the Christian tradition. If someone finds that such identity principles are indeed operative in a tradition, that person may then reasonably abandon or attempt radical reform of such a tradition. Of course, others would challenge such a position by arguing that such practices were not principles of the tradition, but regrettable and remediable distortions of the tradition.

Historical investigations may be necessary but are not sufficient for developing an "interpreted history." Dulles's category of interpreted history was developed in an essay on the historians' uses of the gospels. Dulles argued that there were four patterns for the relationship of faith and history in the twentieth century: history against faith, history and faith irrelevant to each other, history as ground of faith, and the gospels as interpreted history (Dulles 1996, 212-22). Dulles's own acknowledged view (the last of the four) is not limited to the gospels.

Dulles found that historical investigations have values in the light of faith (1996, 222). These values include supplementing the "information that could be gathered from faith and Church teaching," confirming the faith by providing historical support, distinguishing the competencies of faith and history, and contributing to the understanding of and assisting "in the development of Christian doctrine" (1996, 222-223). In this understanding, Dulles seems to place faith itself in a position immune to historical investigation. In doing so, he seems to take a position similar to the one argued here regarding the "immunity" of identity principles to evidential falsification. However, there are significant differences. If we were to offer a more generic rendering of the fourth of his patterns noted above, then, it would be "history as ancillary of faith."

Dulles's typology may be a useful rough sketch of what the relationships of history and faith have been in the modern period. However, it should not be accepted as a sketch of the way we should continue to construe these relationships. If the argument of this book is correct, his account, like all accounts that presume binary problematics, needs clarification and revision. Reflection on Dulles's work allows us to surface three specific factors that need to be considered as we work through the problem of history.

First, the matter for the classification should be particular arguments and positions, not scholars or their works. An author's arguments or positions may fit into different categories at various points in a career of historical investigations—or even in a single work. For example, two historians of the third quest, N. T. Wright (usually seen as a traditionalist or conservative) and Marcus J. Borg (a revisionist), note that both of them—although their methodologies and results differ quite markedly—sometimes support traditional views and at other times are seriously at odds with the tradition (Borg and Wright 1999, ix-x; also see chapter nine below). They do not fit cleanly into any category. Because what is being classified should be specific arguments, the typology cannot be essentialized or petrified. Neither scholars nor works are the items that fit the types. Rather, particular arguments can be fit into the categories.

Dulles, however, tends to take scholars, rather than their arguments, as exemplifying or illustrating each of the types in his typology. Save for "scholars" who have, for non-scholarly reasons, research programs whose purpose is to destroy a tradition or whose work is to defend every jot and tittle of every traditional formulation, many scholars *qua* scholars can at different times be fairly placed in all four types. Their typological classification depends on the particular arguments they make and the particular positions they take in making those arguments. Of course, certain scholars frequently use one pattern of argument and so may be construed as a representative for the type. That is not a problem except that it can obscure the fact that the real issue is the arguments made and the positions taken, not the people who make them.

Second, the typology reinscribed the dualist problematic of faith and history, which in large part created the modern problem of history, as argued above. This is indicated by Dulles's intention "to distinguish more clearly between the respective competencies of faith and history" (1996, 223). At the very least, this formulation effaces the competency of theology, as distinct from the competencies of faith and history. Lindbeck's identity principles, discussed in chapter six, for example, are not merely expressions of faith nor are they only historical reconstructions. They are an interpretation of a very complex history, but Lindbeck's work is a *theologically informed* interpretation of history. Lindbeck's principles and most theological work do not fall easily into either competency if we must choose between history and faith as competencies. It should hardly be surprising that I find this a point at which Dulles's work needs to be developed since a central claim of this book is that the dualistic rendering of the problem must be abandoned in favor of a pluralistic understanding of the problematic if we are to make any progress on the problem of history. Indeed, the problems with Dulles's approach in many ways may replicate the more general problems analyzed herein.

The need to distinguish faith from theology is parallel to the need to distinguish principles from their expression. Lindbeck's principles (not stated as propositions, but as code phrases explicated by rules) are not theological claims, but principles that give identity to a religious tradition, to a "faith." But faith is not inarticulate; hence, expressions are necessary, even though they may vary and they may be disputable. When "faith" is opposed to "history," it is possible to lose the point that doing theology is not the same thing as participating in a faith tradition or having a faith. As we shall see in the final chapters, this is an important distinction; for present purposes, we simply need to note that the obscuring of this distinction is another problem with the bipolar problematic of faith and history.

Third, the dichotomy does not do justice to the gospels. While the gospels are not primarily histories, as Dulles notes, neither are they merely documents of faith. They *are* documents of faith. They are also complex *theological* interpretations of events. The gospels are literary-theological constructs that seek to proclaim the good news and to shape people as disciples. They have major historical components embedded in them. Historians try to unearth them and to distinguish not only what originates from Jesus of Nazareth but also what reflects the ways the early community developed ("under the guidance of the Spirit," a theologian might add). The gospels may not be the results of historical investigations in the modern sense, but they certainly are the result of much sifting and ordering of historical material, of historical reports, as the Gospel of Luke makes clear:

Inasmuch as many have undertaken to set down an orderly account of the events that have been fulfilled among us, just as they were handed on to us by those who from the beginning were eyewitnesses and servants of the word, I too decided, after investigating everything carefully from the very first, to write *an orderly account for you*, most excellent Theophilus, that you may know the truth concerning the things about which you have been instructed. (Luke 1:1-4, NRSV; emphasis added)

The gospels may well be interpreted history, but they are *theologically* interpreted history developed to manifest and proclaim the faith. I take Luke to be admitting to his theological interpretation by his claiming to write an orderly account, to take events as fulfillments or accomplishments, and to show the truth of the teaching that Theophilus (who may be any "God-lover" reading the text) had received.

A response to these three objections could easily be made. One could say that the categories are not essentialized reifications of a very fluid set of works, but simply guides to understanding the uses that historians and others have made of historical investigations and markings of authors' tendencies. The first objection only applies if the categories are frozen into rigidity. That would be a good response to the first objection, but one that would then either accept that the particular items for the typology are arguments or positions, rather than authors, works, or research programs, or admit that the typology is a rather unreliable guide beyond a first (and possibly misleading) approximation.

One might also say that theology is an exercise of faith, so that theology is simply on the faith side of the history-and-faith dichotomy. This presumes that the practice of theology is simply one of the practices of faith, and thus interpreted history would properly fall on the "faith" side of the dichotomy. However, as I have suggested in chapter three, argued elsewhere (Tilley 1995), and will develop in the final three chapters of this book, the role-specific responsibilities of theologians are significantly different from the responsibilities of religious "believers." In brief, theologians are charged to discover (including using the tools of historians and other social scientists), understand (including using the tools of philosophers and cultural critics), and argue for transforming when necessary and proclaim when appropriate (adding rhetoricians' tools) the convictions of the faith community. Believers have to live in and live out the faith tradition and in doing so to witness to and to proclaim the faith. As such, they are not responsible for investigating, analyzing, or transforming the tradition—unless they take the role of theologian, for example, in response to existential challenges to their faith. Hence, I argue that the categorizations by Dulles may be useful for understanding the modern problem of history with its dualistic problematic, but are not useful as a guide to the way forward in understanding the problem of history because this categorization, like other dualisms, unfortunately tends to collapse theology into faith.

Dulles also attributed historical scholars' positive or negative orientation to faith to the scholar's presuppositions. As I suggested in chapter
four, the presumptions of a practice are not necessarily the metaphysical
assumptions of the person engaging in that practice. Here, I want to
extend that contrast further and show that we should not accept the claim
that a scholar's presuppositions control results of investigations.

In writing about historians' approaches to the gospels, Dulles summarized his view as follows:

> It must be recognized, however, that judgments of historicity
> depend in great part upon antecedent presumptions. Even those
> who try to bracket their faith have to use some presuppositions
> about the kinds of reports that are to be viewed as credible.
> Because of differing a prioris, some historians will admit, and
> others will discount, revelation and miracles. Believers who want
> to recover the full truth about Jesus will wish to take advantage of
> the light that faith can supply. They will not assume, even for the
> purposes of argument, that Jesus was less than faith declares him
> to be. (Dulles 1996, 221)

In my judgment, there are a number of points in this paragraph that need
sorting out. As it stands, it leads to some rather unfortunate conclusions.

First, this view equates presumptions, presuppositions, and a prioris.
This conflation accepts the fundamental move of the Troeltschian tradition, rejected in chapter four. Dulles uses the philosophical term "a priori." That term is generally reserved for fundamental ontological or
epistemological claims. His assertion that even those who bracket their
faith (or, presumably, "unfaith") are affected by that faith when they evaluate historical sources reinforces my point. By equating presuppositions
with presumptions and a prioris, Dulles assumed, as the Troeltschians
did, that the presumptions of a practice are metaphysical a prioris and
that some of those a prioris could not really be bracketed.

Dulles is not a Troeltschian. However formally similar his view, mate-
rially there are significant differences. Dulles accepts the Troeltschian
principle that equates presumptions of the practice of doing history with
authors' beliefs. However, he differs on the proper content of those principles in that he does not accept the naturalist presumptions of the principles of analogy and correlation. Rather, Dulles presumes and believes
that God has acted and does act in history. Hence, the logic of his position equating presumptions and beliefs requires him to examine the "presuppositions" of historians as if they controlled the conclusions. His
presuppositions are different from the Troeltschians, but he gives presuppositions a role parallel to theirs.

Van Harvey's proposal to focus not on methods and presuppositions
but instead on the discipline of history and the "moral" demands it makes

on historians to warrant their claims with historical evidence can be brought in at this point. Dulles was quite right to notice how some historians overstep the competencies of their discipline. My argument in chapter five regarding Marcus Borg's work is just another in a series of arguments similar to arguments made by Dunn, Harvey, Schillebeeckx, and Dulles. But such overstepping is not the result of the presumptions one operates with in the doing of historical work. It results from allowing one's metaphysical beliefs about the way the world is control the force of one's interpretation and extension of historical work, as Moltmann did in drawing the fourth axiom against speaking of God's acting in history from Troeltsch's axioms or principles (see p. 47 above). In short, because of the conflation of different categories, this position mislocates the problem by making it a quality of a person rather than a dubiously extended inference from an argument.

Second, this position seems to make miracles and revelation into historical categories. However, historians cannot really, as historians, use "revelation" as a category. They can report that some people found certain events, persons, actions, or artifacts to be revelatory. But the concept of revelation is a theological concept. A similar issue afflicts "miracles." As noted in chapter six, miracles no longer constitute evidence, historical or otherwise, but require much evidence for one to assert their occurrence.

Dulles himself has argued that whether a person finds something revelatory depends on a correlation with her or his faith:

> On the one hand, revelation precedes faith inasmuch as, before anyone can believe, there must be symbols wherein God expresses what he is, and wills to be, for the world. . . .When believers accept revelation, they allow their minds to be determined by the meaning they find in the symbols. Thus revelation shapes their faith.
>
> On the other hand, faith exists before revelation inasmuch as the symbols do not yield their meaning except to religious inquirers or believers who are actively committed to the search for truth. The quest itself involves a kind of implicit faith—a confidence that the search is not a futile one and that God's revelation, if it exists, can be recognized. When the search has succeeded, faith actively receives revelation and provides it, so to speak, with a dwelling place in the mind. Since revelation cannot exist as such outside a created mind, revelation may be said to presuppose faith. (Dulles 1992, 279-80)

If we accept his correlation of faith with revelation, then his finding that some historians preclude discussing revelation is irrelevant. While it may be important that the person doing history have faith, it is not or should not be a factor in her or his properly historical work. Finding an event rev-elatory is within the competency of faith, not of history, on Dulles's own account of the matter. Hence, to fault historians because they have no room for revelation is a category error. To fault theologians or inter-preters of the tradition for having no room for revelation would be an entirely different matter.

What Dulles's argument highlights helpfully, however, is that some scholars who claim to be doing historical work are covertly also doing the-ology. For theologians to deny revelation or miracles is a different issue. To say that "revelation" and "miracles" are not historical categories is legitimate. But to argue that specific texts are not in some sense revela-tory or some acts and events are not miraculous is a theological argu-ment, not a historical one. Once we distinguish faith from theology and recognize that some revisionist theologians ply their trade as if they are "merely" historians, we can take Dulles's point more positively. The prob-lem is not the point he makes, but the structuring of his argument by the bipolar problematic.

With regard to miracles, even historians who are the most critical of introducing faith claims into historical analysis accept that Jesus per-formed healing acts. Marcus Borg, for example, is one who attempts rig-orously to exclude faith affirmations from his historical work. Nonetheless, he affirms that it is historically reliable that "Jesus per-formed paranormal healings and exorcisms" (Borg and Wright 1999, 66). How he performed them is another matter. Few historians affirm the nature miracles, such as Jesus' walking on water or his feeding miracles, as historically reliable. They tend to find them either embellishments of remembered events or imaginative ways of proclaiming early Christians' faith in Jesus. However, historians' acceptances or rejections of Jesus' exorcising and healing acts as historically reliable simply do not necessar-ily track with their being conservative or traditional, on the one hand, or liberal or revisionist, on the other. Nor do they imply acceptance of the reality of the demons being exorcised as minions of the devil. But that some of the healings are properly described as exorcisms is not at issue. That is the way they were perceived and accepted (and in some areas still are; see Cuneo 2001 for an ethnographer's exploration of current prac-tices in exorcism).

The key issue is not whether Jesus performed the actions attributed to him in the gospels. Historians generally affirm some as historically more or less reliable, some as more or less likely to be embellishments, and some as indeterminate. The issue is one of explanation. Are the heal-ings, presuming them reliable, indeed truly miraculous? Well, that depends on what a person means by a miracle. Given the early-modern and modern history of that term, noted in the previous chapter, no sim-ple answer can be given. But if one is asking whether these signs are acts of God, the answer to that question is not within the realm of the historians' work. The discipline is no longer in position (if it ever was) to distinguish the natural act from the preternatural act and either from the supernatural act. Historical investigations may establish some probability that an event or type of event or act occurred. They can say that Jesus did indeed perform healing acts and exorcisms. But they cannot say whether these were natural, preternatural, or supernatural acts. Their disciplinary presumptions limit them to the arena of the natural. They cannot say the acts were miracles.

Historians are limited in what their discipline allows them to do. They can affirm or deny the historical probability that Jesus performed healings and exorcisms, and even that they were taken for miracles by those who witnessed them, but not that Jesus' acts *were* or *were not* miracles. They might sometimes find sufficient evidence to debunk miracle claims by providing evidence that there is good reason to believe that some act alleged to be a miracle was not performed at all. They can work to show what the text of a sacred book is and what it meant to those who wrote it, read it, and heard it at various times. But historical investigations can neither establish nor disestablish whether a text is a revelation, that is, whether God in some sense revealed the text, what was in it, or whether the text is a reaction to, interpretation, or record of God's own self. Those are theological issues and require theological judgments. In short, historians as historians simply cannot say whether something is miraculous or revelatory.

Asking questions about a scholar's hermeneutical presuppositions and methodological foundations does not always enable us to solve problems when history seems to be in conflict with or in support of faith. The question of a scholar's interpretation theory or method may not be the most fruitful question to ask about the works a scholar produces. A more relevant question is whether the scholar has used non-historical warrants to support supposedly historical claims. In fact, what passes for historical debunking is sometimes not done within the methodologically atheistic practice of history at all, but based in substantive, metaphysical atheistic commitments. More importantly, the question about presuppositions often obscures the fact that the investigations themselves may upset the methodologies, presumptions, or a prioris that scholars bring to the investigation, a point mentioned in chapter four as a methodological principle.

This is not only a principle but is also the practice of excellent historians. For example, consider the following methodological point from Elizabeth A. Clark's *The Origenist Controversy:*

> [W]hen I began my research on the Origenist controversy in 1985, before I had encountered Evagrius Ponticus, I imagined that I might explain the controversy with little reference to theo-

logical "ideas" of any sort. But my introduction to Evagrius's *Kephalaia gnostica* in its unexpurgated form challenged my early, purely social understanding of the Origenist dispute. By situating Evagrius as a central force in the Western (i.e., Latin-speaking) Origenist debate, I signal my chastened reconsideration of the importance of both theology and an ascetic spirituality for the controversy. (Clark 1992, 6-7)

Clark did not allow her materialist and social-historical presumptions to control the results of her research. Nor did she allow those presumptions to control the questions she asked of the monuments and texts from the past. Rather, her investigation itself revealed that those presumptions needed to be factored out in order to do justice to the evidence she was uncovering and to construct a narrative of the controversy that did justice to that evidence. Clark fulfilled the role-specific responsibilities of the historian by the standards of the historians' craft because she did not allow her personal presuppositions or her theological views to function as illegitimate warrants or controls in asking her questions, making her arguments, or constructing her narrative. It is not that she had or has or did not have or does not have hermeneutical presumptions or personal beliefs about religious matters, which differ greatly from those involved in the disputes, but that she did not allow them to control or affect improperly her historical questions or warrant her historical claims. While not abandoning a critical perspective, historians do attempt to think in some ways as their subjects did within the horizons of the subjects. The way to evaluate historians' claims, then, is not so much to evaluate their presuppositions but to evaluate whether they have been responsible historians by marshaling the evidence and warranting their claims in ways appropriate to the disciplines of history.

Third, Dulles himself has approved of one effort that looked to many people as an undermining of "the full truth about Jesus." Many Catholics in the past (and some in the present) would have accepted the following syllogism as part of the "full truth" about Jesus: If Jesus is God incarnate, then he has the attributes of God. But one of God's attributes is omniscience. Therefore, Jesus was omniscient. I know of no competent historian who would find that claim sensible on historical grounds. Dulles put this point more elegantly:

Theologians of earlier centuries often spoke of Jesus' infused knowledge in such a way as to suggest that he did not need to learn from other people, from books, or from experience. Modern biblical scholarship has helped to correct this view, and has enabled us to make the psychology of Jesus more intelligible. (Dulles 1996, 223)

Yet it is not clear how one might distinguish between "corrections" to the faith, which Dulles accepts, and "undermining" of the faith, which he rejects, unless one distinguishes, as we did in the previous chapter, between principles and their formulations. In the past, claims about Jesus' infused knowledge may have expressed the principle of christological maximalism, but such expressions are no longer useful or credible expressions of that principle. Theologians, not historians, have the disciplinary duty to make such adjustments in the expression of faith. Again, the bipolar problematic obscures the distinctions between the work of historians and theologians by collapsing theology into faith.

The upshot of these points is that Dulles's approach only implicitly distinguishes what is immune from historical work and what is not. His categories can be sharpened by finding theological construction to be a category distinct either from religious faith or historical investigation. When we do so, we can take a step to seeing how part of the discipline of theology is to distinguish principles from their formulations. If we don't make those distinctions, we can all too readily be confused about crucial theological issues. Indeed, that is just what happened in a painful dispute in which Dulles was involved, one that has turned out to be, I believe, a tempest in a teapot, but a very instructive one.

"An Orchestrated Chorus of Rejection"

In a series of essays published in the spring of 1998, Avery Dulles, S.J., Mary Ann Donovan, S.C., and Peter Steinfels argued whether the Catholic Theological Society of America (CTSA) was really Catholic. This exchange was triggered by the 1997 Convention of the CTSA and the publication of its Proceedings, including full versions of the plenary addresses. The plenary addresses explored current issues in the theology and history of the Eucharist. In his essay initiating the *Commonweal* series, Dulles endorsed Bernard Cardinal Law's claim that the CTSA had become a "wasteland" devoted to "advocacy for theological dissent." Dulles said that an "orchestrated chorus . . . rejected fundamental articles of Catholic belief regarding priesthood and Eucharist . . ." (Dulles 1998, 13). Dulles cited numerous examples of this theological attack. Mary Ann Donovan, then president of the CTSA and responsible for organizing the convention in question, argued that Dulles had misinterpreted the material in the Proceedings (Donovan 1998, 14-16).

Dulles's attack on the CTSA may have been motivated, in part, by the convention's seeming support for ordaining non-celibate men and women. Beyond that, speakers had minimized the role of the ordained priest in the Eucharist, had found the words of consecration comparatively unimportant, and had supported contemporary theological work recognizing the Eucharist as an action of the whole assembly, not the priest alone. While Dulles was certainly not alone in his concerns, the vigor of his opposition suggests that he identified specific positions on these issues as either principles of the faith or formulations of the faith that could not be surpassed.

Dulles had historian Gary Macy, among others, in his sights when writing of the convention. Macy had given one of the plenary addresses, which summarized the meticulous and challenging work he had done on popular devotion to and theologies of the Eucharist in the Middle Ages. In so doing he revealed a true diversity of doctrine and practice in the medieval period. His work (and the work of others) had shown that the Fourth Lateran Council in 1215 used the term "transubstantiation" to say what happened when the bread and wine became the body and blood of Christ, but that proponents of three different views could have legitimately claimed that the term covered their views. All three were taken to be orthodox. One view could be called "co-existence": the bread and wine remained along with the body and blood. A second can be labeled "substitution": the substance of the bread and wine was annihilated and the substance of the body and blood remained. A third was "transmutation": the substance of the bread and wine was changed into the substance of the body and blood (Macy 1999, 82-83). Edward Kilmartin, S.J., made a similar finding, but used the terms "consubstantiation," "annihilation," and "conversion" (1998, 145-46). According to Macy, orthodox theologians held theories of all three types even into the sixteenth century under the general term "transubstantiation." Catholic theologians, however, began to abandon the "co-existence" doctrine, and the Council of Trent (1545-1563) equated the "transubstantiation" term of Lateran IV with Aristotelian-Thomistic transmutation.

Macy's research showed that a view common among theologians and church leaders that an Aristotelian-Thomistic understanding of transubstantiation as transmutation was *the* medieval doctrine is not warranted. Macy claimed that "Thomas's work, interesting as it remains, was an idiosyncratic voice in thirteenth century eucharistic theology and by the end of that century, a voice which ceased to convince" (Macy 1997, 52). Kilmartin would apparently disagree with this point, finding that the thirteenth-century development was a high point of the theological reflection begun in the previous century (Kilmartin 1998, 153). Macy concluded that "despite a surprisingly tenacious belief that a 'dogma of transubstantiation' was promulgated by the Fourth Lateran Council and enforced by the medieval Church, the evidence suggests this was never the case, especially if by this one equates transubstantiation with transmutation" (Macy 1999, 105).

Macy had shown that a verbal token, "transubstantiation," had shifted its meaning substantially: the word remained the same, but the range of acceptable understandings of it narrowed from many meanings in the early thirteenth century to one meaning in the sixteenth century. If one were to take the Fourth Lateran Council (1215) as endorsing only one way of understanding that term, as transmutation, which later theologians and, arguably, the church fathers meeting at the Council of Trent did, that would be a historical error. Whether it is a theological error is a different issue, not entirely unrelated, but nonetheless different; to attack or defend that narrowing as appropriate to the articulation of the faith is a different question from the one of whether they did actually narrow the articulation to one form of words. Kilmartin, despite finding the thirteenth century a "high point," noted that "the teaching of Trent contributed to the suppression of a series of important aspects of the authentic whole tradition of the theology of the Eucharist" (1998, 150).

Macy's work, both in the convention address and in his other publications, can be understood as affirming that, in the past, a plurality of expressions of the essential sacramentality of the Eucharist was legitimate. Indeed, his address goes further by suggesting that once one recognizes that in some theological opinion (and apparently in popular religiosity in the Middle Ages) that "spiritual communion" was construed as a true reception, then the widely believed view that reception of the Eucharist was rare is not entirely warranted. In this sense, the notion of real presence in the sacramental species may well be downplayed; but it is not clear that it was significantly denied or opposed as a principle, even though it was variously construed, especially if spiritual reception indeed was real reception (Macy 1997, 50-52).

John Baldovin, S.J., also sought to reunderstand the agency in the eucharistic celebration. "The Christian tradition has consistently affirmed that it is Christ who baptizes, anoints, offers himself at the Eucharist, etc. The sacraments are acts of Christ, head and members. Thus, they are ecclesial acts" (Baldovin 1997, 68). Baldovin argued that the Eucharist was "fundamentally a communal enterprise in which, since the point of the ritual is incorporation into Christ, the whole Christ, head and members must be the agent" (Baldovin 1997, 77). The fact that the Eucharist is an action of Christ in head and members and that liturgical leadership is thus properly a shared exercise, "the perceived dominance of the ordained presider is an anomaly that needs to be rectified—more in practice than in theory" (Baldovin 1997, 73).

In his remarks, Dulles presumed that the convention presenters were attacking the faith. "These views were set forth with a certain display of historical erudition as though doctrines could be invalidated by tagging them chronologically" (Dulles 1998, 14). But as Mary Ann Donovan pointed out in her response to Dulles's essay, "to adduce historical evidence for earlier stages of doctrinal development is not to attack doctrine" (Donovan 1998, 16). In terms developed in this text, Dulles is arguing that the CTSA presenters had attacked the principles themselves, whereas Donovan claimed that the principles could remain intact even if specific historical formulations were argued to be no longer the best expressions available. The issue was not one of historical claims being used to undermine faith, as Dulles suggested; rather, the question was whether specific doctrinal formulations were necessary to express the faith. The historical arguments can properly be understood as undermining specific formulations and opening the way for theological reformulation (as Dulles had recognized regarding what were taught as doctrines of the consciousness of Jesus). But Donovan also seems to have been captured by the bipolar form of the problematic, for she might have clarified the issue had she distinguished between the substance of the faith and the way in which it is presented.

Baldovin and Macy made some very interesting claims about enduring patterns and remarkable diversity in Catholic sacramental tradition. So far as I know, their claims have not been refuted by historical investigations. Macy's point, that *only* one of the three legitimate meanings that "transubstantiation" had in the thirteenth century was accounted legitimate in the sixteenth century was a historical argument about a problem (seen now, but not then), with a theological discernment made at the Council of Trent. Whether the Tridentine account of transubstantiation was then or is now *theologically* legitimate is a theological argument, another form of "theologically interpreted history," not merely historical argument.

In turn, Msgr. M. Francis Mannion attacked Donovan and her defense of the convention. Mannion found her defense uncompelling, "because, though it appears to refute Dulles, she ends up for the purposes of defense placing herself in a position considerably to the 'right' of the operative convictions of American sacramental theology—a position I do not believe she generally inhabits" (Mannion 1998, 30). In effect, he accused her of dissembling because he assumed both that he knew her positions on sacramental theology and that those positions were the same as the presumptions of doing historical work like that displayed at the convention.

Mannion might have made a similar argument against Macy. Macy noted that a renegotiation of ritual power occurred in the late twelfth and early thirteenth centuries. This is the result of his work as a historian. However, in his peroration, Macy suggested that there is reason to think that there may be a ritual renegotiation occurring today (1997, 56-58), a state of affairs about which he confessed optimism and enthusiasm. His optimism is not a historical claim, but a theological (and sociological) opinion that could be further explored. Whether anyone would be or should be optimistic and enthusiastic nearly seven years later (the time of the present writing) is arguable. That a renegotiation of ritual power is occurring, unhappily fueled by the scandals racking the Catholic Church regarding pedophilia, ephebophilia, and the authorities' cover-ups, is unquestionable; the enthusiasm for such renegotiation seems rare now. But Macy's views reflected in that enthusiasm were not presuppositions that caused Macy's historical investigations to come out the way they did.

Many of the concerns Dulles and Mannion raised are legitimate. Much Catholic sacramental theology has gone far beyond positions that were standard in the recent past. The neoscholastic synthesis in sacramental theology characteristic of much of twentieth-century Catholicism has been left far behind. Whether these advances can indeed preserve the principles that many assumed were preserved in that synthesis is an open question. But it is also an open question whether the synthesis elevated to the status of indefeasible principles a number of defeasible formulations of the faith. Avoiding the bipolar problematic enables a much clearer understanding of what is at issue.

One problem with the way Dulles and Mannion approached these issues was to assume that a scholar's own theological views control the historical investigations. In effect, Dulles and Mannion continued to accept the formal point of the Troeltschian tradition that one's theological or ontological presuppositions are the presumptions of one's historical investigations. In fact, save for cases of special pleading or methodological unclarity, historians *qua* historians do not or should not conflate the two. Indeed, the best historians allow the data they collect to become evidence even against their own particular methodological presumptions and to revise those presumptions if needed, as Clark did in the example noted above. The problem can be exacerbated, of course, when historians fail to note that they are "changing hats" and making theological claims, based in part on the evidence their historical investigations have turned up.

Mannion, in effect, accused Donovan of dissembling about her own views. But her views were not relevant to the issues involved in the disputes. Dulles evidently attributed Baldovin's and Macy's historical claims to their theological stances. Mannion did the same for Donovan.

This approach obscures the issues. Macy's optimism about the (then) present ferment neither substantiated nor undermined his historical arguments. His historical views were based on the evidence he had unearthed from decades of examining the work of famous and obscure medieval theologians. Rather, Macy expressed in a plenary address to a theological society both his appreciation of the present ferment in debate and practice as being as interesting and exciting as that of the thirteenth century, and his optimism for the church in this era. Neither of these is a historical judgment or a presumption for historical work. As part of the concluding peroration, these remarks clearly were not intended to be historical judgments, but rather to show that work on obscure historical matters might even be of use to theologians in the present. Baldovin's comments were more strictly theological, but they were also more status reports concerning contemporary sacramental theology than arguments for specific positions. Baldovin buttressed arguments of the general form—"Despite some twentieth-century theological views, I must tell you we *haven't always understood or enacted* the sacraments in the same way"—with historical references from standard sources.

Mannion conflated Donovan's theological views with the presumptions with which she carries out her historical and textual analysis. Dulles did the same with Macy and Baldovin. Where Donovan stood on issues in sacramental theology was irrelevant; her theological views were not a factor in that argument. No one, to my knowledge, using the tools of the historian's craft, has shown that Macy has failed to substantiate his historical claims. He is a responsible historian, the preeminent American historian of medieval eucharistic theology. Indeed, many of his findings are corroborated by the independent work of Kilmartin (1998). I see no reason to justify a claim that he used his own theological beliefs or religious hopes as presuppositions for warranting historical claims. Nor did he ever claim, so far as I know, that his historical excavations, analyses, and reconstructions showed it unreasonable for us to accept contemporary doctrinal formulae. Baldovin utilized historical sources, but in a rather limited way. He constantly affirmed the sacramental principle and the real presence of Christ in the Eucharist. The issues surrounding the need for an ordained priest to preside at the eucharistic assembly—assumed by the neoscholastic synthesis—come up when one understands the assembly, not just the priest, as united with and representing Christ in the celebration. Similar remarks could be made about Donovan.

The issue is whether the positions alluded to by Dulles and Mannion are the only proper expressions of the sacramental principles constitutive of Catholicism or whether other, more "advanced," theological expressions could also express those principles. Once we distinguish the principles of the faith from the expression of them, it is clear that the participants did not deny or undermine the principles in the tradition, but were suggesting the need for, and occasionally advocating, shifts in the expressions of those principles. Dulles and Mannion might well disagree, but to do so, they need to show that these formulations are not appropriate expressions of the principles that give identity to the Catholic sacramental tradition.

Another factor contributing to the vehemence of the response to the convention Proceedings was the fact that the convention also (by a very large majority) agreed that one of the truly neuralgic issues in this area—the need for males only to preside at Eucharist—was not shown to be a necessary expression of the principle of representation of Christ in and at the Eucharist, and that further research in this area should be permitted. The question is not about the deposit of faith, the idea of Christianity, or the principles that shape Catholic identity. The issue is how theologians in the past offered formulae that embodied these principles and which formula or formulae can effectively embody them today. Few in the theological community are convinced that the issues regarding a male-only priesthood have been resolved.

One of the points at issue can again illustrate what is at stake. A specific understanding of "transubstantiation," the Aristotelian-Thomistic account of transubstantiation as transmutation, is not a principle. It is a formula that expresses a principle of real presence. It "explains" how that real presence is effected. Many scholars have argued that there is a specifically Catholic principle, which David Tracy has labeled "the analogical (or sacramental) imagination" (Tracy 1981; also see Greeley 2000; Tilley 2000, 125-34). What makes this way of construing the world possible is the practice of a sacramental faith and the development of a specifically Catholic principle in theology (as distinguished from what Tracy called the "dialectical imagination" of Protestantism). The operative principle in that sacramental faith regarding the specific sacrament of the Eucharist is the principle of the real presence of Jesus Christ in the Eucharist. "Transubstantiation" is one traditional formula that has embodied that principle. (Whether it still does so is a matter many continue to debate.)

Nor, we can now see, was the principle at stake the words of institution of the Eucharist. Dulles had claimed that a speaker had "attached no importance" to them and that sacramental theology needed "to question the very notion of a consecratory formula" (Dulles 1998, 13). Donovan argued that Dulles had made some selective misreadings of the convention presentations (Donovan 1998, 15). But more interestingly, less than three years later, the Congregation for the Doctrine of the Faith (CDF) had found that the Assyrian eucharistic prayer, the Anaphora of Addai and Mari, was valid despite the fact that it never had a recitation of the words of institution and the fact that "the Catholic Church considers the words of the Eucharistic Institution a constitutive and therefore indispensable part of the Anaphora or Eucharistic Prayer" (Pontifical Council for Promoting Christian Unity 2001, §3). Even a tradition without a consecratory formula could be found a valid expression of the principle (although an exceptional and unusual tradition, from the point of view of the Roman Church). The CDF's remarkable finding suggests that there may be more legitimate theological diversity on these matters than Dulles suggested there was in his comments three years earlier. Certainly, the words of institution are not a necessary guarantee of sacramental validity or a necessary expression of the principle of Christ's presence in the eucharistic action.

Nonetheless, conservative theologians and others properly worry about the contemporary loss of the principle of real presence, a constituent of the Catholic principle of the analogical imagination (see Steinfels 1998, 17). If the analogical imagination is a defining principle of the Catholic tradition and if that principle or a crucial constituent of it, namely, the real presence of Christ in the Eucharist, is lost, then the Catholic tradition has undergone a major transmutation. It no longer would be what it has been. It would suffer what Newman would call a "discontinuity in principles." A Catholic community that did not believe in the real presence would be in discontinuity with the great tradition. It is quite important to raise questions about contemporary acceptance of the principle of real presence; but these are different questions than questions about the necessity of using the term "transubstantiation" (understood as transmutation), the necessity of consecratory formulae, or the necessity of an ordained male to preside in the eucharistic assembly in order to express the conviction of real presence, a constituent of the sacramental principle at the heart of Catholic faith.

What Macy and Donovan have claimed is that there are many articulations of the principle of the real presence. Even the theory of transubstantiation "was developed not in order to secure the fact of the essential change of the bread and wine into the body and blood of Christ. This fact was taken for granted" (Kilmartin 1998, 149). The principle of real presence is, in my judgment, an identity principle in the Catholic tradition. The virtue of the concept of transubstantiation, according to Kilmartin, was the affirmation of the presence of the whole Christ and the overcoming of the dichotomy of "crass realism—subjective symbolism."

But Kilmartin then continues that the doctrine of transubstantiation "has its weaknesses" (Kilmartin 1998, 149). "Transubstantiation" is not identical to the principle of the real presence. "Real presence" is not subject to historical undermining, even though the formulae that express it may be questioned on the basis of historical investigations and thus are debatable within the proper work of Catholic theologians. Specific doctrinal formulae may have to be reformed in light of historical investigations and present needs. By failing to distinguish principles and their formulation, Dulles and Mannion stirred up a tempest where none should have occurred.

The plenary addresses to the CTSA convention, as Donovan put it, presented an authentic, but neglected, strand of the tradition that "emphasizes the entire eucharistic liturgy as celebrated by the whole gathered people of God. To present and explain this growing consensus, in scholarly papers at a theological convention, is the proper work of the Catholic theologian" (Donovan 1998, 16). This is neither an argument against the principle of the real presence nor even against the doctrinal formula of transubstantiation. Rather, it is an attempt to explore ways in which the sacramental principle constitutive of Roman Catholicism can be preserved in the community today, especially in regard to understanding the real presence in the Eucharist, by articulating in ways that can help nurture and evoke the liturgical and other practices that constitute lived belief in, rather than nominal lip-service to, the principle of the real presence.

How to articulate that principle or article of faith has been argued in the medieval and contemporary eras. That the articulation is in dispute does not mean that the principle is disputed, much less opposed or rejected. Or so another correspondent suggested in his comment on the dispute. Roger Cardinal Mahony wrote:

> Theologians are to be commended for continuing the church's efforts to articulate ever more deeply and fully its eucharistic faith—a task that needs to be done in each age. In carrying forward this effort, some disagreement is unavoidable. But how we treat disagreements among us speaks loudly to the entire world about the depth of our faith and our trust in the Holy Spirit working within the church. (Mahony 1998, 4)

Mahony is asking whether the critics allowed their faith and trust in the Spirit to be undermined by historical argument. In the less religiously inflected terms used in this book, the question is whether the critics have indeed conflated a principle of Catholic Christianity with its articulation.

That we are in a period of dispute about the best articulations of this principle is clear. But it is not correct to presume that a historical investigation that shows that there have been diverse articulations accepted as orthodox in the past is motivated by rejection of that principle or is an attack on it. Rather, the problem of this tempest in a teapot—which is, in the end, instructive about other tempests as well—is that the bipolar problematic of faith and history is part of the problem because it obscures the issues, the logic of arguments involved, and the possibilities of finding theological solutions to theological problems involved in religious expressions.

Conclusion

Dulles's category of interpreted history is an important one. His way of working with the category, however, reduces his position to one in which history is almost irrelevant to faith, both in its principles and in its articulations. In the material discussed here, he, like many theologians, continued to construe the problem of faith and history in much the same terms Harvey showed inadequate in 1966. "Faith" and "history" seem to be construed as naming some essential ideas or practices that can be modeled as related to each other in constant and specific patterns.

The problem is more complex than that. Nor is the attribution of the results of historical investigations to non-historical presuppositions very enlightening. Indeed, such attribution can even obscure the real issues.

Dulles's response to the problem of history, given his typology, seems to reproduce the strategies of the neo-orthodox theologians of the past, who wanted to "save" belief by insulating it from historical inquiry (except historical inquiry that supported, enhanced or nuanced that belief), an approach that falls afoul of Harvey's paradox (see pp. 30-31 above). It is an approach that Dulles did not support in laying out his categories in his earlier essay, but it seems to have shaped, at least in part, the arguments he made in 1998 about the CTSA.

While Dulles rightly noted that some principles are immune from historical investigation and that attacks on them are attacks on the tradition, he seems to have identified the principles with customary articulations of them. Donovan rightly noted that doctrines were not being attacked. But both operated in the bipolar framework that prohibited finding a constructive way of working with the issues or of understanding how one could overcome crucial divisions without rancor or scandal, as Cardinal Mahony sought.

Historical work may indeed indirectly undermine confidence about the unchanging character of some specific beliefs or practices. But if a tradition exists, then its principles stand fast even while those articulations may be debated. The issue is discerning whether or not the articulations we propose or use are proper articulations of the principles. And that is not an easy task—since the only way we know the principle is through the articulations. (Hence, working with the difficulties of "following a rule" occupied a significant part of my earlier book, *Inventing Catholic Tradition*, for whether the tradition lives or is deformed or transmuted depends on how and whether the community that carries that tradition follows a rule; see Tilley 2000, 89-122.)

If the articulations of the problem of history continue to be profoundly and irremediably flawed and to warp our theological discourse in unhappy ways, then how can we break through to a better understanding? I have earlier suggested that the concept of "role-specific" responsibilities is crucial. The next two chapters examine the ways in which historians have been carrying out their responsibilities. The final chapters then will lay out the responsibilities of theologians and believers and how they are affected by and may affect the practices of historians. What are the "moralities of knowledge" (Harvey 1986) or the "virtues of the mind" (Zagzebski) needed for engaging in the practices of doing historical investigations, constructing theological claims, and living out religious convictions? The next two chapters will answer these questions regarding historians. The following chapter will bring home these issues to the work of theologians.

CHAPTER 8

Practicing History I

The Battling Secular Historians

> *Social history—the history of the people*
> *with the politics left out.*
> —after G. M. Trevelyan

> *Social history, when it is not a dismal science,*
> *can easily become a sentimental one.*
> —Gertrude Himmelfarb

For nearly a century, proponents of various "new histories" or "histories from below" such as social history, microhistory, psychohistory, economic history, and standpoint (Marxist, feminist, queer, etc.) histories have been battling with traditional, "objectivist" historians for supremacy over the discipline of history. While proponents of each new history sometimes fight the partisans of other approaches, each provides a contested alternative approach to "history from above," "elite history," or, more simply, the "old history." "Old historians" are those historians of ideas and political, national, military, diplomatic, and institutional historians and others who tend to use traditional approaches to writing history. They tend to support objective history as opposed to relativistic history, advocacy in historical writing, or particular standpoint approaches to the writing of history. The old historians tend also to agree "that the natural mode of historical writing is essentially narrative" (Himmelfarb 1987, 1) even though "for those committed to the defense of historical objectivity, a literary or narrativist orientation [is] dangerous" (Novick 1988, 624).

As I suggested in the introduction, the fields of history are highly contested. What counts as "history" is not as clear as it was a century ago, or even some forty years ago, when Harvey was writing *The Historian and the Believer*. As Harvey was finishing his work, the most devastating attack to date was about to be launched against the objectivist synthesis which had held the upper hand in the battle against relativism for at least a quarter century. The ferocity of these battles has had the effect of making the "problem of history" for theology remarkably unstable on the "history" side. The "morality of historical knowledge" that Harvey portrayed (1968) has broken up into many "moralities." No single pattern of "good practice" can cover the varied practices of the historians. This alone complicates any easy solution to the problem of history: many histories present many sorts of problems.

Moreover, the historians' guild has come to substantial disagreement over the principles that shape their discipline and the presumptions of their work. In principle, history remains naturalistic. Its practice presumes that, as chapter six discussed, neither preternatural nor supernatural agents are within the historians' purview. Nor do historians marshal evidence that can be used *historically* to warrant claims about such agents. The relevance of such evidence to theology is another matter, as chapter seven mentioned and chapter ten develops. There is no evidence that the Troeltschian presumptions discussed in chapter four are in play in discussions of the contemporary practice of history. Historians, as we shall see, disagree about what presumptions historians should have as they engage in their work.

"That Noble Dream" Shattered

In *That Noble Dream* (1988), Peter Novick presented a fascinating and insightful history of the professional discipline of history in the United States. Novick organized his astute narrative around how the "objectivity question" was posed and opposed in the historians' guild. The "noble dream" that constituted the "founding myth" of history is the notion that history was and is an objective account of what is past. The objectivity question can be put like this: "Is indeed the practice of history the seeking of the one objectively true historical representation that corresponds to the reality of the events and the patterns of events found in the past, written by a (relatively) value-free, neutral investigator whose interpretation is to be judged on how well it accords with the facts on which it depends?" In effect, Novick asked, "Does the myth hold? Is the dream alive?" His answer was "no."

The academic practice of history in the United States began in the late nineteenth century with an affirmative response to those questions. The "noble dream," as Charles A. Beard had characterized the objectivist ideal in a 1935 essay, was construed at the foundation of the discipline as a constituting principle of the practice of history. Novick shows that this principle was based on a (mis)reading or partial reading of the great German historian Leopold von Ranke. Ranke offered the oft-cited dictum that the work of historians was to present the past *wie es eigentlich gewesen.* Americans read Ranke as an empiricist, dedicated to the facts, to history portraying events, translating that German phrase as "as they *really* were." However, Ranke was something of an idealist and romantic who wanted to open himself to "the flow of intuitive perception" (see Novick 1988, 28) and sought in his own work to understand past events not so much as they really were, but rather as portraying "what was *essentially* happening." Whether Americans creatively misread the meaning of *eigentlich* or caught only part of its meaning, this commitment to objectivity in the American historical community became the founding ideal of professional, academic history in the United States. "Rankean" history was opposed to "subjectivist" history and "Whig history," interpretations of the past which show how we arrived in our glorious present. Competent historians would tell the truth, the whole truth, and nothing but the truth about the past. Such was the "Rankean" "noble dream."

During and after the First World War (an anachronistic designation!) "a changed cultural, social, and political climate produced 'historical relativism,' which, though it never became the dominant view within the profession, did put believers in objectivity on the defensive" (Novick 1988, 16). "The principal argument of the historical relativists . . . was that so far as they could see, historical interpretations always had been, and for various technical reasons always would be, 'relative' to the historian's time, place, values and purposes. They never maintained that historians had a choice in the matter" (Novick 1988, 166). The differences in the presuppositions that the historians brought to the material, the questions that they asked, the purposes for which, and audiences to which they wrote all required that their interpretations be "relative" to (not "relevant" in the shallow sense that would become popular later in the century) the needs of their own times.

Charles A. Beard and Carl L. Becker were proponents of the view that historians simply were always influenced by their own moral, religious, and political concerns and that historians inevitably had to choose from the data they uncovered which data was to be used as evidence—and that their own concerns and purposes shaped their choices of what would count as evidence. "Objectivity . . . can be seen as the founding myth of the historical profession; the pursuit of the objective truth its sacred mission and raison d'être. Small wonder, then, that for many, though not exclusively, those of the older generation, the theses of Becker and Beard were not just mistaken, but anathema" (Novick 1988, 268).

Despite appearances to the contrary, these relativists were not opposing historical objectivity *in toto*, but were challenging three main ideas: that the facts speak for themselves, that any historian could possibly engage in a truly "value-free" investigation, and that the objectivists' ideal of a history that would be a one-to-one correspondence of one "true" interpretation with the way things really were was possible. The relativists were not denying that there were facts or evidence or good historical judgment; they were, however, saying that the facts did not speak for themselves, that historians had to write their history for valuable purposes, and that there might be more than one way validly to represent the slice of the past with which the historian was concerned. Indeed, the very ways in which the historians "sliced" the past indicated that the relativists' claims had some serious warrant.

Today, such a "God's-eye view" that constitutes classical historical objectivism seems an impossible ideal; but an ideal it was—and, in a chastened form, still is. From about 1940 until the early sixties, the ideal of objectivity regained significant footing in the historical community as the old historians co-opted the work of the relativists. As Novick put it:

> Among those historians who attempted to deal with the relativist challenge, the most common attitude was what has been termed, in another connection, "restriction by partial incorporation," though in this case "rejection by partial incorporation" might be more accurate. Becker and Beard were frequently acknowledged to have performed an important service in freeing historians from the belief that "the facts spoke for themselves." (Nozick 1988, 410)

While historians were more chastened about the success of their interpretations to match the ideal, the ideal remained. The "objectivity question" would be answered "yes," even while historians' imaginative contributions to their representations of the past would be recognized.

The sixties, however, saw the ideal of objectivity washed away by wave after wave of challenges. Although various forms of social history (sometimes with the slogan, "history from the bottom up") had been utilized in American historical community for many decades, the maturing approaches developed in the *Annales* school in France and in other locations, influenced by social theory, social sciences, structuralism, and poststructuralist theory, burst upon the American scene. Even though the new histories did not deeply penetrate the American historical consciousness extensively until the 1960s, they had received their most important voice with the founding of the *Annales d'histoire économique et sociale* in 1929. After World War II, the name of the journal became *Annales: Economies, Sociétés, Civilisations*. Although the term "*Annales* school" is still used, it no longer clearly designates what it once did: a certain kind of historical project that had as its purpose the writing of what can be called a "total history" of an event or place. The "*Annales* school" contribution, especially of forms of social history, genealogical history, and microhistory, has helped to transform the disciplines of history. Its journal has become "the most influential historical organ in France, possibly in the world" (Himmelfarb 1987, 3). As one survey of historiography put it, it also is clear that "the creative imagination of its scholars has dissolved any semblance of cohesion" (Breisach 1994, 376). Difference in approach, style, method, and goals ruled history—not only in the *Annales* school, but in the disciplines of history more generally—even to the point of chaos. In 1988 Novick could write, "As a broad community of discourse, as a community of scholars united by common aims, common standards, and common purposes, the discipline of history had ceased to exist. Convergence on anything, let alone a subject as highly charged as 'the objectivity question,' was out of the question" (1988, 628). That the noble dream of objectivity collapsed as a unifying myth was and is obvious; that history as a more fragmented discipline with a host of competing methodologies spread over fields unimagined a century ago has come to an end is not so clear.

There was no single cause for the "chaos," nor was there any determining battle that routed the objectivists. Indeed, the battle goes on (e.g., Himmelfarb 1994, 131-62). Rather, "[t]he collapse of professional historical study as an even minimally cohesive venture was the result of a number of gradual developments—a confluence of evolutionary changes which had accelerated in recent decades and which, both singly and in combination, at some point 'went critical'" (Novick 1988, 579). Socially, the discipline had been the province of white males, mostly Protestant or unreligious (with an increasingly healthy number of Jews, but few Catholics), a hegemony which has been shattered. Intellectually, the emergence of different forms of history as powerful and sometimes intrinsically interesting, as described in the first paragraph of this chapter, has unseated the old historians. As a discipline, history was enhanced (or degraded) by the social sciences. As Novick put it, "As with other developments that challenged the autonomy and integrity of history, the increasing permeability of its borders was not a new development, but rather an acceleration of previously gradual processes" (1988, 584). As history was invaded—for better or worse—by social-scientific and postmodernist discourses and the new histories supplanted the old, the net result was that, "On 'the objectivity question'—as on other questions once of common concern, on which historians, even as they had disagreed, had communicated with each other—discourse across the discipline had effectively collapsed" (Novick 1988, 592).

In this struggle "old historians" like Gertrude Himmelfarb, of course, have continued to fight the good fight. As we shall see later, she offers important lessons to enable non-historians to understand what the fight is all about. But that these are profoundly troubled waters is exemplified by one of Himmelfarb's responses to her critics. Having been accused of attacking social history, Himmelfarb writes, "I find that in the course of the paper I said, no fewer than *seven* times, that my objections are not to social history as such but to its claims of dominance, superiority, even 'totality'—not to social history as it may complement or supplement traditional history, but would supplant it." She goes on to claim that "it is neither the subjects nor the methods of social history that are at issue but their dominance" (Himmelfarb 1987, 26). In other words, the new histories are useful and good, if they can be co-opted by the old histories. Here we see the "containment" strategy of the post–World War II consensus described by Novick continued in the present. But we also see the evident inability to communicate across boundaries, for Himmelfarb was not rejecting social history, but placing it (albeit in a subordinate position). The appropriate rebuttal would have involved showing how other forms of history were subordinate to "social history," a task not clearly undertaken.

But old historians do not make communication easy. They often treat the new histories as exercises in intellectual immorality. While the following comments begin with a brief, clear description of a key difference between modern and postmodern histories, the tarbrush is dragged out yet again in the end:

> Modernism tolerates relativism, postmodernism celebrates it. Where modernism, aware of the obstacles in the way of objectivity, regards this as a challenge and makes a strenuous effort to attain as much objectivity and unbiased truth as possible, postmodernism takes the rejection of absolute truth as a deliverance from all truth and from the obligation to maintain any degree of objectivity. (Himmelfarb 1994, 137)

At best, Himmelfarb is attacking an extreme version of postmodern history as if it were representative of the whole. Himmelfarb reads relativism as rejecting all truth because it rejects absolute truth, as allowing any view to count as "valid" because there is no "God's-eye view" available to humans. But does the rejection of "that noble dream" make all other dreams trash? When old historians overread and take some theorists' rhetorical excesses as if they represented considered opinions, they simply block communication. For who can have intellectual intercourse with someone who denounced one as incurably intellectually licentious?

New historians are not all of a piece. They have turned to all of the other social sciences for methodological models. Weberian and Marxian sociology, structural linguistics, psychological theory, econometrics, and anthropology have provided models. But even those historians "who were attracted to sociological models and modes of inquiry were at odds with those of an anthropological turn of mind; those for whom economistic approaches seemed most fruitful were scornful of those who adopted a psychoanalytic orientation—and vice versa" (Novick 1988, 587). The question of "whose social science" and "which history" have come to the fore.

Some have even found the lines between history and fiction quite blurred. Elizabeth Clark uses a quotation from David Harlan to illustrate the challenge to historical writing: "literature has returned to history . . .

demanding that historians accept her mocking presence right at the heart of what they had once insisted was their own autonomous and truly scientific discipline" (Clark 1999, 92-93; also see Breisach 1994, 333-37; Himmelfarb 1994, 145-46). The strongest challenges came from Hayden White, trained as a medievalist, who embraced radical relativism and aligned history closely with fiction in his 1973 text *Metahistory* (see Novick 1988, 599-607). Historians of various stripes have responded to this last challenge vigorously, insisting that whatever tropes historians used, historical writing was tied to evidence in ways that fiction is not. Historical fiction, such as Ellis Peters's series of Brother Cadfael medieval mysteries, relies on historical investigations to construct plausible narratives and may illumine aspects of life in the eras portrayed. But these fictions are not otherwise closely tied to evidence; their characters and plots are imaginative creations drawn into extant pictures historians have developed, and their portrayals of human relationships and motivations seem to be shaped more by contemporary than by medieval mores.

The "fragmentation" portrayed by Novick continues, even though some historians can figure out how to work within the chaos. Novick suggested that "[p]erhaps the most striking feature of the way in which historians signaled their abandonment of traditional objectivist axioms was the casual, matter-of-fact fashion in which they did so . . ." (Novick 1988, 598). This is rather understated. For example, in her meticulous and comprehensive *History—Theory—Text: Historians and the Linguistic Turn* (2004), Elizabeth A. Clark, historian of late ancient Christianity, is not "matter-of-fact," but clearly portrays the intellectual debates and issues in recent theory and heartily embraces new models of doing history as illuminating, especially for scholars of late ancient Christianity (her own specialization). Her book wonderfully illumines the intellectual debates over the appropriate concepts and theoretical tools for doing the work of history. Once we recognize that all history is linguistically mediated, then we can see that the correspondence-theory-of-truth ingredient in "that noble dream" is an impossibility—for we have no non-linguistic records that we can check to see if they correspond to the histories we write and thus to see if our claims are right or wrong.

Historians must find ways of carrying on representing the past honestly, insightfully, and carefully even though they cannot "verify" their constructions by "checking" them against the (now gone) events of the past. All that is left are records and monuments, many of them preserved by luck or happenstance. Raul Hilberg, a political scientist and author of the groundbreaking historical study *The Destruction of the European Jews*, has written about what his work was like:

> To portray the Holocaust, Claude Lanzmann once said to me that one has to create a work of art. To recreate this event, be it on

film or in a book, one must be a consummate artist, for such recreation is an act of creation in and of itself. I already knew this fact on the day I embarked on my task.

The artist usurps the actuality, substituting a text for a reality that is fast fading. The words that are thus written take the place of the past; these words, rather than the events themselves, will be remembered. Were this transformation not a necessity, one could call it presumptuous, but it is unavoidable. What I say here is . . . applicable to all historiography, to all descriptions of a happening. (1996, 83)

Hilberg goes on to describe his exhaustive work in assembling and analyzing great masses of data to show how the Germans accomplished the Holocaust as "appropriating, transcribing, arranging something. It was not a work of literature but a body of music" (Hilberg 1996, 84). His work was not and could not seem as effortless as Mozart's. Hilberg had to control his work, "as Beethoven had fashioned his music" (Hilberg 1996, 85). "The specific content of my text was given to me, of course, primarily by the records that the Germans had left behind, but there was a problem of rendition" (Hilberg 1996, 86). Whether one tells of the past as if one were an author of literature or a composer of music, the past lives on, not in its pastness, but only in the compositions about it.

Nor can historians any longer claim to have told the whole story *wie es eigentlich gewesen* (in either sense of *eigentlich*). Even the layers of silt, the buried house, or the lost coins we dig up no more speak for themselves than do the documents we discover and interpret. Clark's work satisfyingly accomplishes its aim of showing how historians of late ancient Christianity can utilize the advances in theory that have "fragmented" history. Indeed, she celebrates a revitalized intellectual history, free from the assumption that ancient documents are innocent of interests and can be approached as if they were relatively transparent, free from the anxiety over literary construction that haunted objectivist historians, and free to use poststructuralist literary theory, as well as the other tools created by the many forms of historical scholarship, especially those that constitute the linguistic turn. Yet that "celebration" does not free her or any respectable historian from the obligations to warrant one's claims, to consider all the data when ascertaining what is evidence, to use all the relevant critical tools, and to tell a story (if one is a narrativist) that makes sense of the evidence one finds—acknowledging that meeting the criteria for all these obligations is incredibly difficult.

Novick and Clark, however, touch only lightly the issue of power. Who controls access to knowledge of the past? Who has the ability and authority to understand or explain the forces, events, and actions that shaped both past and present? The erosion of the rock of objectivity also marks the loss of power of those historians who valorized their work by appeals to that noble dream. It is not merely the entry into the profession of "underrepresented minorities." Numerous scholars have persuaded their readers that they have developed tools more interesting than the objectivist, "non-methodological, but very methodical," tools of the masters of the profession, who were committed to "that noble dream." Historians were in the thick of the "culture wars" of the 1980s and '90s; these issues of power extended beyond the realms of history departments and even of academe. If those who write of the past are artists, as Hilberg claims, which ones will receive commissions, have their works shown, and become acknowledged as true artists? The power issues of the culture wars affected history as much as any discipline.

Worse still, it is not only professional scholars in history who undermined the founding myth. Consider the following comments—cover blurbs—on Herman Wouk's World War II novels: Henry Kissinger is quoted as writing, "Brilliant. . . . An outstanding novel and at the same time a great work of history. . . . Wouk has more than recaptured the period; he has given it life" (Wouk 2002b, back cover). An article in the *Political Science Quarterly* is quoted as saying "*The Winds of War* gives more vivid pictures of the principal leaders of the war than military and political history could. Fiction is better than history at showing 'how it really was' where matters of human character are concerned" (Wouk 2002a, back cover). Wouk's "romance" (2002a, ix) is accorded greater authority than "real" history, at least for certain purposes. It is not that history as history is "literary" and even constructed or composed—that argument simmered within the historians' guild. Rather, here were scholars external to the guild valuing fiction over the products of journeymen and masters in the guild.

Analyzing such fascinating power struggles is far beyond the present project (although contestants in the culture wars writing for outsiders provide grist for the present mill, as shown below). But the bottom line is clear: historical work is warranted by its rhetorical persuasiveness for an audience, which includes, necessarily, but is not limited to, the kinds of evidence and argument appropriate for the purposes for which an essay or book is written. And sometimes even fiction can illumine!

In reviewing these battles among historians, I am reminded of a sentence from the introduction to *That Noble Dream*: "And, inevitably, I spend a good deal of time talking about what historians do worst, or at least badly: reflecting on epistemology" (Novick 1988, 15). One crucial issue that underlies much of the debate seems to be a conflation of epistemic *conditions* and epistemic *criteria*. An essential condition that makes a historical representation true is that it actually does, more or less, represent the past for those who take the time to understand it (there are other conditions for truthfulness, too, but limning those is not our task here). There is no reason to think that only one representation can fulfill that condition, any more than there is only one true portrait of Gertrude Stein, or that there is only one way to write the music for and sing the "Dies Irae," or that there is only one true map for any territory (unless, of course, it is God's picture or God's map; but we don't have access to those). There is no reason not to think that some representations truly distort the past so badly that they simply do not fulfill this condition; this indeed seems to be the condition that makes a historical account "Whiggish." But far more importantly, this condition of being true must not be confused with the *criteria for judging* whether a representation is true. How we judge a representation is an issue different from whether it represents. What makes the sentence "It rained in Dayton, Ohio, on October 21, 1994" true or false was whether it rained in Dayton on that date; my claim that it rained on that date in Dayton is warranted or justified not by the occurrence of rain, but by my ability to provide grounds and warrants for that claim and have it accepted by the relevant group of competent and interested investigators.

While this may seem a trivial distinction, getting clear on the differences between conditions and criteria means that the modernist polemics against the honesty of postmodern historians are simply misplaced, but the ludic attitude of some postmodern historians is equally misplaced. The issue is not whether true representation is a goal, but what criteria we have for a representation's being true. That historians do not agree on the criteria is clear; but that they must disagree on the conditions for true representation is not at all clear. A postmodernist is not committed to live in a prison of words and not freed from responsibility for warranting her or his claims, no matter what some poststructuralist theorists write. To accuse them of failing to maintain any degree of objectivity not only is unfair but also occludes any communication (compare Tilley 2000, 152-70).

What historians as a group—whether modernist or postmodernist—tend nonetheless to claim is that they have evidence for their views. While historical novels at their best are based on historians' work and do not knowingly contradict publicly established facts, they are not tied to evidence in the way that historians' writings must be. Wouk, for example, claims much historical accuracy for his work and differentiates explicitly which elements in the sprawling novels were fictional creations (2002b, 1040-42). But he offers, of course, no evidence or arguments for either his facts or his fictions. He simply tells a very complex story, the saga of a fictional extended family and the people, fictional and actual, with whom they interact. Historians marshal evidence to warrant their stories. And part of the function of that evidence is to make those stories rhetorically persuasive for the community of historians who work in the same or nearby fields.

What counts as evidence is, however, up for debate. Historians' use of evidence to buttress their claims has often suggested an analogy with a judicial trial. Yet one of the most successful of the new historians, Carlo

Ginzburg (reflecting on modern historiography and especially on the French penchant for writing the history of the French Revolution more as judges than investigators), has reminded us that the historian is better off "understanding" rather than morally or legally "judging" the past (Ginzburg 1994, 291-93). Indeed, John Tracy Ellis, who was the leading historian of the Catholic Church in the United States, more than once said in classes in the late 1960s that the historian was "not a judge, much less a hanging judge." All historians, new or old, have to attend to evidence. Arguably, their primary point is not to judge the past but to understand it. While historians do tie their work to evidence much more tightly than writers of historical fiction, what counts as evidence differs among them and differs depending on the arguments they construct and the purposes for which they construct those arguments.

Historians' Arguments: An Analysis

It can be very difficult for non-historians to understand what is in dispute among the historians. Partly this is due to epistemological confusions. Partly it is due to a lack of clarity on the arguments historians give (both on their part and their readers'). One way of approaching the issue is by adapting Stephen Toulmin's analysis of argument structures (Toulmin 1958; Harvey 1968, 49-64; Murphy 1994, 3-39). The basic argument structure is illustrated in the following figure:

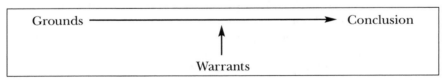

Figure 1

Grounds are evidence. They are based on the data that investigators marshal for making their argument. Warrants are varied and often suppressed. They can be theories that show the significance of the data, definitions of terms, or rhetorical or logical connectors. Warrants function to connect the data with the conclusion. The conclusion begins its life as a question to be answered or a hypothesis to be verified, and, if it is well grounded and well warranted, it winds up as answer or conclusion. An example to illustrate this clearly can be taken from ethics:

> Grounds (G): John, a married man, had an affair with Jane to whom he is not married.
> Warrant (W_1): For a married person to have an affair with someone she or he is not married to is adultery.
> Warrant (W_2): Adultery is morally wrong.
> Conclusion (C): John's and Jane's conduct was morally wrong.

G is data used as evidence. Its accuracy may be established by another argument, but in this argument it functions as data. W_1 offers a definition of adultery and W_2 a moral evaluation of adultery (presumably supported by another argument as well). Given the grounds and warrants, the conclusion simply follows.

Although we often take warrants for granted, and move from grounds to conclusion rather facilely, we rely on warrants to move from grounds to conclusion. We may take it for granted that adultery is wrong, but without that warrant, expressed or suppressed, the conduct of John and Jane alone is not sufficient to warrant a claim of moral wrongness.

Obviously, the acceptability of a conclusion—the claim being made—is vulnerable to attack on its supporting argument. One can attack the evidence used as grounds: one might show that John and Jane were not married at the time of the affair. If so, then the warrant as stated would not apply. They might have been engaging in sexual activity with each other, and that might be wrong, too, but adultery requires a breach of the marriage bond. So if neither party was married, a different set of warrants would be needed to reach the conclusion that their behavior was immoral. One could also attack the warrant: one might say that, in certain circumstances, even adultery could be morally tolerable (see Clebsch 1979, 207, for a summary of one of Jeremy Taylor's arguments supporting this claim). If the warrant is undermined, then the conclusion loses its credibility.

In constructing an argument, one also can marshal *backing* (B) for the grounds and warrants. One might have to show that there was good reason to believe that, in fact, John and Jane were having an affair. One might have to back up one's grounds. One might further have to back up one's warrants and show the reasons that adultery is immoral (and moral theories such as deontological, consequentialist, relational, natural law or divine command theories can be employed to provide this backing—they provide the criteria for judging the adulterous activity immoral). One can also prepare for likely counterarguments or *rebuttals* (R) by the way one constructs one's arguments. Some of these possible rebuttals (like the claim neither John nor Jane was married) may require some "adverbial" *qualifier* (Q) to the conclusion—the conclusion is, perhaps, not certainly true, but so likely true as to be practically indubitable under the circumstances (it would be an odd state of affairs if John had been widowed or divorced and it was not known to the person making the argument).

To see how this argument structure is developed in historical writing, we can consider the following paraphrase (cf. Harvey 1968, 52ff.):

Jesus was crucified under Pontius Pilate (G_1); this is the most likely event to have occurred to Jesus as sources in and beyond the New Testament attest to it with a high degree of reliability (B_1). Rome reserved crucifixion for political crimes (W_1), as historians of Roman law practice have shown (B_2). Unless Pilate was acting to please the Jewish authorities in this exceptional case (R_1), for which we have no reliable evidence (W_2 against R_1), we can assume with a high degree of probability (Q) that it is historically reliable to say that Jesus was viewed as a political enemy by Rome (C).

In this argument, we have evidential *grounds*: Jesus was crucified. These grounds are not raw data that someone collects, but that data which can serve as evidence for the claim which is the conclusion of the argument. There is *backing* for this evidence to show that taking this data from the New Testament is reliable data, indeed a "fact" we can introduce into evidence. This backing could be a claim (warranted by another argument) for the historical reliability of the report of the crucifixion. We have a *warrant* about Roman practices with its appropriate backing by the conclusion of another argument. A potential *rebuttal* is acknowledged, that Pilate acted on the instigation of Jewish authorities in an exceptional case, but this rebuttal is deflected by using as warrant the conclusion of another argument that finds in the gospel narrative(s) of the passion no evidence for this claim (a currently controverted point; see Fredriksen 1999, 8-10 *et passim*). The conclusion (like any conclusion) is *qualified*: the argument does not show that the conclusion is certainly or absolutely true, but that it is probably reliable—in effect acknowledging both that the evidence, warrants, and conclusions are limited and conditioned and that the rebuttal might have some possibility of being true, and thus affecting how historically reliable the conclusion is. The whole argument structure can then be diagramed as follows, with the main structural features in bold type:

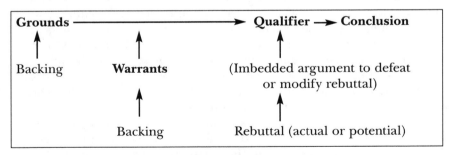

Figure 2

One can read this as saying, "Given these grounds and utilizing these warrants we can (certainly, possibly, probably, or whatever qualifier is appropriate) conclude that *p*" (where *p* is the statement of the hypothesis being proven).

The differences among historians have to do with what counts as grounds, what are proper warrants, and what kinds of conclusions historians can reach. The issue is one of criteria, not of conditions. What makes a specific historical claim true is that it fairly portrays what happened; if it meets this condition, it is true. However, this is not what is at issue. At issue is whether historians establish their conclusions with sufficient grounds and warrants. The criteria for judging that true are not the conditions—the conditions are past and gone—but whether historians have done their work well according to the standards of their profession.

The key issue among the various ways of doing history seems to be what counts as evidential grounds and warrants. As Novick noted, historians are not trained to be good epistemologists. The result is that they tend to blur the issues in their internal arguments with one another. To explore this point, I will use an example neither Novick nor Clark gives much time to, the use of psychoanalytical categories in doing history. Here an argument directed to the literate public—a campaign in the culture wars, rather than within the discipline—by Gertrude Himmelfarb (following an earlier argument by Barzun 1974) is instructive because debates over a well-known piece of work help us see how epistemic criteria for what counts as grounds and warrants is what is at issue. The pattern of argument developed over "psychohistory" is replicated in a number of arguments about the place of the new histories.

Himmelfarb is one of many traditional historians that question the legitimacy of "psychohistory" or "psychobiography" as history. A landmark in this genre is Erik Erikson's *Young Man Luther*. In this text, Erikson attributed Luther's religious rebellion as brought about psychologically by his earlier rebellion against his father and his unresolved adolescent identity crisis. A notorious component in Erikson's analysis is a sort of "anal defiance" transferred from defiance of his father to defiance of the pope and God. Himmelfarb sharply criticized this form of history in general and Erikson's text in particular in the following:

> The boldness of Erikson's thesis is matched by a methodological audacity that leaves the traditional historian breathless. Only certain minimal conditions have to be met for non-facts to acquire the same status as facts. "We are thus obliged," Erikson says, "to accept half-legend as half-history, provided only that a reported episode does not contradict other well-established facts; persists in having a ring of truth; and yields a meaning consistent with psychological theory." Moreover, the stock of facts and non-facts can come from any time or place in history, from any observer or experience, so that a theory about Jesus or an event in the life of Freud are as much the data of Luther's life as those facts (or legends or hypotheses) deriving from Luther's own childhood or career. (Himmelfarb 1987, 38-39; quoting Erikson 1958, 247)

What is important about this criticism of Erikson is that it allows us to unpack the kinds of issues at stake between the "old" and the "new" historians using Toulmin's analysis of the structure of arguments. Himmelfarb shows just what are some of the crucial issues regarding grounds, warrants, and conclusions of historical argument that distinguish them methodologically.

First, there is a profound difference concerning what counts as grounds. For Erikson, facts established as historically reliable by more traditional historians, for example, the details of Luther's life and the significance of his work, are taken for granted. But Erikson also uses material transmitted in legendary form, for example, the Tower incident. Importantly for Erikson, this material must have some probability of being historically reliable by his own methodological lights, including psychoanalytical work (Erikson 1958, 50). Psychoanalysts can use minimal traces as clues for important insights regarding psychological patterns in a person's behavior and thus can give significance to what non-psychoanalysts might find not important. In the quotation from Erikson's work cited by Himmelfarb, Erikson clearly is not proposing to take legendary material as evidence *unless* there is some warrant and backing for taking this material as evidence. Note that Erikson does not propose to supplant evidence accepted by traditional historians with legend, but to supplement traditional historians' evidence with legendary material *if* that material meets criteria of coherence, plausibility, and fit with psychoanalytical theory. These tests amount to backing for his using psychoanalytical clues embedded in "non-objective" documents as grounds in his arguments. So there is a profound difference between Erikson and Himmelfarb in what counts as legitimate grounds. It is not that Erikson in particular and new historians in general do not observe the "elementary rules of evidence" or that they have "transcended the realm of history" (Himmelfarb 1987, 41), but that they have different criteria for what counts as evidential grounds in their arguments—obviously, not uncontroversial criteria!

In their recent textbook in historiography, Howell and Prevenier title one of their sections "The 'Facts' That Matter" (2001, 84). They note that "[e]ach kind of history thus not only privileges certain events, certain kinds of information; each tends to ignore other events and to suppress other data" (2001, 85). Given the selectivity of historians, "the 'fact' as the object of historian's study has . . . been diminished almost to the point of disappearing, at least as our predecessors generally understood it" (2001, 87). The key dispute between Erikson and Himmelfarb is on which data are facts and which facts are relevant as evidence. The argument should be conducted at the level of what the *criteria* are for utilizing theory and acknowledging some data as factual grounds in a historical argument—in Toulmin's terms, the arguments are really about *backings* for grounds and warrants.

The traditional historian tends to prefer evidence that is substantially supported. The more sources, textual and otherwise, that back up the statement of a fact, the better. The traditional historian tends to prefer "commonsense" warrants that have been part of the modern historian's craft (see Himmelfarb 1987, 41); the traditional historian is painstakingly methodical rather than methodological. The psychohistorian utilizes the structure of psychoanalytic theory as his key warrant. By its focus on seemingly insignificant reports, facts, or utterances, for example, the "Freudian slip," the psychoanalyst may well find that minimally backed or attested data are important pieces of evidence for their conclusions. For the traditional historian, the weight is in the evidence, and historians' warrants are taken for granted to be critical common sense. For the psychohistorian, the weight is in the theory, which is not the sort of warrant traditional historians use. Psychohistorians evaluate their data in light of the theory that is not "common sense." Data that intellectual historians dismiss may be crucial evidence when used to support a psychohistorian's claim; data that psychohistorians find irrelevant may be crucial evidence in intellectual history.

Marcus Borg remarked that the historian's craft can be compared to that of the detective's (Borg and Wright 1999, 237). Neither is a "one phase" task, although the same person may work in all the phases. A "street detective" gathers all the data, sometimes without being clear which is factual and available for evidence and which has no evidentiary value. A historian doing archival research is working in a similar way. A "forensic detective" analyzes the data and attempts to discern which of it is likely (certainly, possibly, probably) factual and hypothesizes about what the events might have been that gave rise to the data. When historians reflect on what their archival research has yielded, they form hypotheses, like a forensic detective does at this stage. A detective at the third stage organizes the evidence and appropriate warrants into a case for the most likely conclusion. Historical researchers become creators or composers at this stage, creating an artifact, authoring a history. Himmelfarb faults the psychohistorian for giving little attention to the first phases of this kind of work as done in history. The psychohistorian utilizes the material of the first phase, evaluates the results of the second phase in light of psychoanalytical theory, and constructs a case for a rather different conclusion about at least a substantial component of a major historical event, in Erikson's case, the Reformation, with his heavy dose of theory. The traditional historian rejects psychoanalytic theory as a legitimate historical warrant—it does not meet her criteria. In short, we can say that the traditional historian finds that the psychohistorian overdoses on theory.

Second, Erikson introduces data and arguments that Himmelfarb finds not to the point—they have nothing to do with the sixteenth century. But these are used not so much to warrant data about Luther but to exemplify the use of psychoanalytical theory as warrant in an argument that moves from this data to the conclusion that Luther's rebellion has a psychological explanation. The problem is not with Erikson's data as much as it is his *use* of some data as grounds in his argument that traditional historians find "dubious." His doing this also illustrates the interaction between grounds and warrants. The kind of warrants one uses and the kind of explanation one seeks dictate the sort and weight of data one needs. Indeed, in her own later comments, Himmelfarb implicitly recognizes this point:

> The traditional historian might cite changes in technology and industry as bringing about new patterns of work and family life; philosophical theories positing a novel view of human nature and therefore of socialization and education, the rise of the middle class, the development of political democracy—as well, of course, as changes in breast feeding, toilet training, or any other psychological data for which there is historical evidence, but for which he would claim no necessary primacy or determinacy. The psychohistorian, by contrast, approaches the subject with a prior psychoanalytic commitment. He knows in advance what to look for. His "facts" are psychoanalytic constants. (Himmelfarb 1987, 40)

Himmelfarb, however, doesn't get this quite right. The seemingly irrelevant data is backing not for the facts or grounds, but for the theory that warrants Erikson's move from the data to the conclusions he reaches. But it is important to note that his facts are not mere psychoanalytic constructs, but data available to historians (who might evaluate it differently). Nonetheless, his warrants are indeed psychoanalytical theories. His theory does not tell him what to look for, but it does provide him with criteria to discern what is significant evidence in all the data he and others have uncovered.

The dispute here is not so much about facts or objectivity as about the new historians' finding data that they construe as factual and as grounds for their arguments that the traditional historians have dismissed or ignored as non-objective. The question is not over facts as much as over which data are evidential grounds and what grounds are needed for the conclusion. The key is not whether Erikson's portrayal indeed does meet the condition of representing Luther adequately (at least in part), but whether the warrants he uses meet the criteria of being good historical warrants. In sum, the traditional historian suspects that the psychohistorian's theory does a lot of work in covering for a paucity of facts.

Third, the traditional historian and the new historian also disagree on the nature of historical explanation. Traditional historians want to explain how various states of affairs, events, and human actions brought about other states of affairs or set the stage for certain events to occur or decisions to be made. Many forms of the new history seem to parallel psychohistory in seeking to warrant a "'deeper' level of explanation that goes beyond the empirical evidence of the traditional historian . . . " (Him-melfarb 1987, 41). Quantitative history (sometimes called "cliometrics") attempts to use quantitative data to reach explanatory conclusions. The early *Annales* school attempted to achieve a total history and assumed the theory of structural linguistics (Breisach 1994, 373). Other historians took "scientific" Marxist theory as a very broad, if not universal, warrant. In effect, some of the new histories tend to take the forces which drive human history not as human choices and decisions but as impersonal forces which leave the human agent little scope for her or his actions to have any significant effect. Human choices and actions are ripples on the tidal wave of allegedly more important social, economic, psychological, or historical forces which underlie those choices and decisions.

To a non-historian, an illuminating example of this sort of dispute over the importance of non-personal forces over personal choice is an intervention in the "David Abraham Case," as reported by Novick (1988, 612-21). Reviewers of Abraham's 1981 book, *The Collapse of the Weimar Republic: Political Economy and Crisis,* were generally positive, especially because Abraham seemed to have broken the deadlock between those who argued that German industrialists of the Weimar era were linked to the rise of Nazism and those who argued they were not. Abraham used a "structuralist-Marxist" conceptual approach to warrant his claims. In effect, the industrialists were neither "innocent" nor "guilty" in their choices, but because of the breakdowns of "viable compromises between various sectors of industry, agriculture and labor," elites were left with no choice but an authoritarian solution. "The victory of Nazism was por-trayed as an unintended consequence of systematic breakdown" (Novick 1988, 613). Other historians pointed out a number of significant errors of fact and interpretation in the book, many of which Abraham acknowl-edged. Eventually Abraham was driven out of the profession, by means that were extraordinary at best, unethical at worst.

But the truly interesting intervention in this drama was that of T. W. Mason. Mason had reviewed Abraham's book favorably in the *American Historical Review* before Abraham's opponents had challenged his work. In a later review symposium, after articles by the warring parties, Mason wrote (as reported by Novick):

> Mason noted other errors by Abraham in reporting and charac-terizing some individuals' views (errors addressed by Abraham in his reply) but remained convinced that the book was a largely suc-cessful effort to "raise the argument to a higher plain of struc-tural analysis . . . at which motivations and the choices of individuals are secondary in the sense that they are heavily deter-mined by economic and institutional pressures." (Novick 1988, 614; citing Mason from the *American Historical Review* 88 [1983]: 1144)

Despite recognizing substantial errors of fact in Abraham's work, Mason found that Abraham's argument was substantially warranted. After another scholar found even more errors, in yet another reply, Abraham showed that his argument was "sustained at least as well by the corrected as well as by the original versions" (Novick 1988, 616). Here is a paradigm case in which the weight of the argument is in the theoretical warrant, not the factual grounds.

At this point, we move beyond the bounds of history as a discipline and into the philosophy of history. The issue about what counts as historical explanation is not as much a dispute among historians about grounds and warrants as an argument about whether there are natural forces in the world that are part of the furniture of the universe alongside those ordinary states of affairs, events, acts, and relationships between them that are the "stuff" of traditional history and most non-speculative or non-religious philosophy. The psychohistorian assumed that there are time-transcendent psychological patterns or structures—and that utilizing them on figures like Luther would help us understand his life and work. What Abraham had done, and what his opponents rejected, was to utilize a theory that warranted a claim not only that the Weimar industrialists' choices were not the important fact but that they had no real choice in the face of systemic collapse.

Resolving the disputes between Augustinians, Hegelians, Marxists, Freudians, and a host of other philosophies that offer criteria for writing truly about the way the real world is (and about which historians write) is far beyond the scope of this book. However, leaving this issue in abeyance is a bit too easy. Many of the new histories are claiming, implicitly or explicitly, that there is more to the furniture of the universe than meets the traditional historians' eyes. If there are such forces, then a historical representation of them would meet the key *condition* for being representative; the issue is whether there are *criteria* that would allow us to recognize whether there are such forces and whether appeal to them can be used as *warrants* in historical arguments. Himmelfarb and other supporters of traditional history seem not to "get" this.

But the fault is not all on the traditional historians' side by any means. When Himmelfarb had asked a young social historian about his study of a New England town in the latter part of the eighteenth century, he "conceded that from his themes and sources—parish registers, tax rolls, census reports, legal records, polling lists, land titles—he could not 'get to,' as he said it, the founding of the United States. But he denied that this was the crucial event I took it to be" (Himmelfarb 1987, 13). This glossing over of the American Revolution and the founding of the first modern republic does seem to have had profound and long-lasting effects on the lives of ordinary people from Illinois to Iran. To neglect this historical event seems even more problematical than the traditional historians' attempts to co-opt social history. A theory that would warrant ignoring the American Revolution as a crucial event seems either bogus or misused or misunderstood.

Conclusion

In light of the analysis of these disputes, two conclusions can be drawn. First, even while theologians worked with and in the Troeltschian tradition in their understanding of history, historians were transforming their disciplines. The presumptions of history that led some theologians to assume that historians operated with a specific kind of reductionist naturalism began to crumble. Forces unthought of by traditional historians began to be recognized by some new historians as natural forces which shape history. Just as the concept of what constitutes evidence changed in the early modern period, so the concept of what constitutes "the natural" changed right along with it. But this evolution did not end with the collapse of the preternatural. Marx, among others, challenged the emerging concept of "the natural" by including unseen, material, but occult, forces and historical constants as part of the real world with which historians have to deal. More recent new histories use sources sometimes neglected by traditional historians as relevant evidence and use theoretical warrants that cause them to evaluate and weigh evidence differently. In using the spotlight of generalized (not culture specific) theories, they expanded the realm which is "natural" for historians to explain. While naturalism continues to be presumed by the work of historians and supernatural and preternatural agents excluded from their purview, the operative presumptions in the varied practices of history have become much more diverse than a Troeltschian—or even an objectivist—account would allow.

Theologians should respond to this by recognizing that the reductionist naturalism that made it practically impossible for theologians to assert that God acts in history, in effect, got the "qualifier" wrong. It is not that we cannot warrant the claim that God acts, but that we cannot warrant the claim using grounds and warrants proper to history (which seems to have been Troeltsch's original point, despite the work of the Troeltschian tradition). This does not preclude warranting such claims on other grounds. Nor does the emergence of new histories give religious historians a license to use theological criteria as warrants for supernatural interventions (cf. Harvey 2000, 91-92). Chapter ten will show that, given the reshaping of historical grounds by theories-functioning-as-warrants in the new histories, the shape of theological-historical arguments could be much different from the one historians use. In short, the fragmentation of the discipline of history gives another perspective on the claim of this book that there is no single "problem of history" for theology or for religious faith.

Second, the objectivity question which vexes professional historians seems based in an epistemological confusion between truth conditions and truth criteria. But it is not " 'merely' a philosophical question. It is an enormously charged emotional issue: one in which the stakes are very high. . . . For many, what has been at issue is nothing less than the meaning of the venture to which they have devoted their lives, and thus, to a very considerable extent, the meaning of their own lives" (Novick 1988, 11). The disputes between new and old historians are also about what counts as legitimate in understanding where the nation is. These debates over the warrants historians can presume to use are important. They show the disputes over what are the identity principles (to use a term from chapter six) of the discipline that has been the vocation of many scholars.

History has been a central constituent of the culture wars in this country. The discipline, if it ever was whole, seems fragmented now. But it is fragmented in large part because it has been expanded to include new voices and new methods. How those voices are to be heard and how those methods can be helpfully related to one another remain in dispute. Himmelfarb's attempt to co-opt the new histories will, of course, work in some cases. But it is not a satisfying resolution to all the disputants. These culture wars over the presumptions of historical practice, the principles of the discipline of history, are not over. "Objectivity" may remain a noble dream for some, but others will seek to make true, if perspectival, claims about the past even if objectivity is not their dream.

Despite the inconclusive battles between the new histories and the old, and the acids of postmodern skepticism dissolving any structures of certainty, the historians have at their disposal what Ernst Breisach called a "precious asset." He wrote:

> For at least four centuries generations of scholars have developed a historical methodology—testing, retesting, and absorbing elements from other disciplines—until by now it can act as a wall of defense against the fanciful tale, willful distortion, and honest error, as well as a sufficiently reliable instrument for truth-finding. Even the by now acknowledged omnipresence of the creative imagination in all phases of historical truth-finding . . . does not doom historiography's ability to deliver useful results—useful in the sense of being sufficiently akin to the processes of life to offer knowledge of a high truth value. The presence of imagination leaves intact the need for a critically ascertained factual base as well as the requirements of skill, craftsmanship, and integrity. Only if historians assert such a base for the historical enterprise will there remain a proper gap between the fantasies of visionaries, zealots, and propagandists and the works of historians. (Breisach 1994, 408)

Breisach found the disciplines of history sufficiently supple to accommodate the various forms of the new histories. Yes, we construct or compose history. Yes, it requires imagination. Yes, we are selective. Yes, we are not scientific; quantified data are important, but do not exhaust the human condition which historians study. Yes, we co-opt "theory heavy" studies and by so doing dethrone any pretensions to have the whole story or the "God's-eye view"; that is part of the "precious asset" that constitutes the ongoing discipline. But in the end, Breisach leaves history intact as a discipline distinguished by its dogged methical approach that seems to require no methodological backing, only fair, hard work—while using multiple methodologies as tools for appropriate tasks. And being methical is not a methodology, but the carrying out of a methodology well.

The practices of history neither lead to nor require theoretical relativism, that is, that there are different "truths," none much better than the other (for historians can recognize that these "truths" are often no more than a class's or country's interests puffed up); nor do they require abandoning representational realism in every form—such realism seems to be the condition for crafting historical arguments and narratives (though it is not and cannot be a criterion for judging histories); nor do they require that historians must presume they are making linear progress, that we understand better in some absolute sense than others in the past. Rather, as Clark notes, we have the opportunity to use and be shaped in our thinking by new ways of approaching historical work. Historians *qua* historians recognize their works as conditioned, just as are the works that they studied. What we write is not timeless, but time-bound, and limited by our perspective of the here and now. Historians contribute to warranting with some reliability claims to understand to some degree at least something crucial to being human, "to whom the temporality of life allots the roles of emigrants from the past, inhabitants of the present, and immigrants into the future" (Breisach 1994, 416). For theologians, as we shall see in chapter ten, history is best understood as a constituent of good theology and a stimulus to reformulation of faith claims when necessary, not a veto on faith, even though historical work may sometimes suggest that specific expressions of the principles of faith are no longer credible or useful.

CHAPTER 9

Practicing History 2

The Battling New Testament Historians

History, then, prevents faith becoming fantasy.
—N. T. Wright

Historical description cannot provide theological meaning.
—Paula Fredriksen

Historians of Christianity have attempted to write some histories "from below" and used some "new historical" techniques, such as those discussed in the previous chapter. For example, William Clebsch's *Christianity in European History* is a history of Christian lifestyles and positions; Jay P. Dolan's *The American Catholic Experience* tells the story of U.S. Catholicism not as one of bishops and buildings but of immigrant groups and their inculturations; Albert J. Raboteau's *Slave Religion* approaches its topics in a multidisciplinary manner to account for both the oppressive loss of identity that comes from being enslaved and the creative rebuilding of cultures to keep hope alive; Colleen McDannell's *Material Christianity* explores the practices of U.S. Christians by focusing on items of material culture integral to those practices; social network theory figures prominently in Elizabeth A. Clark's *The Origenist Controversy,* which attempts to account for the waxing and waning of Origen's theological ideas in that fifth-century dispute, and in William Vance Trollinger's *God's Empire: William Bell Riley and Midwestern Fundamentalism,* which attempts to account for the dissemination and perdurance of fundamentalism when fundamentalism in U.S. culture was supposed to be dead; Robert Orsi's *Thank You, St. Jude!* uses conventional historical sources (archives), interviews, and social-scientific theory to show how devotion to St. Jude helped Catholic women form an identity—in some ways harmful, in other ways beneficial—as they negotiated the contrary demands of women's roles in church and culture in the middle third of the twentieth century. Each of these texts utilizes methods from the social sciences to explore the Christian tradition, but each of these exercises in religious history seems to coexist peacefully with other forms of history, rather than to battle with them for hegemony. The historians' battles seem to touch historians of Christianity rather lightly.

Recent debates over the historical Jesus are the place in which the issues that affect the disciplines of history appear in religious history most acutely. Mendenhall and Gottwald, mentioned in chapter five, have offered new histories of ancient Israel, but have not evoked responses as wide or as well publicized as the research on Jesus. Jesus research in general, and the third quest in particular, has been a prime battlefield for disputes over method. Some criticisms even brim with vituperation. Walter Wink, for example, in 1996 presented to the Society for Biblical Literature annual meeting his review of the disputes as if he were scoring a boxing match between the belligerent Luke Timothy Johnson (1996) and the members of the feisty Jesus Seminar (Crossan, Borg, et al.). However, this presentation mocked the sometimes bilious exchanges in a side-splittingly funny manner (Wink 1997).

A few years later Marcus Borg and N. T. Wright jointly wrote a book that illustrates more constructively the differences in historical methodology in two strands of contemporary studies of the "historical Jesus." This chapter analyzes the issues at stake. The chapter concludes by claiming, in brief, that Harvey's bipolar portrayal of the relationships between the "morality of historical knowledge" and the "morality of religious belief" needs to be expanded into a multipolar relationship. This especially applies not only to history generally, but to that central modern exercise in the history of Christianity: the quests for the historical Jesus.

Questing for the "Historical" Jesus

The primary data in the quests for the historical Jesus are the synoptic gospels of the New Testament. Positivist attempts to say that the gospels are simply records of facts sink on the shoals of the contradictions among them. The gospels are theological, literary creations for specific purposes in specific contexts that reflect on profoundly important (to their communities) events and actions of the past. At best, they are interpreted history (as suggested in chapter seven). These texts, like many ancient texts, provide data which contemporary historical investigators can use to establish factual claims about the past and to marshal evidential grounds for their conclusions.

Yet these data are not evidence. Historians can argue how the data of the New Testament yields facts that can be *used* as evidence in the context of supporting or undermining hypotheses about what Jesus did and who he was. Recognizing the difference between relics of the past as data to be evaluated for its evidentiary value, not as evidence to be "read off" the texts and monuments of the past, is one way of acknowledging the autonomy of the historian, discussed in chapter three. Historians do not merely accept the data of the past as facts to be put into evidence, but confer the authority of evidence on the data that has survived, been retrieved, and been evaluated (see Harvey 1968, 39-42; compare Murphy 1994, 134-35).

What constitutes evidence and what weight the various forms of evidence have are highly debated, as the last chapter showed. Many New Testament historians, for example, strongly prefer earlier written materials to later written materials, other things being equal. The presumption here is that sources closer to an event are more likely to be accurate than later sources. Yet a "second generation" writer may have a better perspective on events and their significance than someone closer in time to the events narrated. Hence, many find that there is little or weak evidence for the "empty tomb," especially because the stories are found to be written late in the composition history of the gospels. Others can reply that, although the writing of these stories may be late in the process of composing the gospels, the stories themselves may be quite early, preserved in oral lore and only written late in the process of transmission as their significance became clearer, perhaps because all the empty-tomb stories valorize women as the first witnesses—and are reliable just because they utilize women as witnesses. Moreover, in a patriarchal culture that distrusted women as witnesses, why would anyone make up a story utilizing the witness of that supposedly unreliable and hysterical half of humanity when he or she could make up the story utilizing the testimony of robustly reliable males? That the written stories are late in the tradition may not count against their reliability. And that women are the prime witnesses to the empty tomb paradoxically gives the stories more credibility.

Like the disputes between the traditional historians and some new historians, the issue is what data count as evidence and how much evidence is enough. Historians' views on evidence are influenced by which warrants the historians accept. Traditional historians ignore feminist theory, even the minimal recognition that patriarchal cultures shape texts patriarchally (see Schüssler Fiorenza 2000, 33). Feminist historians find different data to be key evidence than do traditional historians because they utilize feminist theory to help construct their warrants. Unfortunately, more traditional New Testament historians tend to ignore or reject some of these new historians because of their rhetorical style or their heavier dose of theory in their historical work (see Schüssler Fiorenza 2000, 34-55 for an argument about some of the problems in the third quest for the historical Jesus).

Even if we presume that earlier sources are preferable, there may remain disputes about what counts as "early" and about whether the presumption stands in certain cases or is not relevant. What a historian allows to be evidence depends in large part on the ways that a historian evaluates the data. The methods a historian uses will determine, in large part, which data counts as (relatively) reliable evidence and which data is not reliable.

Here I analyze two distinctive ways of approaching the data of the New Testament by analyzing the methods used. The present analysis needs to be distinguished from what Harvey has called the "presuppositions gambit," often utilized by conservative Catholic and evangelical apologists. Harvey described the gambit as follows:

> It begins with the indisputable assumption that every historian has his or her presuppositions and hence is not neutral. But it then proceeds to equate these presuppositions with "faith" so that it can move to the conclusion that even secular historians who reject appeals to supernatural intervention in history are no less acting "in faith" than are those believing historians who accept them. (Harvey 2000, 91)

As Harvey demonstrated, the issue is not "faith"; some committed Christians work naturalistically when a discipline calls for that approach. Moreover, the historian as historian may recognize events as extraordinary or mysterious or astonishing. But that would not license a historian as historian to attribute such events or acts to a supernatural intervention or to construe them as a miracle. That an act or event is miraculous is not within historians' discourse, a point chapter seven made. To attempt to validate or undermine historians' claims on the basis that their naturalistic or supernaturalistic faith is incorporated into their presuppositions is a gambit that fails because it wrongly assumes that a person's beliefs must function as presumptions of their work, as chapter four noted.

Nonetheless, historians' methodological approaches, including their presumptions, can determine what data counts as evidence. This difference about how to treat the data and what counts as evidence is illustrated by the methodological differences usefully explored by Marcus Borg and N. T. Wright as they seek the "historical Jesus."

Wright describes his fundamental method, which I will dub a "holistic hermeneutics," as follows:

> The researcher, after a period of total and sometimes confusing immersion in the data, emerges with a hypothesis, a big picture about how everything fits together. The hypothesis is proposed, spelled out as fully as possible. In the process, it is tested against three criteria: Does it make sense of the data as they stand? Does it have an appropriate level of simplicity, or even elegance? Does it shed light on areas of research other then the one it was intended to cover? (Borg and Wright 1999, 22)

Wright describes a method in which one moves from the part to the whole and back again, and again, and again. It doesn't matter so much where one begins. Rather, one allows the analysis of each and every part to shape and reshape the analysis of the whole, and one's vision of the whole to place each and every part. The method is not so much like sifting and evaluating evidence as a jury does in a trial but more like the work of the detective who moves back and forth from first-order data gathering to second-order hypothesis formation, returning to the data to find evidence to support the hypothesis or modifying the hypothesis in light of new or reevaluated evidence. A similar form of dialogical discernment is involved in moving from ethical theories to moral cases and back again in an effort to settle into an equilibrium in which cases can be used to illustrate the theory and theory can be used to guide subsequent cases—all the while recognizing that new cases can require adjustments of theory and theory can spotlight significant factors in new cases. Wright's warrants are analogous to those criteria that help us discern whether an ethical theory or principle is good to adopt: simplicity, elegance, fit with data, and fecundity.

In contrast, Borg proposes a "genetic" method in which one isolates elements in the narrative and traces them to their origins. He finds that the gospels contain "history remembered" and "history metaphorized." The former is the realm of fact; the latter is the realm of faith (although Borg does not rule out the possibility that facts may be buried in the latter). His approach is to differentiate which data reliably record events remembered, for example, the crucifixion, and which data do not record reliable memories, but are explicable as creations of the authors of the gospels, for example, the miracle at the wedding feast at Cana, or "metaphorical narratives using imagery from Israel's" saga, for example, the miraculous feedings (Borg and Wright 1999, 5-6). This discrimination requires a two-step process.

The first step is to discern what is early and what is late in the developing tradition about Jesus. Borg accepts the mainstream biblical scholars' reconstruction of the history of the tradition in the "two-source hypothesis": after a long stage of oral transmission of stories about and sayings of Jesus, the earliest layer in the gospels is the hypothetical Q document, reconstructed on the basis of analyzing material shared by Matthew and Luke, but not found in Mark; Mark is the earliest gospel (about 70 C.E.). Mark and the hypothetical Q are the two earliest documents we have (even though both are apparently amalgams of earlier sources, some of which can be discerned, at least in Mark). Matthew and Luke had copies of Mark and Q and amalgamated them with their own distinctive traditions later in the century. Borg finds that Paul's epistles (the earliest written documents in the New Testament), the Gospel of John, and the collection of Jesus' sayings called the *Gospel of Thomas* are not major sources for remembered events. Given this analysis, a useful warrant is obvious: if events or sayings are attested in two or more early sources, then they are more likely to be historical. Those events or sayings that are mentioned once and that fit with the multiply attested material and are not likely to have been added on by the developing tradition are more likely to be historical. Hence, the genesis and attestations of the individual pieces of data in the gospels indicate what kind of qualification (unlikely, possibly, probably, almost certainly) we need to give to a claim of their historical reliability.

The second step is to understand the social contexts in which Jesus lived (and in which the gospels were written). This involves the study of ancient Judaism, the multidisciplinary study of Christian origins, and the crosscultural study of religion pursued in the academy (Borg and Wright 1999, 8-14). The first suggests that if something belonged to the ancient Judaism of Galilee and Judea of Jesus' time, it may well be attributable to Jesus; contrarily, if something belonged to the early church, but not to the Judaism of Jesus, it is not reliable. A prime example of this is the evangelical attribution of virginity to Jesus' mother on the basis of the quotation of Isaiah 7:14 from the Greek Septuagint, which uses *parthenos* (virgin) to translate the Hebrew *ʾalmah* (young woman, girl). It is less obvious that the Aramaic or Hebrew would support the church's claim than would the Greek. The crosscultural study of religion has developed categories and constructed patterns for various types of behavior and social movements. Although these sorts of warrants can be overused (see Schüssler Fiorenza 2000, 108-14), they can function, like the psychoanalytical and other social-scientific theories discussed in the previous chapter, to suggest to the researcher what data might be more likely to be useful as evidence than traditional historians would allow. Obviously, these two steps are not sequential, but influence each other.

Borg and Wright agree on at least three key points. The practice of history should not be fettered or bolstered by faith (but this agreement is done in terms that presume the dualistic faith-and-history dichotomy that this book finds problematical). The primary sources for evidence about Jesus are limited to part of the New Testament. The study of the contexts in which Jesus lived and worked and in which the Christian movement developed is essential. Nonetheless, Borg and Wright disagree on numerous points.

First, Wright rejects Borg's acceptance of one view of the evolution of the traditions about Jesus: "[A] century of research has failed to reach anything like a consensus on a single one of the stages in question, let alone on the hypothetical developments in between" (Borg and Wright 1999, 21). The content of supposedly oral transmissions of stories and sayings, the existence of the Q document, and the temporal priority of Mark are hypotheses which are not to be construed as the grounds for historical investigations because they are the more-or-less warranted results of gathering historical data and marshaling appropriate data as evidence for the hypotheses. Second, the "genetic" method of breaking up the texts we have into components such as miracle stories, parables, sayings of Jesus, and so on, requires two "unproven" assumptions: "(a) the belief that isolated fragments of Jesus material circulated, and developed, in the early church divorced from narrative frameworks; (b) a quite well worked out theory about Jesus and the early church which actually dictates the rules proposed for assessing material" as earlier and later (Borg and Wright 1999, 21). Third, Wright claims, "We are not in a position to solve one part of the puzzle first and then to use it as a fixed point from which to tackle the rest" (Borg and Wright 1999, 23). While scholars can discern different patterns in the material about Jesus, Wright is right to claim that there is no evidence or clear warrants for discriminating the stages or for the circulation of units of material. We can reasonably assume that oral transmission did change the units of material transmitted, but when and how that was done or how large collections of material were changed are difficult claims, at best, to warrant, although historians have built hypotheses about the units circulating and changing over time. Nor can we assume that there is a gulf between the "pre-Easter Jesus" and the "post-Easter Jesus." We may come to that as a conclusion, but it cannot be part of the warrants we use in doing our investigations (Borg and Wright 1999, 24). To do so would be to engage in a viciously circular argument.

Borg responded to Wright's argument. We will take up each of these issues.

First, although the hypothesis of Markan priority is not universally accepted by biblical scholars, it is accepted by a vast majority of them. "In the case of the priority of Mark, it seems to me that the probability is very high indeed, even though I am aware that highly intelligent scholars (though relatively few) have reached a different conclusion" (Borg and Wright 1999, 236-37). Borg also found that the existence of a written Q document was quite probable (although he did not find that the various layers of earlier and later material in Q identified by some other scholars were warranted sufficiently for use in historical-Jesus research). While it is possible, of course, that the common understanding among scholars about these issues is wrong, Borg found them sufficiently well warranted to be of use in understanding the material in the gospels.

The issue between Borg and Wright is whether the scholarly hypotheses on which Borg relies yield warrants "fine-grained" enough to be of use in establishing historical reliability. The "two-source hypothesis" in general has a high degree of plausibility (but not certainty, by any means). We can probably, in the case of Q, accept that some of Jesus' sayings were collected after his death. There may have been a document assembled about twenty years after Jesus' death, although this is less sure. Matthew and Luke may have known Q as a written document, rather than as a remembered set of sayings (about two hundred verses) orally transmitted. Although the arguments do not, in my judgment, decisively warrant a claim that Q existed as a written document, it is better warranted than the other candidates that purport to explain the similarities and differences in the synoptic tradition.

In the case of Mark, we can recognize some of the units of material that Mark used as he composed his gospel some forty years after Jesus' death. But even if we accept the two-source hypothesis in general, it is difficult, if not impossible, to back up warrants for finer-grained claims about what was written early and what was written late (a point Borg explicitly acknowledges about Q). Nor can we warrant on indisputable evidence what originated in oral form early in the tradition and what originated late. Nor can we warrant claims concerning what meanings or force sayings attributed to Jesus had for Jesus and his initial audience if they circulated as aphorisms stripped of their context (as Fredriksen demonstrates regarding the saying on not serving God and mammon; 1999, 23-24). All we can warrantedly show, at best, is that some unit of material entered the written record at a specific point. We can say in some cases that a unit of material seems to have been elaborated or changed (such as the baptism of Jesus by John) as it migrated through the tradition. To warrant such further claims requires that we can marshal evidence to show that a saying or event was later because it was "metaphorized." But to do so, as Wright argues, presumes something not in evidence: that we know enough about the early churches and their contexts to show how in detail they edited the material they inherited.

That the early Christian communities edited the material is a given. How they edited it requires that we know their tendencies to change the material. But we only know those tendencies from the material that was supposedly changed. Such an argument would be circular; and since it requires focusing on one gospel text and the community that produced it, the sort of corroboration and nuancing that would characterize the "holistic hermeneutic" method of Wright ordinarily would not be fine-grained enough to warrant such conclusions strongly enough to rely on them. Occasionally, we can see the development, as in the baptism of Jesus by John. As Fredriksen put it, "Mark states the fact outright; Matthew, Luke and John offer various obfuscatory scenarios" (2000, 94). Luke and John also stress John's inferiority to Jesus in their gospels. Hence, we can say that a genetic approach can warrant particular claims about the later writers "obfuscating" events. But that we can see it in a few particular instances does not make this very problematical warrant into a methodological rule.

Borg suggests that by refraining from using the genetic method, Wright may give the status of "fact" and "evidence" to data that are not really independent evidence, but versions of the same evidence. Thus, Wright would be open to finding an item much more reliable (by multiple attestation) than the evidence (as Borg construed it) warranted. And of course this is possible; but it is equally possible that the genetic method would throw out reliable material. But the issue between them is, in the end, whether the genetic method can deliver sufficiently fine-grained warrants to get us to be able to reliably affirm what is earliest and "remembered" rather than "metaphorized." It is not clear that it can reliably deliver the goods it promises.

In effect, this first dispute comes to a stalemate. The question cannot be settled. There is no decisive evidence or warrant to show that the genetic method yields reliable results or that the holistic approach fails to be precise enough about evidence to be reliable, any more than we can say, as a general rule, that what was written later is less reliable than what was written earlier. Methods generally do not provide warrants sufficient to demonstrate the reliability of specific claims.

Second, Borg does not respond to Wright's claim about the circulation of sayings and stories independent of a narrative structure. However, at least one pericope, the cleansing of the Temple, seems to have circulated without being definitively placed in a narrative structure: the synoptics place it in the story so that it is an instigating factor in the arrest of Jesus, but John places it at the beginning of his ministry (see Fredriksen 2000, xxi-xxiv). Moreover, choosing between the timeline of Mark (singly attested) and the timeline of John (singly attested) for Jesus' ministry is arbitrary. Given the general point that all the final editors of the gospels purposefully shaped their material into narratives with different rhetorical points, the common reliance on Mark's timeline, which moves Jesus breathlessly in about six months from Galilee to Jerusalem, is unwarranted. This timeline may well be Mark's construction. It is not multiply attested and does not cohere with material that is multiply attested. Even if the material the gospel writers used did not circulate without a narrative structure, we cannot on the basis of the evidence available, and using the criteria of the genetic method, warrant a preference for either of the two basic narrative structures—Mark's and John's—which have come down to us.

In effect, historians are left with three choices, none of which can be warranted on historical grounds. They can accept something like Mark's narrative structure and the embedded timeline (most do). They can accept something like John's narrative structure and the embedded timeline (few do). They can factor out the timelines, but this option leaves them with an assumption *de facto* identical to the one for which Wright says there is no evidence: that we have no narrative structure to help us understand what isolated sayings or narrative could have meant. That such a choice of temporal sequence in the events of Jesus' life is fundamentally arbitrary means that historians who use the genetic method can only arbitrarily reconstruct an image of Jesus and his work that can help explain how this man was deemed worthy to be crucified by the Romans (while his followers were not).

There is another version of the "earlier-later" criterion that Borg does not cite, but that could help warrant claims like those he made. Historians do not really need to know clearly the evolution of the challenges to the faith in each of the early churches. Rather, historians as historians are naturalists. Their discipline means they can properly find that claims about actions within the range of human abilities are more historically reliable than those which attribute superhuman abilities to Jesus or which call for divine intervention. Both Borg and Wright, for example, accept as historically reliable that Jesus was a healer, although this had not been a major issue in Wright's writing (Borg and Wright 1999, 66-68, 222-25). Borg does not need to distinguish between the "pre-Easter" and the "post-Easter" Jesus. Rather, what is needed is a discrimination of historical probability. Historians who are explicitly naturalistic like Borg can find warranted the claim that Jesus did some remarkable healings, which his disciples accounted (and account) as miracles; but few, if any, historians, even those with traditionalist religious leanings, find warranted a claim that the nature miracles are reliable—not because they were created by the early church but because they are so extraordinary that there is no obvious or even likely actual historical basis for them. As chapter five showed, Borg's use of the distinction between the "pre-Easter Jesus" and "post-Easter Jesus" is dubious at best. Rather, the naturalistic presumptions of historians and the warrants which derive from them—which may not apply outside the realm of historical research—are sufficient to make discriminations between which events and acts are historically probable and which events and acts cannot be affirmed as factual on historical grounds. Using both Borg's warrants and the more generic historical warrants noted here, we find the list of events and acts found to be historically likely and those unlikely to be rather similar. However, it may still be problematical to demonstrate the links between them, especially those that must have led to Jesus' execution. Thus, the second point regarding historical sequencing, both within the story of Jesus' life and death and within the developing Christian communities, has no clear historical resolution sufficient to warrant a fine-grained chronicle of the sequence of events and acts in Jesus' life, work, and death, even though an alternative, non-chronological, more generic criterion can be of use in warranting some of the genetic historians' claims.

Third, Borg noted that "some judgments are so probable as to be certain; for example, Jesus really existed, and he really was crucified" (Borg and Wright 1999, 236; also see A. E. Harvey 1982, 8). Moreover, Paula Fredriksen notes that it was *only* Jesus who was crucified—his followers were not, and they evidently were not even pursued with great vigor by any authorities (Fredriksen 1999, 8-10). These judgments are so highly probable that they can be taken for granted as facts. Indeed, E. P. Sanders, whose method is a form of "holistic hermeneutics" rather than a "genetic method," listed eight historical facts (which he seems to have listed chronologically in the life of Jesus—but note the problems of chronology discussed above) that are almost indisputable:

1. Jesus was baptized by John the Baptist.
2. Jesus was a Galilean who preached and healed.
3. Jesus called disciples and spoke of there being twelve.
4. Jesus confined his activity to Israel.
5. Jesus engaged in a controversy about the Temple.
6. Jesus was crucified outside Jerusalem by the Roman authorities.
7. After his death Jesus' followers continued as an identifiable movement.
8. At least some Jews persecuted at least parts of the new movement . . . and it appears that this persecution perdured at least to a time near the end of Paul's career . . . (Sanders 1985, 10-11; compare Perrin 1974, 277-78 for a similar list).

Fredriksen (2000, xxii; 2003) has argued rather persuasively that #5 cannot be affirmed on historical grounds to be a cause of #6; she also attributes #5 to the early church, but I am not persuaded that she can sustain an argument that the Temple incident never occurred (see Tilley 2003, 275-76 n. 18). Other scholars might reformulate #3 (to exclude reference to the twelve) and #4 (as not quite as probably reliable as the others). While #6, #7, #8 are clearly in sequential order, the sequencing of #1-#5 may not be well warranted.

What Sanders has shown is that there is a way out of the stalemate noted above. By focusing first on Jesus' actions, Sanders took a new tack in historical-Jesus research, in effect inaugurating the third quest. Some of Jesus' actions are practically indubitable, even if we cannot warrant claims so firmly about the meaning of what he taught.

Sanders noted that for many scholars the key issue is to understand what Jesus taught—whether about God's kingdom, his own role, or the moral and religious practices of Judaism of his time—and that pursuing this issue requires "the unspoken assumption that what he really was, was a teacher." As Sanders pointed out, it is "difficult to move from 'Jesus the teacher' to 'Jesus, a Jew who was crucified, who was the leader of a group which survived his death, and which formed a messianic sect that was finally successful'" (Sanders 1985, 4). Hence, beginning with Jesus' teachings—so many of which evidently came down to us separated from the specific contexts in which and purposes for which he uttered them—is perhaps not the best way to understand the significance of Jesus in and for his time. If Sanders is correct, and I think for the most part he is, we do have practically certain warranted facts that can be a "fixed point" to guide us in understanding the "rest of the puzzle," *pace* the point Wright made. As Sanders notes, the issue is not one of building from the "certain" facts upward, but of being "careful to enter the circle at the right point . . . a point which is secure historically and whose meaning can be established with some independence from the rest of the evidence. One must also, of course, avoid circular arguments" (Sanders 1985, 10).

Wright's objection to a foundationalist and genetic approach, that is, to attempting to establish some facts and building up from them, is side-stepped by Sanders, a "holistic" interpreter, though not by Borg.

There is a final dispute between Borg and Wright. In commenting on Borg's identification of Jesus as a "Spirit person, healer, wisdom teacher, social prophet, and movement initiator" (Borg and Wright 1999, 230) Wright writes, "I myself prefer to use as far as possible language that reflects the culture under discussion rather than importing categories from elsewhere, useful though that sometimes is" (Borg and Wright 1999, 35; also see 226). Wright argues that the categories of Jesus' social world are the primary way to identify who he was and what he meant. Wright goes even further than this and argues that "Jesus . . . believed himself to be Israel's messiah . . ." (Borg and Wright 1999, 49). Borg, however, finds that such an emphasis on Jesus' identity is a post-Easter development and historically unreliable (Borg and Wright 1999, 58). Borg discusses this difference in his summary:

> We both agree that Jesus was a deeply Jewish figure, but we follow different strategies as we seek to describe him; Tom uses emic categories (categories from within the culture), I am using etic (categories from outside the culture) categories. And I can translate my etic categories back into Jewish categories, just as Tom presumably could also translate his Jewish categories into more etic language. (Borg and Wright 1999, 230)

Borg rightly goes on to note that the choice of audiences for whom one writes and the purposes for which one writes are the major factors in making this choice (230-32). Borg does not see Jesus as conceiving his vocation in terms of messiahship, but Wright does.

Borg's easy presumptions about translation are rather misleading. Whichever way one goes, from etic to emic or emic to etic, much is lost in translation. First, it is practically inconceivable that either Jesus could have thought of himself or those who responded to him and formed the first Christian communities could have thought of him in such etic terms. While claims about any historical person's self-consciousness are inherently debatable, use of etic terminology not only precludes such investigations but also may obscure more plausible claims about a person's presentation of himself or herself in the community in which she or he lives. Second, Borg's uneschatological "spirit person" who "mediates the sacred" may be far more a product of Borg's crosscultural and anachronistic method than of the historical investigations undertaken about this particular person. As Peter Novick noted, "Anthropology, in the 'etic' mode, addressed its subject from an Archimedean point" beyond and above any culture (1988, 549). Even if one could get to a position "beyond culture," George Tyrrell's pithy diagnosis of Adolf Harnack's ahistorical historicism, first published in 1909, could be applied *mutatis mutandis* to any who choose "etic" categories for interpretation: "The Christ that Harnack sees, looking back through nineteen centuries of Catholic darkness, is only the reflection of a Liberal Protestant face, seen at the bottom of a deep well" (1963, 49). The use of etic categories is more open to misuse, conscious or unconscious, than categories from the time and place of the subject being studied. Third, whichever way the translation goes, from emic to etic or etic to emic, the meanings of the terms are not wholly translated back and forth. The set of terms Borg generates from crosscultural study of religion simply cannot be translated without remainder into the contexts of the New Testament, nor can the concepts articulated in those writings find an exact equivalency in the crosscultural concepts.

Conclusion

The debate over emic and etic approaches parallels the debates between traditional and new historians sketched in the last chapter. Like psychological theory, etic approaches do not create facts but help us to see which facts are significant. But to use etic approaches in any significant way as warrants in historical reconstruction runs the danger of being reductionist, of losing the particular in the general. While there may be transcultural forces that are tidal waves to the ripples of particular events or actions, if what one wants to understand is the particulars, one needs to use such warrants very carefully. In the present dispute, to identify Jesus as a spirit person makes him an exemplar of a category rather than an individual to be investigated on his own terms.

Borg also wants to make Jesus accessible to contemporary people. In this, he is at one with many of those who have been involved in the quests over the last two centuries. However, this is not a historical task, but a properly theological task. It is important to note this point because many (not all) involved in the quests are disguised theologians who use the practices of history to warrant claims about what people ought believe today. As Fredriksen put it, the historical Jesus stands "with his back to us, his face toward the faces of his own generation." To make Jesus "morally intelligible and religiously relevant to" modern believers is not a *historical* undertaking, "the critical construction of an ancient figure," but a *theological* project, "the generation of contemporary meaning within particular communities (2000, xxvii). Etic warrants are inevitably freighted with meaning for contemporary consumption; they may be important, but in the end, we must recognize, with Novick, that it is difficult to use them as properly historical warrants. Moreover, etic warrants and the desire to make Jesus accessible in the present also run the danger of minimizing the differences between the subject of etic comparison and readers of those comparisons. If Jesus is strange to modern ways, as Schweitzer argued a century ago, these approaches tend to make him all too familiar, practically a contemporary. At its most extreme, this danger is realized in the WWJD ("What would Jesus do?") movement in evangelical Christianity which seems sometimes simply to reinforce by appeal to "Jesus" the inclinations of those who ask WWJD.

The battle between Wright and Borg was fought over a particular field, the historical Jesus. Despite substantial agreement documented above on what the data were, on the principle of historians' autonomy, and on the necessity of seeing Jesus in his socio-political context, insoluble differences remain regarding key issues of methods of investigation, genetic vs. holistic, etic vs. emic, and regarding what counts as evidence. Sanders, battling on the same field, suggests that a different approach may sidestep the problems. In effect, however, Sanders sides with Wright on issues in historical methodology, but with Borg on warrants for claims about Jesus, for Sanders does not claim to know anything about Jesus on the basis of faith, while Wright does (see Borg and Wright 1999, 15, 17, 24-27; Sanders 1985, 2). Moreover, the reconstructions of the historical Jesus, as noted in chapter five, are so various that it is hard to see just how scholars could have drawn such dissimilar conclusions from the same evidence.

This reminds us that the issue is not individuals' presuppositions or worldviews. These do not control the data. Rather, the disputants' understandings of the discipline of history is crucial. Some scholars (see Padgett 1997) continue to assert that scholars' worldviews shape their historical work. In an indirect sense, this may be so. But worldviews factor out when one attempts to warrant historical claims. To do so credibly, one cannot rely on metaphysical claims or assumptions, but on the ordinary practices of the discipline. Everyone may have one's own personal commitments, whether theistic, atheistic, agnostic, and so on. But if one lets these commitments, rather than the rules of the discipline, control what data and warrants count, one cannot properly engage in the discipline. One ignores the role-specific responsibilities of historians and substitutes one's own views.

The problems of methods and warrants affect all of the contemporary efforts in the production of history (Certeau 1988, 21). In one sense, the battles over the historical Jesus simply refract very similar battles over historical methods and warrants found in secular historiography. In short, the problem of history has given way to the problems in history, the morality of historical knowledge to the moralities of historical practices. What this means for theology is the topic for chapter ten.

CHAPTER 10

Practicing Theology

The theologian's task is faithfulness,
not the creation of the new.
—Stanley Hauerwas

St. Anselm's classic definition of theology is "faith seeking under-standing." Yet the ways of spelling out the sort of work theologians are to do, the standards they are to meet, and even the communities they are to serve are nearly as numerous as the theologians who do the spelling out. Pithy proposals like Anselm's can be both profoundly insightful and pro-foundly misleading. It is, in one sense, just as simple as Anselm's defini-tion suggests. Yet in another sense, it is far more difficult. Both "faith" and "understanding" are extraordinarily complex practices.

As a protest against the individualistic, entrepreneurial free-for-all that passes for theology among modern and postmodern academics, Hauerwas's point in the epigraph above is deep and rich. Theologians are properly measured not in terms of how clever and original they are, but by whether they represent faithfully and well, in word and deed, the tra-dition that they serve. Yet fidelity requires creativity. It is not merely throwing "fresh perspectives on traditional commitments" (Hauerwas 1988, 1), but developing new ways of articulating the convictions of a reli-gious tradition so as to help participants live in and live out a tradition. If the problem of history has had no other effect over the last two centuries, it has forced theologians not to take their traditions for granted (see Tilley 2000; Thiel 2000). Our traditions are not fields open to easy explo-ration. We must work as critical historians to retrieve our traditions and as faithful scholars to construct them anew.

Although the term "theologian" is used predominantly in Christian-ity, and less in Judaism or Islam, I will continue to use it to designate those whose work, in whatever tradition, is defined by the tasks discussed here. Muslim "theologians" may be better called philosophers, theoreticians, jurists, or scholars, but Islam needs such "theological" work as much as Christianity or Judaism. John Esposito put it this way:

Muslim societies have experienced the effects of rapid change, and with it the challenges in religious, political, and economic development. Muslims continue to grapple with the relationship of the present and future to the past. Like believers in their sister traditions, Judaism and Christianity, the critical question is the relationship of faith and tradition to change in a rapidly changing and pluralistic world. As Fazlur Rahman, a distinguished Muslim scholar, observed in *Islam and Modernity* (1982), Muslims need "some first-class minds who can interpret the old in terms of the new as regards substance and turn the new into the service of the old as regards ideals." (Esposito 1999, 690)

Those "minds" are among those denominated "theologians" herein.

Theological creativity is essential to the life of any religious tradition. Traditions are incarnated in different times and places. Participants cannot simply recite the formulae of the past nor perform the rituals of the past to preserve continuity with the past. Rahman's point, quoted by Esposito above, makes this clear. A particular example is the Catholic acceptance of the Aristotelian-Thomistic account of transubstantiation. This account presumes a philosophical system that provides insight for the few who understand it. But those formulae may no longer clearly articulate the principle of the real presence to the many Catholics who don't understand it. The system itself has been tried and found wanting by numerous Catholic scholars. Similarly, the first public reading of the daily Scripture passage by a boy who becomes *bar mitzvah* may have profoundly different significance in an Hasidic community's synagogue in nineteenth-century Poland from what it has in a reform community's synagogue in twenty-first century Palm Springs. How can and should these be related? Those are practical theological questions. For our present connections with the past to be a real "carrying on" of the traditions rather than simply nominal links to a romanticized past, we cannot merely engage in rote repetitions of what our ancestors did in wildly different intellectual, social, and political contexts. The twenty-eight-year-old curate in a Catholic parish in the United States who parades around in biretta and Roman cassock after Christmas Masses in 2003 is more a figure of fun than a statement of fidelity to a religious tradition. Fidelity requires practical and theoretical creativity. The past cannot simply be replicated in the present. It must be retrieved for the present.

Another way of putting the matter is that a theologian's work must contribute, indirectly or directly, to identifying and articulating the principles of a religious tradition. Even those who do not fully support Lindbeck's work recognize it as a creative account of Christian doctrine, an expression of creative fidelity. His three identity principles are clearly necessary in the Christian tradition. One aspect of theologians' work, then, is to discover and understand those principles and the convictions that express them. But there are other principles that constitute the various Christian traditions and other convictions that Christian communities hold, even if they are not obviously expressions of identity principles. These also require retrieval. And as noted in chapters six and seven, various formulae embody those identity principles. No one embodied formulation of them is the absolute or the final embodiment of them. Moreover, the articulations of principles alone are insufficient to flesh out a religious tradition rich enough to endure over time.

Theological retrieval means discovering how the tradition in the past articulated and lived out its principles, understanding what those convictions and practices meant, and proposing transformations of them as needed in the present. The tradition's identity principles and their expressions in some of the specific narratives, shared practices, and concrete convictions that shape convictional communities must be discovered, understood, creatively transformed if needed, and proclaimed when appropriate. Such discovery, understanding, transformation, and proclamation are the theologians' tasks for their religious convictional communities (and the parallel task of theoreticians who work in other convictional communities, e.g., political movements; cf. McClendon 1986, 21-24; Tilley 1985, 11-16). These tasks constitute the practices of the theologian as theologian—they delineate the realms of responsibility appropriate for the theologians' role.

The theologians' tasks require creativity. The formulations of identity principles function as rules, as Lindbeck argued. Classics require response and interpretation, as Tracy showed. But principles may be embodied in varying rules. Yet rules don't apply themselves. Nor do classics give their own interpretation. The principle of monotheism, for example, does not itself give us substantive rules for how to worship God, how to conceive of God in every cultural context, or how to recognize and respond to God's will. Nor does it assure us that monotheism does not entail patriarchy even though monotheistic traditions (perhaps like almost all traditions) are patriarchal. Rules do not tell us when and where to apply them—unless "always and everywhere" are parts of those rules. "Christians are monotheistic" may articulate an identity principle. But how that principle is understood and applied in practice has varied widely over the centuries, from social trinitarianism to deism. This identity principle needs to be fleshed out—simply to state it as a principle leaves it too vague to be put into practice.

If Jesus of Nazareth is in some sense a "classic" person in the Christian tradition, the previous chapter shows that the precious texts we have that detail what he did and said require interpretation and are open to different interpretations (compare Tilley 2000, 92-101). Indeed, much of the work of the quests, as Paula Fredriksen has noted, has not been as much historical as it has been theological construction informed by historical investigation. In attempting to retrieve what we can know of Jesus in ways we can understand today, the theologians discussed in chapter nine participated in the theologians' task of creative fidelity. To what extent they were successful in their work, of course, is another matter. Creative fidelity is a constituent of theologians' faithfulness; mere repetition of formulae of the past is neither creative nor faithful (or so argued Tilley 2000).

Creativity may not be a goal of doing theology, but it is a condition for doing theology well. Liberal Christian theologians made proposals for living in and living out the Christian tradition by following Jesus in the face of the challenges of the Enlightenment and the collapse of the biblical narrative. Jewish theologians have made proposals for ways to live in and live out the Jewish tradition and continue the saga in the wake of the *Shoah*. Muslim scholars make various proposals for walking the straight path prescribed by God by interpreting the Qur'an, debating the meanings of *jihad*, uncovering various ways to engage in almsgiving (one of the five pillars of Islam), and arguing over how people are to dress in societies increasingly colonized by Western materialist culture. They proffer various answers to questions about ways of walking in God's path as Muslims in the modern world. So although, in one sense, the theologians' task is not to create the new, in another sense, theologians fail to be faithful if they are not creative, if they do not come to understand the circumstances in which the community finds itself, and if they do not say and show how to live in and live out the tradition in new ways in these new circumstances. So if one were to think that because creativity is not a *task* of theology it is not a *component* in faithful theologizing, one would be wrong.

It is important to distinguish the obligations of theologians from those of other believers. Theologians must discover (including using the tools of historians and other social scientists), understand (adding the tools of philosophers and cultural critics), argue for transforming when necessary (adding rhetoricians' tools), and manifest and proclaim when appropriate (adding activists' and apologists' tools) the convictions carried in the practices, narratives, and codes of the community. Believers are obliged to live in and live out the faith tradition and in doing so to witness to the faith they live and believe. Obviously, the obligations typically overlap; but participants in the tradition take different roles and have different role-specific responsibilities.

As noted in chapter three, one of the problems of the dualist problematic ensconced as the "problem of history" was that it failed to note that theologians have different role-specific responsibilities from other participants in a tradition. Participants' responsibilities vary widely from tradition to tradition. The few generalizations one can make about religious participants generally are either rather vague ("Do good, avoid evil") or delimited by contrast: only Christians follow Jesus, only Muslims are to make the *hajj*, if possible, and so on. Other participants in a tradition do not have the responsibilities of theological investigation that theologians have.

Distinguishing theologians from other participants does not imply that "ordinary" believers can be or should be "mindless" in their religious practice. That would be a caricature. Believers have to respond to challenges to their beliefs. Simply being part of the modern world may force non-theologians who participate in a tradition to reflect on how to meet the challenges of modernity faithfully. Given the spread of advanced education and the explosion of information technology in recent decades, ordinary believers, even in remote locations, are often faced with the challenges of modernity.

Although this is a finely drawn point, it is important to note that such responsibility is not role-specific, but much broader: it is a person-and-situation specific responsibility (cf. Stout 2004, 192, who construes these as unconditional obligations). However it may have been in other times, contemporary people do not derive their identity from one community or tradition. We are formed by and participate in distinct civic, national, social, familial, religious (and other) communities (cf. Shea 2004, 23-27; Shea prefers to say we belong to many "tribes," which he details deftly). We have access to an uncountable number of images, unimaginable amounts of information, and incredibly quick communication with far-distant people. Such participation and access contribute to our identities. We are compelled, as persons, to negotiate our identities because of such multiple belongings and such inundation with information and communication. We did not choose to have to negotiate our identities. This is not a role we take up but is part of the situation in which we live. Given this situation, we each have various roles to play in it. But it is important not to collapse the challenges that our situations present to us and the responsibilities called for by our roles in those situations. Contemporary Christian ethicists, for example, have to meet all the challenges that any Christian does in the present situation; but their role-specific responsibilities have to do with the specific responses to ethical challenges that they develop in and for the Christian community.

I also use the term "situation" advisedly. Theologians often work with a dualistic understanding of "the church and the world" or "the church and culture." In doing so, it is easy to reify any of the terms in these dichotomies. James Wm. McClendon, Jr., working within the Christian tradition, has provided a compelling alternative way to think about this issue:

> The world (or "culture") has appeared for us not as one smooth global unity, but as an indefinite congeries of powerful practices, spread over time and space, so that any number of these practices may impinge upon believers in a variety of ways, while our witness to them will necessarily take a corresponding variety of forms. . . . Culture . . . is not monolithic; "the world" is itself divided. Meanwhile, "the church" is exactly the realm in which

responsibility to Jesus Christ is the hallmark of discipleship, so in it the call to be "responsible" can only be defined in terms of his Lordship over all, not by some worldly measurement. (McClendon 1986, 231)

All participants in a religious tradition live not in a reified entity called "culture" or "the world," but in the context of multiple practices and multiple traditions. McClendon identifies discipleship as the hallmark of the Christian community; other communities would have other hallmarks. The point, then, in this complex situation with so much impinging on one is to find out how to live in and live out the tradition both without succumbing to the "congeries of powerful practices" present in our situation and without ignoring that they, as well as our religious commitments (which should be ultimate), shape our identities.

Given this situation, some of us did choose or were called to take up the role of theologian. Practicing theology is not the same thing as practicing religion. Theologians are the physicians of the tradition, diagnosing the difficulties participants negotiate, recommending remedies, and expanding the understanding of the tradition. But theologians cannot make a faith healthy or cure a believer's maladies. The theologian has the role-specific responsibility to marshal resources (discovering, understanding, and arguing for transformation when necessary) that participants (including themselves) can use to proclaim and manifest the convictions that give shape to a tradition. The non-theologian can use those resources, but is not obligated by her or his role as a participant to marshal those resources.

Some Christians may have been forced by the problem of history or other modern challenges to reflect on their faith and its credibility. It is not that they were fulfilling role-specific responsibilities to investigate the tradition. The problems were thrust on them by their situation. But theologians had and have the role-specific responsibility of meeting those challenges. In the eighteenth and nineteenth centuries only an intellectual and social elite among believers found that the biblical narrative was eclipsed by the moon of the Enlightenment. Many continued to live in and live out the world of the Bible. But because they are part of the "culture establishment" as well as of the religious tradition, theologians had the responsibility to meet those challenges and to respond to the eclipse. Their responses could then be resources that others, not theologians, could utilize in formulating their own responses to challenges to their convictions. The present chapter, then, addresses the role-specific responsibilities of theologians.

The social locations of theologians also shape their work. As part of his important argument against the privatization of religion and special pleading in theology, David Tracy has very helpfully identified three "publics" in which theologians carry out their constructive work: the soci-

ety, the academy, and the church (Tracy 1981, 5-6 *et passim*). These publics
are more than the audiences that theologians address. Rather, they are
multiply specifiable contexts that shape who the theologian is and what
the theologian does. Theologians are citizens of a nation, members of the
academic profession, and participants in a religious tradition. Each of
these roles is a constituent of a theologian's identity. Yet as a citizen, one
might be a stranger in the land, an immigrant or bicultural person, a
member of a disadvantaged group, or a willing participant in hegemonic
practices. As an academician, the theologian might work in a parish, a
divinity school or seminary, a university, an institute, or in other locations
where teaching and research is fostered. As a participant in a religious tradition, a theologian might be lay, ordained, officially authorized or not; a
theologian may also hold an authoritative office in the religious tradition's institutional structure. These different social locations shape not
only the theology we do but the practices in which we engage and the very
persons we, who are called to do that work, become. While many, perhaps
most, people today have to "negotiate" their identities, theologians have
to do so not merely because of their multiple social locations but also
because of the work they are called to do in those social locations. The
interests we have as theologians are conditioned significantly by the
places in which we do our work as well as by those with whom and for
whom we work, our collaborators and audiences in religious community,
academic institution, and socio-political realms. But our responsibilities
are given by the nature of our work and the specific set of practices which
are appropriate in our places.

Theologians who are also ecclesial authorities have their work shaped
differently from those whose work is shaped by being in research universities. Theologians who work in parishes, grassroots movements, or community service organizations have work that is different from those who
work in seminaries or divinity schools. Theologians working in the U.S.
environment find different political and economic issues shaping their
work than theologians in Latin American, European, African, or Asian
contexts find. Ethnic differences, gender differences, differences in sexual orientation, and status (laic versus cleric) differences are also factors.
These differences can be multiplied.

But the point is not merely to admit one's social location. The point
is to see that one's social location inclines one to be interested in specific
problems and to develop specific patterns of insight and oversight. The
problem of history addressed in this book, for example, is a distinctive
problem addressed in Euro-North American theology. This problem
might not be a main concern of many in other social locations. The analysis developed and the solutions proposed here emerge in and from the
author's location. While authors always hope their work has an impact on
other scholars, they also recognize that those in other locations may not
be interested in the work they do. For example, the present text might

have no discernable impact on the work of a bioethicist who is a patients' advocate in a medical center. Our locations condition not only what we see, but what we find of interest, and what we think significant and insignificant.

The present author has a responsibility to be aware that his work is particular, not universal. It can aspire to making universal claims, or at least claims that are true for a large number of contexts; but in so doing, he must listen carefully enough to voices from other locations so as not to run roughshod over concerns central to those in other contexts or to expect that the problems he addresses are burning problems for all theologians or theoreticians. For example, U.S. Latino/a theologians have identified numerous blindspots in mainstream theology: liberal individualism, blind communitarianism, monocultural hegemonism, intellectual, commercial, and cultural colonialism, racism, sexism, and the hegemony of elites who work all too hard fiddling around to enforce theological conformity while communities burn because authority is seduced and healthy diversity repressed. While one cannot occupy the social locations of others, one can and must hear the voices of others, especially when they speak of the oversights common to one's own location. Acknowledging one's particular location is crucial, then, for understanding the limits of one's own work and for allowing it to be influenced by work done in and from other places. For if one is deaf to the voices of others, one cannot fulfill one's responsibility to be of use to the community and tradition that one serves. (Whether the present author actually does what he says should be done in this matter is another question!)

Discovering and Understanding

The first task of the theologian is discovering the principles of the tradition and their articulations in the convictions and in the practices of the community that carries and is carried by the tradition. One might think that this is the easy part. All one would have to do, one would think, is to look at classic texts, catechisms, handbooks, instructional materials, and so on, to find out what a given community believes. And in one sense, this is true. But each of these provides only a snapshot of belief at a particular time and place. When one examines, for example, the canons and decrees of the Council of Trent (1545-1563), one finds that "transubstantiation" is a key belief about the transformation of the bread and wine that occurs in the celebration of the Mass. Yet as discussed above in chapter seven, it is clear that transubstantiation did not always have a fixed meaning and that the Catholic tradition had been—and now is again—more varied in its accounts of the transformation. What the theologian has to do is to "read through" the texts in attempting to discover the convictions that articulate the principles of the tradition. The conviction of

the real presence of Christ in the sacrament of the Eucharist, as opposed
to the conception of Holy Communion as an ordinance that memorial-
izes the redemption wrought in Christ, distinguishes the Catholic and
some Protestant traditions from other Protestant accounts. But "real presence" is a principle of the Catholic sacramental tradition that is allied
with a more pervasive principle of sacramentality identified by David
Tracy as an "analogical imagination" (see Tracy 1981; and Tilley 2000,
125-34).

The key, then, for the theologians' tasks of "discovering and understanding" is not merely historical investigation, but theological analysis
of the "classics" of the tradition to articulate the convictions they carry
and the principles those convictions express so as to retrieve them for
the present community. In this context, the understanding required is
different from historical understanding. In general, historians do want to
enable their audiences to understand what happened in the past. They
squabble over which methodological principles and differing practices
make this understanding possible. Theologians do this—whether as historians or as those who use critically the work of historians—and have
the added task of getting their audiences to accept an understanding of
the past that provides a pattern for religious practice and belief in the
present. This is not to say that historians sometimes step beyond the
boundaries of history proper in their work. At least parts of the campaign for objectivity against the relativists, described in chapter eight,
and some of the attempts to make Jesus "available" for the present, discussed in chapter nine, are more partisan than historical. And even if historians are always advocates—whether theological, social or
political—we can distinguish their properly historical accounts of what
has been from their advocacy of what should be.

The theological task is neither repetition of the past in the present
nor repristination in the present of the past. Christian theologian Edward
Schillebeeckx describes the historical theologians' tasks of understanding
and presenting the tradition this way:

> The identity of meaning can only be found *on the level of the cor-*
> *responding relation between the original message (tradition) and the*
> *always different situation*, both past and present. The fundamental
> identity of meaning between subsequent periods of Christian
> understanding of faith does not concern the corresponding *terms*;
> it concerns the corresponding *relations* between the terms (mes-
> sage and situation; then and now). (Schillebeeckx 1991, 313)

Similar claims could be made for other traditions. Repetition of the past
is not fidelity to the past. What is required is not discerning y ($x=y$), where
x is the past term and y is the present term, but following a more complex

formula, $x{:}a{::}y{:}b$, where x is an articulation of a principle in context a and b is our present context. The point is not simply to replicate x, but to solve for y. This is the key creative work of the historical theologian in any tradition. That it can evoke controversy goes without saying.

The question then becomes "what" is to be analyzed. For Christianity, the Scriptures are central. Catholics would add tradition. Methodists would add reason and experience. Jews would focus on the Torah, the Writings, the Prophets, and also the Talmuds and the rabbinic commentaries as well as contemporary experience. Muslims traditionally find the "Qur'ân, the example (*sunna*) of the prophet [and, one might add, his followers as both are recorded in *hadith*], the consensus (*ijma*) of the community, and analogical reasoning or deduction (*qiyas*)," as Muhammad ibn Idris al-Shafii put it in the ninth century, to be the sources of the law that govern the community in seeking to walk the straight path prescribed by God (Esposito 1988, 78). Custom and the religious practices of Shi'i and Sufi Muslims are also important for various branches of the Muslim community.

Modern theologians of most traditions have sought to analyze "experience" as a source for discovering the convictions of a community. The generic appeal to personal, individual religious experience sustains little, if anything, beyond what William James was able to sustain in the *Varieties of Religious Experience* a century ago (see Tilley 2004; Bagger 1999). However, contemporary U.S. Hispanic theologians (e.g., Espín 1997, 164) have recovered a concept of "social experience," or "*experiencia*" relevant to contemporary theology. This use of "experience" does not authorize religious belief in general, but identifies patterns of practice in specific communities. Attending to *experiencia* can help theologians understand concretely how a tradition is lived in and lived out.

While individual religious experience is often cited as if "anyone" might have had such experience, *experiencia* is qualified adjectivally by "who" has the experience. *Experiencia* is the shared experience or practice of a group, such as "women's experience" or "the U.S. Latino/a experience" or "mestizo experience" or the "U.S. Catholic experience" or "the experience of the poor" or "the experience of immigrants." In practice, recognizing social experience as a theological resource can give marginalized groups privileged status. In using such experience as a resource, the theologian can qualify or challenge the normativity of mainstream articulations of the identity principles of a tradition. The multiple ways in which a tradition has come to life in varying cultures provides data that theologians can and should consider. Hearing these new voices—whatever one's location—helps restore the variety in traditions often effaced in the past. It must be admitted, though, that there is no general answer to the question, "What weight should be given to alternate voices in a religious tradition?" than there is to the question, "What weight should old historians give to the social sciences and the new histories?" Part of the work of theologians is to make such discriminations on an issue-by-issue, case-by-case, basis using the tools theologians normally employ.

Listening to the voices of others is important for the purposes of uncovering and overcoming blindspots in mainstream theologies. What Orlando O. Espín notes about Catholicism could be applied *mutatis mutandis* to other traditions: "Theological study of popular Catholicism is indispensable to the study of doctrines and their development within the Catholic tradition, and this Tradition has been profoundly affected and shaped by the people's faith and daily experience" (Espín 2002, 152). Indeed, Gary Macy's use of popular religiosity as a resource for discovering what the community has believed was an important constituent in his understanding of the variety of eucharistic devotions and eucharistic theologies in the Middle Ages (Macy 1997, 43ff.).

Among Christian theologians, the turn to praxis is an example of listening clearly to the voices of others. But the point is not to listen merely to their words but to listen to what they say in the context of their lives. Schillebeeckx put it this way: "Personally, I would call religions wisdom schools. . . . Religions are not systems of truth constructs; they try to trace a way of life, albeit not without truth and insights" (Schillebeeckx 2002, ix; I have elsewhere made a similar point: Tilley 1995, 29-57). To discover and understand the past of a tradition is not to understand the propositions that people uttered or believed. It is to understand how their practice gave substance to those beliefs.

Historians can contribute to the discovery of the tradition in important, if limited, ways. As noted in chapter six, the classic problem of history has history functioning as an authorizing discourse. History was the ground on which our religious traditions could show their credibility despite the eclipse of the biblical narrative. We could attempt to base our claims on "historical investigations." In the past, theologians could even presume that they knew "the assured results of criticism" (Tyrrell 1963, 19) as a basis for their claims. That presumption is no longer operative, if it ever legitimately was. It is important to understand the issues involved with construing history as an "authorizing" discipline. Three points can surface those issues and show how history does and does not function as an authorizing discourse.

First, historical investigations of the Bible, both Jewish and Christian, do not authorize or undermine a tradition, but they may authorize or undermine claims within a tradition. Historical investigation of the Exodus may force us to rethink the facts about the Exodus or to reconceive the shape of the saga of the Jewish people. However, the rejection of a tradition that includes a principle of God forming a covenantal relationship with Israel is a different issue, as chapter five's discussion of Rubenstein's work showed. The remarks of scholars from Reimarus to McKenzie and later to Mendenhall and Gottwald show that the ways we imagine the Exodus need revision, but not necessarily that belief in the God of the Exodus needs to be abandoned. Some Jewish scholars would find the founding of the nation of Israel in 1948 yet another historic event in the saga—one requiring a renarration of the story.

Principles that give identity to a religious community are not directly vulnerable to historical investigation. In this, they seem parallel to the invulnerability of acceptance of historical forces by some historians which evidently are not directly vulnerable to errors concerning historical facts (as shown in chapter eight's discussion of critical reactions to the work of David Abraham, who used Marxist-influenced categories to understand the emergence of the Third Reich). One accepts or rejects the identity principles of Judaism, for example, by accepting the saga of Judaism as a saga of a covenantal relationship even if the specific facts about the events narrated in the saga have to be reformulated in light of critical investigation. The *formulations* of identity principles in theology and the religious imagination may require significant amendment as the result of historical investigation, just as particular understandings of the effects of political and economic forces leading to the collapse of the Weimar Republic may need amendment in light of the uncovering of errors regarding historical facts.

The same sort of point also applies to the New Testament. In asking whether critical scholarship has undermined the historical reliability of the gospels, James D. G. Dunn answered in two ways:

> Yes!—but only for the person who comes to the Gospels with expectations they were not designed to fulfill. Whoever looks for chronological accounts, detailed conciseness in every episode recorded, pedantic precision in reproducing Jesus' teaching as given, word for word, and such like *will* be disappointed. But *not* because of anything scholars have said or done. Rather because the evangelists themselves were not concerned with such matters. The fault here, if fault there be, lies not with the scholars or in their findings, but in the false expectations with which so many have come to the Gospels. (Dunn 1985, 27)

That is, because the gospels are not stenographic transcripts in the literary genres of the court reporters' records or the daily newspapers with their expected (but not often achieved, it seems) accuracy, one can find historical elements in the gospels, but only by reading them "against the grain," by looking in them for materials that are retained for the evangelists's purposes of manifestation and proclamation of the good news. The evangelists had purposes other than those found in modern reportorial writing. The items that one can establish by reading "against the grain"—

a possible listing of which appeared above on page 138 above—are too frail to provide the sinews for a robust faith. But that is not the whole story. As Dunn put it:

> No!—because all these traditions . . . go back to Jesus and his ministry. All are firmly rooted in the earliest memories of his mission. In conveying the traditions of Jesus' words and deeds the evangelists were concerned to present the tradition in ways that spoke most powerfully to their readers. So while it is ever the first memories of Jesus which they retell, they do so in ways often shaped by the circumstances and the needs for which they were retold. (Dunn 1985, 28)

Dunn here rejects Marcus Borg's attempts to separate "history remembered" and "history metaphorized." It is not that one deals with facts and the other with faith. The gospels are faithful retellings of the earliest memories of Jesus' acts, including his teaching, and of the significance of those acts. To attempt to separate which parts of which pericopes that reliably record events "remembered" from those parts of pericopes that are created as faith expressions by the evangelists is confused. Such sorting neglects the point made by Dunn. Such attempts to use "reliable" material to authorize or undermine the principles of the faith tradition are confused. Borg tends to presume that retrieving "history remembered" authorizes new ways to think about Jesus. Perhaps it does. But the wild variety of portraits of the historical Jesus suggests that no one of them presents pictures that clearly do not fall foul of Tyrrell's critique of Harnack's seeing his own face reflected at the bottom of the nineteenth-century well of Catholic darkness. The variety also suggests that we do not need to supplant the patterns preserved in the gospels.

We need to remember an important distinction here, between principles and their formulation. Historical investigations may bring up facts that "force" theologians to rethink their formulations, but not that force them to reject their faith. Critical scholarship has forced theologians to far greater reticence on the knowledge of Jesus, as Dulles acknowledged. Historical work has shown that questions such as "Was Jesus conscious that he was divine?" are difficult, at best, to ask, much less to answer, in historical investigations. The work of Macy and Kilmartin, among others, cited in chapter seven, may "force" Catholic theologians to rethink the necessity of using one understanding of transubstantiation as the only or best way to express the sacramental principle of the real presence of Christ in the eucharistic celebration. Although it is clear that the expressions have had to change, and often become less grandiose, it is not clear that the principles have had to change.

There are various ways to understand the continuity of principles. Imagine, for example, that currently ongoing and inconclusive arguments surrounding the historicity of the Last Supper eventually force theologians to rethink the status of the institution narratives. The synoptic gospel tradition has an institution of the Eucharist at the Last Supper (and no foot-washing scene). The Johannine tradition does not have an institution narrative (but narrates the foot-washing in witty detail). Hence, the tradition of the institution of the Eucharist at the Last Supper is not multiply attested in the gospels. Some would find it, therefore, not reliable as a historical fact about what Jesus did. But Paul also writes of the institution in 1 Cor. 11:23-26 and places it on the night Jesus was betrayed. Some would take this to be "multiple attestation." But someone might ask, "to what?" Does this attest to a ritual that emerges very early in the Christian tradition or to a ritual that recaptures accurately the memory of an act of Jesus? Whatever claims are eventually (if ever) warranted on historical grounds as answers to this question, would those claims, if they were negative about the historical reliability of the institution narrative, undermine the sacramental principle of Catholicism or warrant the rejection of the sacramental principle by some Protestant traditions? In the unlikely event that a scholarly consensus were to conclude that the institution narrative does not reliably convey a historical act, that would require neither Catholics nor Protestants to abandon their principles. Catholics could simply note that, even if the narrative is historically unreliable as a depiction of Jesus' act, it is clearly a historically reliable reflection of a ritual of the early church. That the inspired writers included it in the New Testament is sufficient reason to accept it as part of the tradition, an expression of the sacramental principle. Non-sacramental Protestants could agree about the scholars' consensus on the reliability of the depictions and still claim the ordinance as attested in Scripture (without the elaboration of the sacramental system that they would find their forebears had properly rejected in the sixteenth century). James D. G. Dunn's suggestion that we may be asking the wrong questions or seeking what we do not need is cogent. It may not really matter whether we can amass historical evidence for the occurrence of the institution by Jesus or for the development of the communion ritual from Jesus' practice of commensality (multiply attested and probably rather historically reliable as such claims go). Historical investigations may make reformulations of principles necessary, but they are not sufficient to undermine or authorize those principles even if the reformulations are sometimes painful to the community living in and out of that tradition.

Historical investigations are not sufficient to warrant claims about what are the principles that give a tradition its identity or whether specific proposed formulations are legitimate. As chapter six noted about the ways we can construe God's acting in history, these are difficult issues. But they are not primarily historical issues, but theological issues. Theologians must undertake historical investigations as historians do and must account for the results of historical investigations in their own proposals to articulate the principles of the tradition. The difference is not one of the historians' lack of faith and the theologians' faith or even a difference in method (though there may be such differences). The key difference is that historians and theologians have different role-specific responsibilities and are responsible to different communities. Theologians have multiple social locations that structure their responsibilities while historians are primarily responsible to the academic community.

Historians interpret records of events, actions, states of affairs, and so on. If there are no discoverable records, there is nothing for the historian to work on. In their work, historians are responsible for presenting clear and well-warranted claims about events, acts, states of affairs, persons, and communities in the past. The complexity of historical warrants and the difficult epistemological issues discussed in chapter eight are part of the story here. But consider the religious principles discussed at various points in this book: monotheism, historical particularity (with regard to Jesus), christological maximalism, and (for Catholics) a sacramental church (and world, I might add; see Tilley 2000, 125-44). The facts are that Christians' practices and creeds are said (by contemporary theologians) to exhibit those principles. But those principles are simply not the objects of historians' investigations. They emerge from what Avery Dulles has called interpreted history, a reflection on the claims that historians warrant. As noted above, even in the task of discovering and understanding the convictions of a community, the theologian goes beyond the proper role of the historian. To use the detective metaphor from chapter eight, the theologian is a third-stage detective whose purposes are not merely warranted re-creations of the past.

A historian of ancient Christianity, for example, might acknowledge that in the fourth century, the Arians did not accept christological maximalism, at least in the ways that the Athanasians did. That historian might warrant the claim that powerful political and economic motives were at work, that the Athanasian party, in cooperation with imperial wishes, sought to dominate the Arian party by imposing a specific theology on the whole church. A theologian might accept both the factual claim about the Arians and the more controversial claim about the Athanasians' motives and the forces at work in the dispute while also finding that the principle of christological maximalism was and is constitutive (in part) of the Christian tradition. That theologian might also find that the understanding of those principles was defective, if not among the Athanasians in the fourth-century controversy, perhaps in a fifth-century controversy between orthodox Christians and Nestorians. Indeed, Pope John Paul II and Mar Dinkha IV, catholicos-patriarch of the Assyrian church in the East have, in their "Common Christological Declaration," paved the way for rapprochement between their two churches and declared that Nestorians and Catholics have expressed the traditional faith in different for-

mulae. This religious accord is not based merely on historical investigations but on theological analyses of earlier disputes and theological judgments that those disputes were not about the principles of the faith but
about their formulations in the conviction sets of the communities (see
Thiel 2000, 134-39).

In sum, historical work may be useful and even necessary for understanding religious principles, but it is not sufficient. Nor can historical
investigations affirm or undermine those principles directly. In some circumstances, historians might undermine or affirm the reliability of
expressions of principles. But, since the principles are not simply the
result of historical investigations, but emerge from reflections undertaken in the properly theological realm of theologically interpreted history, it would take theological, not historical, arguments to undermine or
affirm them—such as the arguments about "sacraments" and "ordinances" in the Christian traditions.

Second, historical conclusions are textured. They may be strongly
warranted or weakly warranted, but they always have degrees of probability, not certainty, as the sketch of the practice of history in chapter
eight reminds us. Yet the multiple perspectives in the historians' practices
render it possible that strongly argued and even solidly warranted claims
may be undermined by later historians uncovering new data or using new
methods that revise the sorts of conclusions drawn from the data at hand.
One example of this need to take historians' conclusions tentatively is the
ongoing debate about the survival of African cultural elements among
African Americans in the United States, especially in African American
religion.

In 1941 anthropologist Melville J. Herskovits argued that Africans
brought to the United States as slaves had carried with them cultural traditions that they preserved even in slavery. He argued that it was a myth
that the "Negro is thus a man without a past" (Herskovits 1958, 2).
Among other cultural elements, Herskovits attributed distinctive African
American religious practices, for example, the "ring shout," antiphonal
responses to sermons, as well as views about the interdependence of
divinity and humanity to retentions of African religious elements (summarized in Herskovits 1958, xxxvi-xxxix). In 1953, E. Franklin Frazier,
then Chief of the Division of the Applied Social Sciences in the Depart-
ment of Social Sciences of UNESCO in Paris, argued in a lecture that
enslavement had indeed stripped Africans of their culture. In an
expanded version of this lecture, first published in 1963, he argued that
the cultural vacuum thus created was filled in large part by Christianity—
not a syncretized form of Christianity as in Latin America, but an "invisible institution" inspired by Baptist and Methodist preachers (Frazier
1964, 2-19). This institution, along with the family, became the key cultural institution for black Americans, "the major form of organized social

life among Negroes . . . . the church communities in the South became a sort of nation within a nation" (Frazier 1964, 83). When Albert J. Raboteau came to publish *Slave Religion* in 1978, he found they were both right—and wrong—because of their different perspectives. He wrote:

> Herskovits was right in demolishing the myth of the Negro past. . . . He did succeed in demonstrating that elements of African culture survived slavery in the United States. . . .
>
> On the other hand, Frazier . . . was right in challenging excesses in Herskovits's argument, in posing the question of African survivals in terms of significance or meaning and in keeping sight of the real differences between Afro-American cultures in the United States and elsewhere in the hemisphere. . . . In the United States the gods of Africa died. (Raboteau 1978, 86)

With regard to voodoo in New Orleans, Raboteau claimed "that the rich pantheon and complex theology of Haitian *vaudou* did not survive in New Orleans voodoo; the panoply of gods was attenuated and the rites of worship corrupted" (Raboteau 1978, 80). Yet Jessie Gaston Mulira argued that in the conglomeration of African rituals and beliefs in New Orleans voodoo, two Dahomean deities, the Ogun of the Yoruba Orisha, and other deities also survived (Mulira 1990, 64), and a tradition of "hoodoo," of medical and magical conjuring based in African ritual practice, also arose.

While Raboteau's mediating view seems to provide a new baseline for further research, it is clear even from this brief sketch of the controversy about African American religion that social scientists and historians are still debating the significance of the retentions of Africanisms in African American religion. While all the participants recognize some retentions, the significance they give to those retentions varies. Their judgments, even when strenuously expressed (as by Herskovits and Frazier), need to be recognized as "not final." Van Harvey summarized the principle of the varying "texture" that historians give to their conclusions in the following:

> [The historian] indicates what he believes can be affirmed with practical certainty, what can be asserted only with caution or guardedly, and what is to be asserted as possible, given the present state of his knowledge. The historian's assent, so to speak, possesses a texture. He does not traffic in mere claims but in qualified claims ranging from tentativity to certitude. (Harvey 1968, 62)

Yet given the developments in historiography in general and in this one example in particular, certitude seems a distant ideal for significant historical claims.

Even more importantly, the perspective of the historian moves. Sometimes, the past is imagined as a "moving target" which is never quite settled; some of the postmodern historians mentioned in chapter eight seem to presume this. However, what is moving is the point from which the historians approach the past. What this means in historical terms is that the picture of the past can become unsettled as one's social location changes. Justo González, describing the shape of the history of Christianity past and future, put the point this way:

> Still, as I look at the picture of the worldwide church and try to divine what the third millennium might bring, I become increasingly convinced that in our evaluation of the sixteenth century the Reformation will eventually take second place to the Spanish and Portuguese invasion of the Western Hemisphere, and to the ensuing colonial expansion of Western Europe. That was the first of two momentous stages in the birth of a worldwide church— and in many ways the birth of such a church will be proven to be more significant for the future history of the church catholic than the birth of the Lutheran, the Reformed, the Tridentine, or any other tradition stemming from the Reformation. One could say that the cataclysmic change that has affected our view of the sixteenth century is such that, although that century still looms large and must still be listed as such, an entire new mountain chain has emerged that tends to overshadow the older—much as in the North American continent the younger Rockies overshadow the Appalachians. (González 2002, 44)

Even if one lives east of the Appalachians and finds the Rockies obscured in the distance, one must recognize González's point: as Christianity becomes more a world church and less a Eurocentric one, the way the history of the church is narrated must change.

Historical claims are always probable at best and vulnerable to revision by recovering new data, reanalyzing old data, reevaluating the significance of established facts, utilizing new forms of warrant, and so on. Yet even if it is probably established that African retentions are significant in African American religion or that the Reformation is dwarfed by the concerns of the world church, the question (if any) of their being appropriate ways of expressing and enacting Christian convictions is not an anthropological, sociological, or historical question, but a theological one.

Raboteau has argued that the "ring shout" was not limited to African Americans but was adopted by European-descended Americans as well, for example, in the camp meeting (Raboteau 1978, 66-73). Clearly, this practice was "baptized" or adapted beyond the African American church. Theophus H. Smith has argued that the practice of conjure ("hoodoo") among African American Christians became a form that did and properly could fit Christian images and convictions—to my mind about as well as James P. Mackey says the forms of Greek philosophy fit early Christianity (see Smith 1994; Mackey 2003). If there are issues about these or any other "baptized" practices or forms being appropriate for Christians, these are properly theological questions—each answered positively by Mackey and Smith. Even though historians can help theologians understand what the tradition was, their conclusions are tentative and probable and cannot unequivocally form a basis for theological discernment of whether a practice or belief is either an expression of or compatible with Christian principles. Much the same could be said about other religious traditions, especially the ways in which Islam has adopted and adapted indigenous practices and expressions as it expanded into West Africa, South Asia, and Oceania; but the point is clear: theological questions are not simply reducible to historical questions, even though historical evidence may be extremely important for answering those questions.

Historical investigations do not always strongly authorize conclusions. The conflicting claims of Herskovits and Frazier demonstrate that point. However strong their authors' claims, the evidence is open to a number of interpretations. Following Stephen Toulmin's analysis of arguments, Van Harvey (1968; and chapter eight above as well) emphasized this need to "qualify" conclusions from investigations. Of course, some claims are well warranted and practically certain, for example, that Jesus died by crucifixion. Other claims historians make about Jesus are not quite so certain, as chapter nine showed. The claims that historical investigations tend to warrant most strongly are hardly in dispute or in need of authorization. In sum, this "texturing" of historical claims means that the sorts of authorizations that historians can supply are quite limited. Indeed, it almost seems as though the more we would like authorization for our religious convictions, for example, Christian belief in the resurrection of Jesus, the less authorization historical investigations can supply.

Third, there are situations, however, in which historical investigations can undermine a principle. The basic issue is simple: if a principle cannot be reformulated to account for the results of historical work, then that principle can be undermined. One example of this is Richard Rubenstein's theological judgment that "we are faced with a choice that can neither be evaded nor glossed over: *Either Scripture's account of the covenant is credible, or, however we understand God, Divinity is not the biblical God-who-acts-in-history-and-chooses-Israel*" (Rubenstein 1992a, 178-79). I have argued in chapter five against the necessity of Rubenstein's dichotomy and his rejection of the God of history. Many Jewish thinkers have opposed Rubenstein's view while recognizing its importance. Yet, for Rubenstein and for many others in both Jewish and Christian traditions, the dawning of the significance of the *Shoah* rendered a key principle of the Jewish tradition incredible in any formulation, however revisionist. One can respect and admire the courage of this theological judgment even if one disagrees with it.

Counterfactual questions do not admit of certain, or sometimes even clear, answers. But we can ask, "Had the destruction of European Jews not occurred, would Rubenstein have rejected the God of history?" The point of this question is not to psychoanalyze Richard Rubenstein. The point is to note that his writings show that it was the profound impact of the irrefutable historical evidence of man-made mass death carried out systematically and "conscientiously" in "civilized" Europe that rendered the theological claims of divine election of the Jews incredible for him. A more straightforward point could be made. Had there been no Holocaust, there could be no post-Holocaust theology, and Richard Rubenstein could not have practically invented "post-Holocaust theology *de novo* in 1966 with the publication of *After Auschwitz*" (Braiterman 1998, 8). There is no way to know if Rubenstein might have traveled a similar theological course had there been no Holocaust. But he could not have taken the same journey because testimony to and the historical record of the Jewish experience in Europe were and are central factors that led him to reject belief in the God of history.

The Jewish tradition, however, carries on. Rubenstein is even recognized as a part of it, if a maverick, having been honored by various Jewish institutions with doctorates *honoris causa* and other accolades. Historical evidence and/or social experience had undermined an identity principle of Judaism for some Jews while not undermining it for others. Because people disagree about this crucial theological issue does not mean that one can or should find one's opponents irrational or morally weak. Traditions are malleable and, perhaps, the very fact that there are battling theologians working in, with, and on the convictions carried in the tradition indicates that the traditions are alive and well enough to recognize that some evidence and experience require them to be reformulated.

Historical investigations can in certain specific cases undermine religious conviction. For some believers in some situations, no formulation of an identity principle can withstand the evidence historians and others marshal. If few or no believers can formulate an identity principle in a way that a tradition can acknowledge the historical evidence, then that tradition will wither away, undermined by historical investigations. This is the issue that the classic problem of history recognized. It is an issue of the credibility of religious traditions.

In a very influential essay published half a century ago, Antony Flew issued the "falsification challenge." In the light of the ambiguity (at best) of the world in which we live, he asked, "Just what would have to happen not merely (morally and wrongly) to tempt but also (logically and rightly) to entitle us to say 'God does not love us' or even 'God does not exist'?" (Flew 1955, 99). Flew had claimed that if nothing would falsify a religious belief, it could not be meaningful. That claim has been found wanting for a number of reasons, including ones like those made in chapter six argu-ing that identity principles are not falsifiable by historical investigations but are nonetheless meaningful. Yet the challenges from history render belief in God incredible for many. This does not make the monotheistic principle incredible; for those who don't believe, it is simply inoperative, irrelevant, uninteresting—or perhaps abandoned. It is also possible that the critical historical work on the historical Jesus has also undermined not merely overdrawn beliefs about Jesus, but convictions about Jesus as the incarnate son of God and savior. This does not make the principle of christological maximalism incredible as a principle of the Christian tra-dition, but it may render it incredible or irrelevant to people who had been committed Christians. Religious convictions are not, *pace* Flew, fal-sified "in general," but in specific situations for specific persons; only if those situations are general and those persons typical (not claims that are clear enough to know how to warrant) are beliefs falsifiable "in general."

The issue, then, is not a generalized problem of history or one of role-specific responsibility, but the responsibility of persons in situations. If historical investigations render religious principles or the convictions that express them incredible, they do not do so for "anyone" or "everyone," but for specific persons in specific situations. Their challenge is not to the credibility of religious convictions, but to their plausibility.

Theologians committed to the principles of a tradition must recog-nize such challenges and respond to them as well as they can. These chal-lenges, and others discussed below, cannot simply be sidestepped by construing relevant historical investigations as done only within the prin-ciples of a tradition. This aspect of the modern problem of history can-not simply be avoided. If nothing else, the historical evidence regarding authorities' failure to cope with priestly sexual misconduct with minors that have surfaced in recent years, the settlements consequently paid to some victims, and the conviction of dioceses in criminal courts have "scandalized" members of the Roman Catholic community. For some, the principle expressed in and through a hierarchical and sacramental church has been falsified. It is not that the role of the bishop is meaningless in Catholicism; far from it. It is that, for many, the evidence has made con-fidence in a hierarchical principle underlying the Catholic tradition implausible and thus incredible for them. Theologians, including those consecrated and serving in the episcopacy, have role-specific responsibil-ities to respond to these and other challenges to the credibility of the principles of the tradition, especially as the challenges become more gen-eralized and the people responding negatively become more typical (again, generality is a useful guideline, but hard to measure clearly).

Historical investigations can contribute to the work of theologians in discovering and understanding the past practices and beliefs of a reli-gious tradition. But historical work cannot of itself authorize the acceptance, rejection, or reformulation of the convictions embodying the principles of a tradition. Yet the results of historical investigations can be the straw that breaks the camel's back of faith. The issue is not merely one of holding a belief, but of sustaining a commitment to living in and living out a tradition. I have outlined the issues involved in the wisdom of making or abandoning such commitments elsewhere (Tilley 1995).

In sum, the acceptance or rejection of a formulation is the responsibility of participants in the tradition. Insofar as theologians are participants in a tradition it is their responsibility. But the role-specific responsibility of arguing for formulations and reformulations of principles in theory and practices is ordinarily the responsibility of theologians. Historical investigations discover evidence and warrant claims that challenge our understanding of inherited practices and beliefs. It is the role-specific task of the *theologian* to respond to those challenges. It is the person-specific task of the *participant* to continue or to abandon a tradition.

The issue of history as an authorizing discourse, then, requires nuancing. Historical work, while necessary for understanding and discovering the convictions of a religious tradition, can never give us certainty nor can it alone bring participants to or away from faith. The debates discussed in chapters eight and nine and the examples in the present chapter show that history yields no certainties. The modern bipolar problematic of faith and history made it seem as though history could function as an "authorizing discipline" in a strong sense. In our era, then, the problem of history has evolved away from one in which appeals to history were meant to resolve problems of authority and thus either validate or undermine faith. Once we distinguish principles from their articulation, and theological construction from religious conviction, historical work no longer in some sense authorizes belief, though historical investigations may, for some, contribute to the undermining or acceptance of the convictions of a religious tradition.

Transforming

The second role-specific responsibility of the theologian is arguing for transforming the convictions of a tradition. Some of these convictions express identity principles. Other convictions may be held by members of a tradition even though they are not identity principles of a tradition. Numerous examples could be developed, but a current controversy in the Christian traditions provides an example that shows the complexities of this theological task.

Many Christians believed that there was "no salvation outside the church." St. Cyprian of Carthage is usually given pride of place in originating this assertion, although Francis A. Sullivan, S.J., finds its roots at least a century earlier in the work of Origen (Sullivan 1992, 18-24). Some Protestant Christians have used John 3:16 as a "proof text" for this position. Since this position finds that only those who specifically respond to Christ can be saved, it has been dubbed "exclusivism." Many find that it was a mighty incentive to the missionary movements of Christianity: all those who were converted would have a chance at salvation, while those who had never heard of Christ would be left behind.

A contrasting view, "inclusivism," appeals to many. In this view, people who live a good life by their own lights are "included" in salvation. There are various forms of inclusivism that expand the range of those included and the criteria for inclusion. Recent philosophy of religion and theology have also seen the development of "pluralism," which recognizes many paths bringing salvation (or its equivalent) to the members of the various religious traditions. Such pluralism comes in at least three varieties, reductive pluralism (all religions are saying the same thing and achieve the same salvation), phenomenal pluralism (all religions are saying different things but provide different paths to one salvation), and radical pluralism (all religions are saying different things and lead to different ends, e.g., heaven, rebirth, nirvana, for their followers). It is beyond the scope of the present book to investigate these options; indeed, lively debates over the legitimacy of the various ways beyond exclusivism characterize contemporary Christian theology (see Knitter 2002).

The problem at least some Christians have with accepting inclusivism and pluralism is that they seem to be violations of the sense of the tradition. For centuries, the Catholic Church, for example, has taught *extra ecclesiam nulla salus.* How could this tradition be changed?

Francis A. Sullivan has argued that a transformation is legitimate. His claim is that the Second Vatican Council made a decisive shift away from exclusivism. His thesis is that the slogan "outside the church, no salvation" is neither a necessary nor a felicitous way to talk of a Christian belief that "God has given to his church a necessary part to play in his plan to save the world" (Sullivan 1992, 204). Rather, this formulation expresses not a claim about those "outside the church," but more fundamental convictions about the love of God for all humanity, God's desire that all be saved, and the role of the church in God's plan for effecting that salvation. Even Cyprian's harsh dictum, understood in its social and theological context, does not have the rhetorical purpose of articulating a doctrine of salvation, but of warning people not to leave the church and urging others to return. Sullivan undertook a meticulous analysis of this idea as it was used in the tradition, and found that there were other formulations of these more fundamental convictions. He summarized one recent approach to this issue as follows:

Perhaps even more striking is the optimism which characterizes the approach of Vatican II to the question of salvation for the great majority of people in the world who have neither Christian faith nor baptism. We have tried to show that this optimism does not mean that the church has no role to play in the salvation of those who will never be her members on earth. Not only are they related to the church by the grace which the Holy Spirit offers to them, but the church is also the sign and instrument of their salvation. The necessity of the church for the salvation of humanity, which the axiom "No salvation outside the church" expressed in so negative and misleading a way, is the same truth that has received positive and profound theological expression in Vatican II's presentation of the church as the "universal sacrament of salvation." (Sullivan 1992, 160-61)

Sullivan found that the formulation of the tradition had been changed by the Second Vatican Council. What was needed, then, was a way to account for the changes and to say what was changed. Sullivan's analysis is that the formulation of an important Catholic ecclesiological principle was changed. The principle had been expressed negatively; it could, and should, be expressed more positively.

What form that positive expression should take is still hotly debated among Catholic theologians. It is too easy to attribute theological differences about such formulations to the varying social locations of the theologians. Theologians working in academic institutions in the United States and Europe or developing theologies in South and East Asia have different locations from those who work in the Vatican. The issue among them is not whether a traditionally exclusivist doctrine can be reformulated. The issue is rather *which* reformulations are the best expressions of the principles of the tradition that also respect the integrity of the other living religious traditions.

Few, if any, theologians, at least in the Christian tradition, would accept claims that religions are all essentially the same. Yet an article by Dave Shiflett in the *Wall Street Journal* has recently reported that a poll by George Barna shows that over one-fourth of "born-again" Christians believe that religions "teach pretty much the same thing" and that half of "born-again" Christians believe "that a life of 'good works' will get you through the Pearly Gates" (Shiflett 2003, 2) The headline for another article reporting this research reads, "Research continues to reveal a steady theological collapse among professing Christians in America" (Veith 2003, 1). With regard to religions teaching the same things, the worry about Christian participants' beliefs seems warranted—and if this is true for the "born again" segment, what of the rest? However, the "inclusivist" or "pluralist" belief seems at least to be dealing with the sorts of challenges theologians are facing. While this group of Christians seems to be ignoring theologians on one reformulation of the traditional views in response to the situation of pluralism, they may be finding theologians helpful in another way of responding to the pluralistic situation.

The numerous examples used throughout this text suggest that theologians are prolific simply because they are trying, from their various social locations, for their various audiences, to reformulate the convictions of the tradition in response to problems that arise as the tradition evolves in different times and places. This is not to say that individuals will not transform the expressions of their own beliefs as well. Far from it. This work is a role-specific responsibility of theologians working in and for a religious tradition. Given that theologians' roles are instantiated in various social locations, the responsibilities are multiple.

Theologians as Participants

The final task of theologians is the proclamation and manifestation of the tradition. Although theologians have role-specific responsibilities in this work of witness, they tend to carry them out in the first two tasks. Proclamation and manifestation is a task theologians share with participants. Yet, frankly, at this point the problem of history becomes less of a factor. It is not that participants are immune from the effects of historical investigations. As we have seen in this chapter, historical work in certain contexts for certain people can have a profoundly negative effect on one's commitment to a tradition. But that is not a direct result of historical work, but a consequence of a number of factors—after all, not all monotheists came to abandon traditional forms of faith after the historical evidence of the extent of the Holocaust was revealed. Other factors are involved. But historical investigations seem not to have a strong effect on the practices of proclamation and manifestation. Or so chapter eleven argues.

CHAPTER 11

Practicing Religiously

> *How do you stay faithful to the religious tradition*
> *in an age which we describe as modern, which means . . .*
> *skeptical, not given over to authority, fragmenting*
> *of community, agnostic in method.*
> —R. Scott Appleby

Scott Appleby articulates the key question that faces religious participants today (Patterson 2003). As suggested in chapter ten, the issue is not merely the critical (skeptical?), methodologically agnostic practices of historians. The problem is more complex. Indeed, the contemporary challenge to fidelity is also complicated by the material wealth of so many. As Vincent Miller notes in *Consuming Religion*, even our religious traditions have become commodified. Religion becomes an item of consumer choice. Marketers compete for market niche in the spirituality market. The church growth movement dominates evangelization. Megachurches provide an hour of Sunday entertainment and label it "worship"—while serving up Starbucks coffee. Spiritualities are on sale for consumption and personal growth—just pay the trainer in spirituality as one pays the trainer at the local spa or health club. It does not take much of a jaundiced eye to note that the commodification of spiritual realities has reached epic proportions when spiritual corporate entities resort to litigation to preserve their intellectual property rights so no "unauthorized" (that is, "non-paying") person can have the spirituality they sell (Effross 2003).

The response to the challenges of modernity has been, at least in the United States and much of western Europe, a turn away from institutional religion to spirituality. But as Miller notes, "Spirituality as the emergent form of religious life is consonant with the workings of commodification" (2003, 106). Our desires are shaped to be satisfied by goods we can buy in the spiritual marketplace, use, and discard, not by the Good that can be "bought" only by a life of commitment that we give our lives to and for, and that we cannot discard without discarding our selves. How can modern folk live in fidelity to their religious traditions?

Obviously, there is no single answer to that question. Yet reflecting on the foundational texts of the Western traditions can help us see the shapes the answers can take. Chapter two noted how the different forms of the central texts in the Western religious traditions give rise to different problems of history. One aspect of each of them is relatively immune to undermining by historical investigation. Jews, Christians, and Muslims believe, respectively, that the Hebrew Bible, the Christian Bible, and the Qur'an were each, in some sense, authored by God. Each of them also had human authors or scribes. Historical investigations—Appleby's agnosticism in method writ large—can challenge traditional claims about human contributions to the text, about the accuracy of the text's representations, about the process of its development, and about formulations of basic principles of a tradition. But historical investigations alone can neither undermine nor support the claims that one or more of them is a divinely authored revelation. That texts are inspired or revelatory or divinely authored is a judgment that historians *qua* historians cannot make.

Theologians can argue about the ways a text can be authoritative. They can propose new interpretations of texts, new accounts of their status as human products (as well as divine), and new ways believers can understand the authority of the texts. Of course, if someone believes that a specific version of one of the texts is the miraculously delivered words of God without human contribution, then well-warranted historical claims might undermine beliefs about the process of the delivery of the text. Historical investigations could show that variations in texts are best understood as introduced by human authors, redactors, or transcribers of the text. Such investigations could possibly undermine some specific formulations of fundamentalist principles. But the principle that a text is God-given, articulated in a variety of other convictions specific to each tradition, is, like other identity principles, immune to direct undermining by historical investigations. Those who would preserve an inerrant text can seek to formulate different versions of their principle or ignore historians' work altogether.

Each of the traditions that valorize these texts also creates different fundamental patterns for practicing religiously.

The Hebrew Bible both tells a saga of an ongoing covenantal journey with God in which Jews continue to live and provides an extensive law code by which to live. The 613 *mitzvot* apply to those old enough to be *bar* or *bas mitzvah* (although not all laws apply indiscriminately to both women and men). Those laws are interpreted in many ways, including *kashrut* regulations, in the annual ritual cycle of Jewish feasts, fasts, and holy days, and in the weekly obligation of the community to gather a *minyan* to pray, if at all possible. The Jew who is said to fail in his or her religious practice is said to be non-observant. God's laws are ignored.

The Qur'an is both a record of prophecy and revelation and the source of law for the community. The Muslim who walks the straight path in submission (*islam*) is a slave or servant of God. The devout Muslim participates in regular, daily prayer and lives a life in submission to God's will. To fail as a Muslim is to fail to submit to God's will. The arrogant and disobedient one can become an apostate or heretic.

For Christians, the ways of practicing religiously and failing to do so are varied. One way of noting the variations is to notice how those who fail to engage in the practices of the tradition are described. The perfectionist Christian, typical of participants in Baptist and Methodist traditions, seeks to live a perfectly sanctified life. To fail is to "backslide." The Catholic is active in worship and in the local church. Catholics avoid sin, but are not described as "backsliders" if they sin, for all people sin—and all can be forgiven if they repent and confess. To fail to live a Catholic life is to be "lapsed," to fall away from participation in the sacramental life of the church. For those traditions in which right belief is primary, especially in some branches of the Reformed tradition—and in all of these traditions in a more general sense—to fail to believe is to cut oneself off from the community of believers. One becomes an "unbeliever." These different foci in living out and failing to live out one's tradition roughly indicate differences in what, in practice, is considered "good practice" in each of the traditions.

Given the wide variety of ways people practice their religion and can fail to practice their religion well, writing a chapter on participants' religious practices in light of historical investigations is almost impossible. Either the chapter would be so vague as to be useless or so long as to be another whole book (even if it were devoted to just one tradition). For instance, just playing the variations on Muslim *jihad* as a religious practice would involve examining the multiple ways *jihad* is understood: as one's spiritual struggle to submit to God, as the individual's and community's struggle against oppression and injustice, as the community's struggle to spread, by violence if necessary, the realm of peace where God rules (*dar al-islam*) into the domains where God does not rule and there is injustice and war (*dar al-harb*), and even the corruption of *jihad* by some into a cover story disguising political imperialism and personal greed (cf. Esposito 1988, 16-17, 40, 95, 170-71, 173-74). Adding to this the other ways Muslims submit to God's will, the ways Jews seek to observe the law, and the patterns Christians develop for discipleship would make this chapter practically interminable. (Indeed, I plan to devote a whole book to examining patterns of Christian practice just to see what they can teach Christians about how to construe the person and work of Jesus Christ.)

Nor are the religious practices of these traditions static. Contemporary problems can evoke creative responses. For example, given the difficulty and cost of litigating disputes in courts, numerous patterns of binding arbitration have appeared. In Canada, Muslim leaders formed a judicial tribunal (Darul-Qada) to set up legal panels across the country to arbitrate civil disputes between Muslims under Muslim law, the *Sharia*. A similar process has been set up for Jews with the acceptance of a *beth din*, a panel of three rabbis who can sit in judgment in matters of Jewish law and can be recognized as giving decisions that Canadian courts accept, in at least some provinces (Coday 2003). These responses by Muslim and Jewish communities to the modern situation indicate not only theological creativity but a way of carrying on the tradition by understanding how to utilize elements from the past in new ways in the present.

Historical investigations have more of an impact on theological construction than on everyday religious convictions and commitment. Obviously, historical and theological work does become practically important in numerous ways for participants. The Canadian adaptations noted above are one example; to make them work requires both historical investigation and theological construction. The scholarly rejection of the patterns of Christian anti-Semitism and the increasing real recognition of the Jewishness of Jesus, especially among the third questers for the historical Jesus, are reshaping Christians' ways of thinking about Jews. No longer is the *contra Iudaeos* tradition, especially in Christology, normative, however much its hangovers continue to blight Christian theology and Christian life (Fredriksen 2003, 12-14). Because theologians are also participants in the traditions, they are also called upon to manifest and proclaim the convictions of their tradition as other participants are. Even though historical investigations affect theological work more directly than they affect religious conviction, history can and does impact the expressions of faith.

At the risk of unutterable vagueness, I shall use a typology of ways of being faithful to structure this chapter. This chapter argues, at least in general terms, how believers can and should respond as believers, and also suggests the relevance of historical investigations to their responses. I have suggested above ways in which historians' work can affect the reception of canonical texts. Beyond the practice of reading and interpreting texts, there seem to be two kinds of practices in which people participate when exercising their religious commitments. The first is a pattern of sustaining and gathering in. Living in and living out a religious tradition requires mutual support. The second is a pattern of extension and going out. Whether in forms of witness, service, action, evangelization, or expanding the territory of *dar al-Islam*, "gathering in" is balanced with "going out." The underlying assumption of this work, as noted in the introduction, is that being religious is a matter of participating in a practice or set of practices that give one's convictions meaning and enable one to live under the governance of a religious vision. Hence, the question is how participants in a tradition, including theologians, are to engage in the practices that constitute their tradition and how historical investigations can affect those engagements.

Gathering In and Sustaining

Traditions are passed on through local communities embedded in enduring institutions. Participants are responsible as participants for participating in the community, nurturing its life, and for supporting the institutions that enable the tradition to endure through changes in time and place. A religious *tradition* requires both a *local community* and an *enduring institution*. It is important to distinguish the institutional from the communal and traditional elements of religion. It is difficult, however, to do so, for they are so complexly intertwined as to be inseparable in practice, even if they can be distinguished in analysis. It is unfortunate that these distinctions are so often ignored in both popular and academic writing. The significance of making such distinctions is crucial for understanding the issues of participation in a religious tradition.

Above we suggested that different ways of "falling out" of religious traditions and practice indicate some differences in what counts as "good practice." Similarly, a rough and ready understanding of the differences of these elements can be seen by describing the way each divides. *Communities* split or separate or send out colonies; fissures in *institutions* are schisms; deviations from *traditions* are heresies. Often heresy and schism are linked (many, but not all, apostates are both heretics and schismatics), but they are not identical. And communities often split (e.g., congregations or parishes grow so large as to be unwieldy and split) even though there is no heresy or schism. The importance of making such distinctions suggests that the communal and institutional elements of a religious tradition can and must be distinguished, even if they cannot be separated.

An institution is an enduring communal authority structure. These authority structures function to maintain a tradition over time. Max Weber described institutional authority in religions as the routinization of charismatic authority. Weber was concerned with detailing patterns of authority and patterns of transition in authority. (Of course, with authority comes responsibility, a point not highlighted in Weber's work, but noted here.) A religious community can be formed around the authority of a charismatic figure and can exist without formal institutional structures so long as that leader is effective and remains the center of the community. But communities organized around the authority of a charismatic leader cannot endure beyond the leader's death or loss of charisma unless that charisma is routinized into an organizational structure with identifiable offices and responsibilities. This office gives persons who succeed the leader in guiding the ongoing community a certain measure of authority and responsibility. Weber put it this way:

> In its pure form charismatic authority has a character specifically foreign to every-day routine structures. The social relationships directly involved are strictly personal, based on this validity and

practice of charismatic personal qualities. If this is not to remain a purely transitory phenomenon, but to take on the character of a permanent relationship forming a stable community of disciples or band of followers or a party organization or any sort of political or hierocratic organization, it is necessary for the character of charismatic authority to become radically changed. Indeed, in its pure form charismatic authority may be said to exist only in the process of originating. It cannot remain stable but becomes either traditionalized or rationalized, or a combination of both. (Weber 1947, 363-64)

Weber delineates two types of institutional religious authority. Institutional authority based on "legal patterns of normative rules and the right of those elevated to authority under such rules to issue commands" is *rational* authority; institutional authority "resting on an established belief in the sanctity of immemorial traditions and the legitimacy of the status of those exercising authority under them" is *traditional* authority (Weber 1947, 328). Both sorts of authority create offices, one of whose main responsibilities is to replicate a pattern of practices and beliefs inaugurated by the charismatic figure, that is, to guide the formation of a tradition. In so doing, the institutional authorities play a crucial role in the endurance of a tradition.

These structures make possible a transmission of tradition to second- and third-generation members who do or wish to live in and live out a tradition. These participants and fellow travelers are distant from the leader in time or in location. The origins and development of institutional authority and authorities in Christianity, in the various Islamic traditions, in the Jesuits or any other religious order with a charismatic founder, and even in the enduring institutions, such as the National Baptist Convention, are merely a few of the historical examples that illustrate this Weberian "charisma and routinization" thesis.

Weber's understanding must be read "dialectically" rather than, as it often is read, "monodirectionally." Institutional authority is not necessarily merely a successor to and a degeneration of charismatic authority. Moreover, the charismata of charismatic figures are constituted, in part, by institutional authorities, communal relationships, and inherited traditions. Charismatic figures' contributions are never, and could never be, purely original, as a monodirectional reading of the relationship between charismatic and institutional authority would suggest. Charismatic persons respond to specific social, cultural, and religious situations by reshaping the given tradition and social context, by discerning meaning in it in new, unconventional ways, and by communicating that meaning to others. The quests for those fascinating historical figures such as Kung Fu Tzu, Jesus, or Muhammad are possible only because their charismatic powers have been routinized and preserved in practices and texts in an enduring institution. It may be obvious, but it is often ignored: institutions are not necessarily "deteriorations" of charismatic authority or real religion. Institutional authority and responsibility are *necessary* for later access to that charismatic figure. Once the charismatic figure and the immediate memory of her or him is gone, no practically possible continuity of his or her distinctive gifts and insights in a religious institution is possible without official authority.

It is a commonplace that institutional patterns of authority and responsibility are enormously varied and complex. In the Christian traditions, institutional authorities have usually been clerics. Among Shi'i Muslims, for instance, the *imam* is properly not a cleric but a lay prayer leader. Although he has authority for the local community gathered in the mosque, he may or may not have institutional authority beyond the local community. In both traditions, political rulers often have tremendous institutional authority, demonstrated, for instance, when the Emperor Constantine convoked and set the agenda for the Council of Nicea in 326 C.E. The power of the clerical *ayatollahs* in Iran represents another form of political-religious authority; indeed, many Shi'i Muslim traditions have rejected the separation of religions and political institutions characteristic of the secularized West. There are many institutional patterns creating social locations in which authority is exercised in multiple ways in passing on a tradition.

These institutional structures do not have to be "strong" in their authority. Over the last two centuries, the Roman Catholic Church has increasingly centralized its authority in the papacy and the curia in Rome. This process has skewed the image of institutional authority in religion. Authority may be very dispersed as in Judaism, or more centralized as in Catholicism. It may be inherited or elected, strongly hierarchical or inclining toward egalitarianism, rational or traditional.

So given that there are religious institutions, what do religious people have to do with and for them? Participants in the tradition have the responsibility of sustaining the tradition. How to do this is, of course, very tradition-specific. At minimum, a certain respect for the teaching, findings, rulings, or other pronouncements of those in office is required. Typically, for many traditions, supporting the offices of the institution, if not the current form of the office or the present officers, is key. Institutional authorities can become corrupt or ineffective in sustaining the tradition. An obvious example of institutional corruption undermining effective communication and sustenance of a religious tradition is the late medieval church. The need for institutional reform was obvious, and reforms were attempted before the Reformation of the sixteenth century. However, definitive reform occurred only after the institutional schism of the Reformation in which new institutional authorities were developed, ones that the reformers and their successors expected would be better able to sustain the pure message of Christianity than had the Catholic institutions. Another example of corruption was revealed with the collapse of some of the televangelistic ministries in the United States. Corruption in institutions or of its officers can destroy a community and undermine the ability of a tradition to be sustained.

Historical work can often point out the problems with the present claims of an institutional authority. Historians may uncover corruptions of the past. They may show that institutional authorities have not always had the authority they presently have. Understanding past corruptions, however, can have a prophylactic effect in the present. Religious people can see how the institution has veered off course in the past and work to prevent similar occurrences in the present. Understanding the evolution of the authority of an institutional officer can show how present patterns have developed. For example, understanding the history of the papacy in Roman Catholicism from a primacy of honor to a primacy of jurisdiction (see Schatz 1996) has shown that the present pattern of authority may not be the only legitimate one, even in a church with strong authority (see Quinn 1998).

What a participant's responsibility would be in the varied cases of institutional reform or collapse cannot be laid out in the abstract. Perhaps a principle can be suggested: the institution is the servant of the tradition and the gathered community. Its service is to sustain the tradition and support the communities that carry it on. When such service becomes domination or the institutional authority is valued over the tradition it was instituted to carry on or valued over the appropriate freedom and responsibility of the local communities and their members, then communities and their members need to discern how better to carry on and preserve the tradition, perhaps by changing the officers, if not the official structures. To further specify the participants' responsibility would require particular investigations far beyond the scope of the present work.

Institutional authorities, even strong ones, may occasionally be ineffective. Perhaps the most obvious example here is the contrast between the personal and institutional authority of Pope John Paul II and the simultaneous refusal of Roman Catholic communities to accept the institutional authorities' finding that "artificial" contraception is intrinsically evil. In the American branch of the Roman Catholic Church, laity are far more willing to have married men and women ordained priests than are the official authorities. How the church will change in light of these resistances remains to be seen. But in general, although the function of institutional authorities is to sustain the tradition, traditions may be transformed whether or not the official authorities support the changes.

Enduring traditions have both institutional and communal elements. But the key point is that this is not a merely nominal distinction: their function is different. While institutions sustain the tradition through time, communities gather together in mutual support, prayer, worship, and reconciliation in a specific place and typically at a specific time. If institutions are fundamentally diachronic and translocal, communities are synchronic gatherings in particular locations.

A significant characteristic of a community formed around a charismatic leader is that it is gathered. "Gathering" marks the communal, as opposed to the institutional, aspect of enduring religions. The Catholic Church as an institution is worldwide; the Catholic Church as a parish or base community or religious house is gathered and local. Islam is a worldwide movement; but Islam in Iran is quite different from Islam in Bali or in the United States. Ashkenazi Judaism is as much Judaism as Sephardic Judaism, but the patterns of life are different. Relationships in communities are typically interpersonal, while relationships in institutions are typically structural.

In some cases, the community simply is the institution. A Baptist church with a thoroughly congregational polity may be necessarily local, but that does not mean it is not both a community and an institution. The "First Baptist" churches in many towns or cities of the American South have become enduring bureaucratic, even hierarchical, institutions. Having a deeply communitarian ideology and local autonomy does not preclude a church from simultaneously being a hierocratic institution. Such local institutions may also have some difficulty in distinguishing the kinds of relationships appropriate to various situations.

Edward Farley has helpfully used Emmanuel Levinas's notion of the "community of the face" to define "community" in this sense as "a social group in which face-to-face relations are valued and pursued for their own sake. Face-to-face relations are part of the raison d'être of a village, therapy group, and some kinds of schools. Accordingly, in most instances, a small village is a community and a staff of researchers is not" (Farley 1990, 290). For Farley, Christian and Jewish communities have been prime examples of such gathered, face-to-face communities. Face-to-face relations are central and distinctive of communities, not institutions. (It is too soon to tell whether dispersed or virtual communities linked electronically fall more on the communal or institutional side of the distinction; can gatherings be "virtual"?)

Generally speaking, a person is raised or initiated into a religious tradition in a local community. Communal leaders and familial authorities teach a person; their authority is traditional, in Weber's sense. One's father, one's mother, one's aunts, one's uncles, the local shaman, the monk, the missionary, the rabbi, the minister, the director of religious education, or some other traditional or official authority may initiate a person into religious practice and belief. Although these authorities may be officially designated, the tradition is learned face-to-face, in community. All of the people who have such authoritative positions (however that authority is given) have a responsibility given them by their position in the community, which may or may not be an official institutional position.

Converts generally learn the tradition in a gathered community. They may be converted by individuals whose authority is more rational or traditional than charismatic. Conversion is not necessarily induced by a charismatic figure. Missionaries even learn recipes for reaching potential converts, and revivals become routinized. When learners are tested to see if they have understood the tradition, the testing is done by designated individuals who function as institutional authorities charged with preserving and extending the tradition. One person may assume both roles of teacher and tester. But the teacher primarily functions "face to face," while the tester primarily functions as an officer empowered to decide if the learner has understood the tradition sufficiently to be a full member. Whether one is born into a religion or is converted into a religion, generally speaking, a gathered community shapes one's religious life and one's entry into the religion.

Leaders of a local community may have their formal authority from their office (institutional authority). However, their effective authority for initiating others into the tradition requires a face-to-face relationship. Obviously, these relationships, although interpersonal, are not necessarily friendships between equals. Various modes of relationship may be appropriate depending on the circumstances. As local, then, a religious community *gathers face-to-face* and is constituted by interpersonal and social relationships. This does not preclude translocal gatherings, such as revivals, missions, camp meetings, the *hajj*, and so on. The key is the face-to-face gathering.

That an individual ordinarily learns how to participate in a tradition through participation in face-to-face relationships does not deny the importance of official authority in a local community. Communities can certainly exhibit and even be constituted by routinized authority. However, especially in a pluralistic society, where members may find that leaving a community is a "live option," local, gathered communities flourish where face-to-face relationships are valued and strong. It is these sorts of relationships which make official authority effective in a gathered community in a pluralistic social context.

Face-to-face religious communities form themselves when and where folk join in the practices of realizing (making real) a religious tradition. These places may be called churches, mosques, worship centers, synagogues, monasteries, ashrams, and the like. A gathered community may constitute itself for a brief time and then evaporate, as happens in some revivals in the United States when charismatic authority is not routinized. People with official status may participate in and may well have authority in local communities, but that does not mean that local communities necessarily are institutions.

The participants have the responsibility of creating and re-creating the gathered community. Many Christians identify a church as a place, typically one for worship. Yet a Christian can ask, "When is church?" A Jew might ask, "Do we have a *minyan* yet?" The gathering of a religious community is an event. The sense of church or worship or group meditation as an "event," more common in evangelical than in Catholic traditions, means that the participants have a responsibility for making the event happen, for making it possible and desirable for the community to gather. With regard to Christianity, Avery Dulles described this responsibility as follows:

> The idea of discipleship, as we know it from the New Testament, makes ample room for both freedom and failure. Unlike the bare notion of community, discipleship brings out the demands of membership. The Church is not a club of like-minded individuals, but a venture in which all depend on the community and are obliged to make contributions to the community and its work. The possession of the Spirit is seen as the mark of a mature disciple and as a prerequisite of responsible, creative ministry. (Dulles 1982, 15)

What Dulles writes of the church applies to all forms of vibrant religious communities. The gathering of the community for worship and prayer, for instruction and guidance, and for restoration and healing of rifts does not happen automatically. Religious participants have the role-specific responsibility of gathering for the purposes of sustaining the community in the tradition. In the Western traditions, prayer and worship are the fundamental reasons for gathering.

Historical investigations again have, at most, an ancillary role for delineating the responsibilities of participants in religious communities. A historical sociologist like Max Weber can discern patterns, such as the evolution of charismatic into institutional authority. Such patterns can provide guides for understanding how communities can be maintained. As a historian, Weber would be a "social historian" whose patterns might seem not so well warranted to more traditional historians (thus replicating the patterns noted in chapter eight). Yet even as some religionists cast aspersions on the use of social theory in theology (e.g., Milbank 1991), it is clear that Weber's work is useful for understanding the dynamics of most religious communities and institutions, even if it needs modification (as suggested above, the relationships between authorities are more dialectical than monodirectional and responsibility needs to be correlated with authority).

But communities are not only maintained and gathered, they are also "sent out."

Going Out: Witness, Service, Expansion

As with the patterns of sustaining and gathering in, the patterns for "going out" are as varied as are the traditions. For better and for worse, belonging to a religious tradition creates a division. In Christianity, this division has often been dualistic, the division between church and world. The church, then, is to go out into the world. In Islam, the distinction between the reign of God (*dar al-Islam*) and the reign of war and injustice (*dar al-harb*) is often taken to require the expansion of Islam, where God reigns, to external (or enemy) territory.

However, such divisions are not necessarily external to communities. In commenting on the situation of Christians in the United States, James W. McClendon, Jr., once wrote that "the line between the church and the world passes right through each Christian heart" (McClendon 1986, 17). This sort of insight has been part of the Christian tradition at least since St. Augustine. The division is as much internal to the participants and the community as it is external to either. Nor is the division simply "dual"; rather, it is multiple. Religious practitioners engage in a wide variety of practices and have a wide variety of allegiances. They are not only Jews (or Christians or Muslims), but may be socialists (or capitalists), politically liberal (or conservative), and so on. Because these divisions are multiple and both internal and external, rather than dualist and external as the church-and-world or religion-and-culture rubrics suggest, the division is not necessarily between us and them. Of course, some religious rhetoric asserts otherwise, but this rhetoric is typically used in an effort to cement and ossify religious identity, often in a religious community that tends to understand itself as under siege from its enemy or enemies.

How can a religious community and its participants sort out these competing loyalties? Three patterns of practice respond to this situation. First, participants witness to their tradition and to its primacy of place among their loyalties. Second, participants may engage the world by service, social action, and other efforts at transforming the world in which they live into something close to the way their tradition says it should be. Third, participants may engage in explicit missionary struggles to bring others into the tradition they live in and live out. It should be noted that not all religious communities engage in all these patterns of going out. And the impact of historians on these practices may be minimal; but, as noted above, historians can teach participants about "what happened" when similar paths were followed in the past. But participants must choose how to follow those paths in the present and, presumably, armed with historical understanding, be aware of at least the "classic traps" into which their engagements with the world can fall.

First, the practice of witnessing. Witness is diverse. It can be simply living out in disciplined fidelity the way of life that constitutes the tradition. Avery Dulles understands this as part of the sacramental life of the church: "Authentically sent by Christ, the disciples make him present anew as they live under the direction of his Spirit. Thanks to the sacramentality of the Church, . . . the members of the Church experience his power as they are remade in his image" (Dulles 1982, 16). Stanley Hauerwas put it this way:

> The truth of Christian convictions can be known only through witnesses because the God Christians worship is triune. If the truth of Christian convictions could be known without witnesses, then that truth would no longer be the work of the Trinity, and those who espoused it would no longer be Christians. . . .
>
> Witnesses must exist if Christians are to be intelligible to themselves and hopefully to those who are not Christians, just as the intelligibility of science depends in the end on the success of experiments. (Hauerwas 2001, 211-12)

The lives of witnesses, then, exemplify what it means to live in and live out a tradition.

The root meaning of the Greek word we transliterate as "martyr" is "witness." In the era of postbiblical expansion, the first distinctively Christian pattern of life emerged as martyrdom. Inspired by the tales of the martyrdom of the Maccabees and of the stoning and vision of St. Stephen (Acts 7) and seeing their Lord and savior as a martyr unjustly killed, they witnessed to the truth they found in the Christian tradition by their martyrdom. Clebsch describes the period as one in which Christians sought "dual citizenship": to be citizens of Rome and citizens of the eternal city. In many instances, these dual commitments could be lived out with little or no conflict. However, when the commitments became irreconcilable, for example, when the legal authorities demanded that the Christians turn over their Scriptures and/or worship the Roman divinities, the martyrs witnessed unto death their commitment to the community and its God. Ultimately, their city was the eternal city.

But martyrdom is not a "sectarian" or "withdrawn" form of witness. In discussing the martyrdom of Anabaptists in the sixteenth century, McClendon makes this clear:

> The baptist martyrdom was neither sought nor self-chosen; it came at the hands of state authorities. . . . The civil arm enforced the banishments, jailings, drownings, and burnings-at-the-stake; many church officials encouraged these actions but normally they did not execute them. Put more broadly, it was society, or, as we say today, it was the surrounding *culture* that imposed these cruel penalties. *See, though, what follows: the costly work of the martyr as such **engaged** both believer and culture, both "Christ" and*

"world." . . . [I]n martyr Christianity, the opponents of the faith
are as fully involved as their victims. Thus the radical work of
martyrs cannot be primarily inward-looking—disproving the
often-heard charge that the practice was "sectarian" and self-
preoccupied. Their focus required disciples to engage the spiritually needy other, to confront the antagonistic other.
Martyrhood is of necessity a work of *witness.* (McClendon 2000,
347)

To be a witness is always "transitive." One witnesses *to* another *about* something. Sometimes one's life is a witness to members of the community;
other times one's life testifies to others outside of the community. Sometimes one witnesses for the tradition to the community as well as to those
outside by exemplifying how to live in and live out a tradition. To live a
life of witness is not to withdraw from engagement with others outside the
community or from opponents within the community, but to engage
them not with force or political action to change structures in the society,
but with confronting them with someone who does actually place the tradition to which he or she witnesses at the determining center of his or her
identity.

Another form of witness, not only in the Christian tradition, has been
the witness of asceticism, of a commitment to supplant in their own lives
the (evil) practices of the world with the graced practices that would allow
them to focus on witness to God alone. Ascetics, however, are also not
withdrawn. Even though early Christian monks withdrew from the city to
the desert, people flocked to them. There they showed people how to
overcome the passionate vices that threatened to distort their love of
God: "piggishness, lechery, greed, depression, hatred, inability to care,
bragging, and egotism" (Clebsch 1979, 76). They served as exorcists, as
arbitrators of disputes over tithes, water rights, and property rights, and
as physicians for ailments such as infertility (Brown 1971).

Martyrs and monks show that what is good enough to live for is good
enough to die for; if one would not die for what one lives for, whatever
that might be, one has failed to live one's life as one ought. Only what is
great enough to die for is great enough to live for. This does not mean
eschewing enjoyment or pleasure; rather it is shaping one's desires so that
what one desires fundamentally is God. Ascetics do not snuff out desire
but channel their desire to the divine. The ascetics' witness is not a withdrawal but precisely a witness to the rest of the members of their community and to others who sought to understand what they were doing, a
witness about the practices of living in God's love, of living in the tradition. While all might not be as spiritually athletic as the ascetics, they can
and should witness to one concerning how to order one's desires to what
one really desires.

Witness is not sectarian; it is one way for engaging the world. Sometimes a gathered community or sacramental church can be "inward-look-ing." Sometimes religious communities can withdraw, insofar as it is pos-sible, from communication with those outside the camp. But these are not so much witnesses as failures to be witnesses *to* others *about* one's ultimate commitments.

One increasingly persuasive account of a crucial difference between Christian and American traditions illustrates this point of the importance of witness. The question is not whether to witness, but, as McClendon put it, given the situation, how to witness:

> At least at one point, though, [the American master story] con-trasts sharply with the biblical master story. . . . In the story Americans tell themselves, every great problem from indepen-dence to slavery to totalitarian threats is finally resolved by the *ultima ratio* of war. . . . Not even the best bearers of the American legend (Lincoln?) have escaped its inbuilt savagery. In surprising contrast, the biblical master story pivots upon a slave people who ran away "in urgent haste" (Deut. 16:3), upon a Savior who enters the capital city riding on a donkey and who is called the Prince of Peace; today it demands a living witness to that peace. (McClendon 2000, 361-62)

To put it more harshly, the biblical tradition asks one to be willing to die as a witness to God's love and justice; the American tradition asks one to be willing to kill to get our way in the world.

Our witness, then, reveals which tradition we ultimately live in and live out.

There are many who would refuse the stark opposition here por-trayed. They might recognize the ultimate differences in the traditions and the lives they inspire and shape. But some would find that "witness" is not the right "tactic." They would argue that the point is not merely to witness to the world, but to engage it in order to change it and to bring it closer to the way God would want it. These folk would work to transform the world.

Second, the practices of transformation. Often, "witness" slides over into "transformation." The traditional Christian dichotomy between char-ity and justice is too easy. Transformation on a small or individual level may be called charity, but it is work for justice nonetheless. Transforma-tion on a social or structural level may be called justice, but it is intimately connected with charity nonetheless. Many religious groups operate shel-ters for the poor. This is typically identified as charity. This witness to hos-pitality comes closer to work for justice in some of the activities of the Catholic Worker movement. Dorothy Day, for example, did not merely extend hospitality, but also demonstrated against war and publicly sup-ported striking unions in both New York and California. Michael Goldberg reflects on Jews as a "kingdom of priests" by noting that Jews are to minister to God by "bringing the whole world into his service" (Goldberg 1995, 15). McClendon reflects on Goldberg's comments by noting that Jewish communities have done that to a significant degree. "On six continents Jews have been agents of morality, of civility, of literacy (witness the role of *Torah*), of clean living (witness the food laws) and pure worship (witness the synagogue). Despite some failures and with interruptions, Jewish people have continued to live out the story of the Exodus" (McClendon 2000, 360). While this is only part of the story, such witness to "how to live truthfully with God, that is to the terms of the covenant made between God and their ancestors at Sinai" (Goldberg 1995, 162) is to live out a tradition that is at least distinct from, even though it can be compatible with, political traditions like the American tradition. Whether this is done as witness or as an attempt to change the individuals and families through charity or a culture by bringing justice to the culture seems to vary from time to time and place to place. The point is that witness and charity are not separable from justice and transformation, but distinctive ways to seek to bring the vision and the reality of the community to those who will benefit from such work.

As noted earlier, the U.S. Catholic bishops have called for an economic transformation. In their pastoral letter *Economic Justice for All*, the U.S. Catholic bishops proposed a key moral criterion for the formation of just economic policies. They wrote:

> Decisions must be judged in light of what they do *for* the poor, what they do *to* the poor, and what they enable the poor to do *for themselves*. The fundamental moral criterion for all economic decisions, policies, and institutions is this: They must be at the service of *all people, especially the poor.* (National Conference of Catholic Bishops 1986, §24)

Echoing the words of the judge in the eschatological parable of the sheep and the goats ("Truly, I say to you as you did it to the least of these you did it to me"; Matt 25:40), the bishops have argued for a transformation of the common understanding of how to judge economic fairness and thus for changes in the way the society distributes its wealth and income. They claimed, in effect, that economic decisions are not to be judged by what they do to or for the whole nation. In doing so, they reject the common, but implicit, moral norm: what the policy does for the "average person." This "averaging" norm is rhetorically useful and can easily be a cover story for economic injustice. It can be applied in so many different ways that it is nearly useless; witness political debates about tax cuts where both sides say their approach is better for the "average person" or the "middle class."

The bishops sought to transform economic ethics. Economic policies are to be judged by the ethical standard of what they do to and for the poor and how they enable the poor to do more for themselves. In the tax cut debates, the question must be what the cuts will do for the poor and which pattern gives better benefit to and for the poor—and enables the poor to do for themselves. In other policy debates, the issues are to be focused not on what a policy does for the successful, but on how it affects the underclass. Clearly, any policy that tends to create a permanent underclass, however much it may benefit "the average person," is immoral by the bishops' standards.

The bishops derive their criterion more proximately from liberation theologians. Gustavo Gutiérrez, for instance, has noted the need for transformation of economic structures. However, that is not the only form of transformation needed. He recognizes the "liberation from social situations of oppression and marginalization" that oppress and destroy people, forcing the poor to live in subhuman conditions (Gutiérrez 1988, xxxviii). These situations may be structured by political, economic, social, or other patterns that oppress people. Christians need to work for the transformation of these structures. Gutiérrez also sees the need for a "personal transformation by which we live with profound inner freedom in the face of every kind of servitude" (Gutiérrez 1988, xxxviii) and for "liberation from sin, which attacks the deepest root of all servitude; for sin is the breaking of friendship with God and with other human beings" (Gutiérrez 1988, xxxviii). Because these transformations are accomplished not by human effort alone but by the grace of God acting in and through human actions, Gutiérrez's theology seeks multiple transformation in those areas where we need liberation: social, personal, spiritual. In so transforming what is now to what it should be if God were to reign, activists "activate" God's grace by their work for transformation.

Activism is distinct from witness. Witness exposes others to what the good life can and should be and provides a model for the community to live in and live out. Activism seeks to transform the social structures that can deform the people of a society and make it practically impossible for them to be able to live in and live out the way of life the community valorizes. Nonetheless, some patterns of witness are "activist," and some active interventions clearly "witness" to what it means to live in and live out a tradition.

A third way of being sent out is to engage in missionary work, to attempt to convert others into participants in one's own religious tradition. Judaism has not, so far as I know, been a strongly missionary religion, but both Christianity and Islam are. Of course, missionary expansion can be indistinguishable from some forms of activism. For instance, the remarkable two years of 632-634 C.E. saw Abu Bakr expand the control of Islam to the entire Arabian peninsula and set the stage for the establishment of a new empire. The effort was an interesting mix of activism by the sword and missionary effort. As Fred M. Donner put it:

Property and wealth—as well as political power—were redistrib-
uted on a grand scale. Most important, the newly emergent state
provided the political framework within which the religious ideas
of the ruling Believers, who were but a small part of the popula-
tion, could gradually spread among the conquered peoples. The
many captives taken during the conquests came to be integrated
into the tribes and families of their captors as clients (*mawali*), a
fact that facilitated the transformation. (Donner 1999, 13-15)

Contemporary Muslims have undertaken various approaches to expansion and reconstitution of their traditions. They have resisted Western
colonial and neocolonial hegemony to keep their traditions alive in historically Muslim countries. "Consequently, conformity to Islamic culture,
traditions, and norms is not only a source of pride in Muslim contributions to civilization, it has become a divine imperative, a cure for what ails
Muslim society and the world" (Haddad 1999, 632). Muslims have "created a variety of missionary outreach activities in various countries. They
have also created a corpus of literature geared toward proselytizing"
(Haddad 1999, 608-9).

The linkage of colonialism with the Christian missionary movement
is an oft-told story. The point for religious participants, however, is that
they do not have to replicate the hegemony of the West as they reach out
to those of other traditions or of no religious commitment at all. Historical investigations can help Christian missionaries to be aware of practices
that carry the danger of inappropriate hegemony. Avery Dulles's account
of the "herald model" of the church recognizes a different way of evangelization for Catholics. As he put it:

Evangelization . . . should not be seen primarily as the communication of doctrine or even of a "message." It means introducing
people to a blessed and liberating union with the Lord Jesus, who
lives on in the community that cherishes his memory and invokes
his Spirit. To evangelize . . . is never a matter of mere words. It is
an invitation to others to enter the community of the disciples
and to participate in the new consciousness that discipleship
alone can bring.

Evangelization is too often seen by Catholics as the responsibility of a small body of "professionals," who alone are presumed
to be competent to unravel the complexities of "Catholic doctrine." . . . [E]very Christian can be called in some way to become
a missionary. . . . Wherever they go, convinced Christians will
seek to extend the way of life revealed by God in Jesus and thus
to gain new disciples for the Lord. (Dulles 1982, 17)

And so evangelization returns us to witness. By the way participants live
in and live out a religious tradition, they engage in missionary activity.

History, Theology, and Faith

Chapters ten and eleven have shown some of the ways in which historical investigations can be supportive of or a challenge to theological construction and the living out of religious convictions. Obviously, much more could be written and numerous additional examples cited. However, the point I have wanted to establish should now be clear: History as a practice does not yield results that are necessarily antithetical to theology or faith. Historians cannot as historians undermine or support the principles of a tradition. Yet historians can show that articulations of those principles or that practices of participants have been and are now problematical. And participants can be swayed to eschew their tradition in part because historians have contributed to rendering it implausible for them. Theologians have the role-specific responsibility to cope with such challenges. Other participants may have to face such challenges, but that is a context and situation-dependent responsibility. The theologian is responsible to assist the religious community and its members (and even those who are not its members but who are colleagues in the social locations of the theologians) in meeting those challenges. Participants may accept such assistance as they seek to form their own minds.

Some, then, may come to the judgment that they should abandon the tradition or seek to revise it radically. The practices of the tradition may have become intolerable or meaningless. The principles of the tradition can no longer be articulated. Theologians have the role-specific responsibility to undertake the tasks of creatively transforming and appropriately proclaiming the traditions they have discovered and understood. Individual believers have other role-specific responsibilities—to live in and live out the tradition, to proclaim it in community, and to witness. But most of their responsibilities regarding dealing with historical investigations are more person- and situation-specific, rather than role specific. "While an ordinary believer may justly assume the prudence . . . of religious commitment unless there is reason to doubt it, the theologian has the role-specific duty to investigate the assumptions and warrants ingredient in those commitments" (Tilley 1995, 140). The problems historical investigations create are multiple. So must the responses be.

CHAPTER 12

History, Theology, Faith

We have undertaken a long journey of multiple investigations. Where has it brought us?

The first goal was to dissolve the modern problem of history in its dualistic format of "history and faith" or "history and theology" which often really meant "history versus faith" or "history versus theology." We traced the development of the problematic and some responses that took the problematic for granted. In the second chapter we argued that the various sacred texts of the Western religious traditions created rather different "problems of history." Assuming that there was a single problem was possible only by obscuring the variety of narrative forms central to these canonical texts. Indeed, even in the classic bipolar formulation, there were multiple problems. The Niebuhrian distinction between "internal" and "external" history was too simple to cover all the problems. While Van Harvey made important progress in his attempt to shift the terms of the discussion away from methodology and to the practices of historians and believers, his preservation of the bipolar problematic was not satisfactory. However, his later analysis of the "ethics of belief" in terms of "role-specific" responsibilities opened the way for a more nuanced approach. The Troeltsch-tradition's approach to the problem was analyzed in chapter four. Its account of historians' presumptions extended the range of the presumptions beyond the bounds of historians' practice. Moreover, the presumptions the tradition described were simply not the presumptions that historians worked with in their practice. The Troeltsch-tradition worked more with the philosophy of history than with the practice of history. But it was historical investigations, the result of practice, that gave and give religious traditions difficulties; the issues were important as philosophical issues, but not entirely germane to addressing the challenges of history. While many have argued that history required radical revision (or abandonment) of traditional religious faith, chapter five showed that two exemplary practitioners of this approach, Richard Rubenstein and Marcus Borg, did not make their cases. That is not to say they were personally wrong in their revisionist views; not at all. It is just that the arguments that they used to support those shifts can be sidestepped rather easily without resort to incursions of the supernatural or other forms of special pleading. These five chapters, then, represent the main argument for dissolving the classic problem of history.

The second goal was to understand how history related to religious traditions. Some conservative theologians and believers had argued that historical-critical approaches to sacred texts were either blasphemous or irrelevant. Ignoring the blasphemy claim, chapter six sought to show how at least some of the basic identity principles of a tradition were immune from undermining by historical investigation. Rather than seeing historical criticism as merely an attack from outside the tradition, the chapter argued that there were good reasons within Christianity for historical criticism to arise. And even within the tradition, expressions, articulations, formulations, applications, and other practical embodiments of the principles of the tradition were shown in chapter seven to be vulnerable to historical undermining or amenable to historical support. Ignoring the distinction between principles and their formulations has led to problems; whether Catholicism as a tradition can be sustained by the theological articulations advocated at the 1997 CTSA convention or require the more traditional formulations that Avery Dulles supported is an open question. The conclusion is that historical investigations were relevant to particular theological claims and religious practices and that some claims and practices might be amenable to revision, reformulation, or rejection as the result of historical work, but that the fundamental identity principles of a tradition were not vulnerable to historical investigation. Nonetheless, individuals might come to a theological judgment for or against a traditional formulation or even for or against a tradition by using, in part, historical analyses.

The third goal of the book was to attempt to stay close to what historians actually do in the practice of their discipline, that is, how they exercise their role-specific responsibilities as we attempted to give an account of the relationships of history, theology, and faith. Previous investigations tended to use what philosophers of history said about history. But if we are considering the practices of history as well as the practices of theological construction and living out a faith tradition, then we need to look at practices. The debates about what constitutes grounds and warrants in historical investigation and the use of theory in history are very contentious subjects. Chapter eight showed the contentions about the nature of history among secular historians in the United States in general, and chapter nine turned to a very particular dispute relevant to religious history. The upshot of this investigation is to show that history can no longer be considered an authorizing discipline in the sense that it can "authorize" a tradition; its results, at least at the level of solving controversial questions, did not admit of anything approaching certainty or even, sometimes, high probability. Within a tradition, historical work has a contribution to make to authorizing or undermining specific claims, but the judgment of which claims best articulate the principles of a tradition is finally a theological one. While, as chapter six showed, we should not accept the dualistic typology that Dulles proposed, his insight that there are different competencies at work is clearly sustained. The competencies, though, are not the competency of faith and the competency of history, but the various competencies of those who engage in historical investigation, theological construction, and living out and living in a religious tradition.

The final two chapters then related the practices of historical investigations to theological construction and participation in a religious tradition. In so doing, we expanded and deepened the insights of the first seven chapters: the relationships of history to theology are piecemeal and particular. Although the author's social location is religiously Catholic and professionally academic, it seemed worthwhile to attend at least in passing to the problems of history as they appeared and appear in the other Western monotheistic traditions, not merely to hear the voices of others in the author's social location but also to realize that despite the differences, the monotheistic principles of our traditions make it possible to share challenges and develop analogous insights. There are multiple problems and challenges to theological work in Judaism, Islam, and Christianity from historical work, but not one overarching problem of history.

The role-specific responsibilities of theologians bring them necessarily into the arena in which history is practiced. Historical tools are necessary for understanding the tradition that has been handed on to the present. When we sketched, all too briefly, the sorts of practices participants—whether theologians or not—engage in as they live in and live out a religious tradition, a similar result occurred: there is no systematic relationship between faith and history. More precisely, I argued that the "non-professional," that is, the "non-theologian" participant in a religious tradition, may have person- and situation-specific responsibilities, but does not have the role-specific responsibilities of theologians. Theologians by trade are to deal with the problems of history; circumstances, not professional or vocational practices, may bring the problems of history into the lap of the participant. The final goal of the book was thus reached: the problem of history was dissolved as a systematic problematic and replaced with a plurality of challenges that would have to be resolved *ad hoc* by theologians and participants depending on their circumstances.

Some might say that this was a wasted trip. Was it? I would argue "not at all."

First, some intratextualists (Frei, perhaps) might argue that the point is not to allow historical work to interfere with accepting the biblical narrative. Historical investigations can make us modify the narrative, understand it more clearly, rectify misapplications of the narrative, and so forth. But history is finally irrelevant to the faithful acceptance of life lived under the governance of the biblical vision. Chapter six, of course, mounted an argument against this view. It was not that the biblical narrative was eclipsed in and by modernity, but it collapsed because of internal issues within Christian communities as much as from external pressure from rationalist historians. Chapter eleven supplied a further argument against this view. The biblical narrative is not merely in external competition with other narratives, whether secular, consumerist, Americanist, or otherwise. Rather, these narratives are at battle in the hearts of those who practice Christianity as well as those who live out other traditions as well.

Such battles, however, may be quite subtle. Sometimes people live in multiple worlds, or perhaps, take on multiple roles which may not be fully compatible with each other. It is not that our lives are watertight compartments. Rather, it is because the traditions in which we live are partly compatible that we can live within each of them without noticing the conflicts among them. McClendon's invaluable discussion of the conflict of stories (2000, 358-70) is followed by his own confession of his acceptance of the pattern of racism of the culture of his youth, a pattern his understanding of Christianity as given him by his parents and community did not confront (2000, 370-72). Many of us accepted both the Christian story and the story of white superiority. Many of us accept today the Prince of Peace as we go to fight wars to establish and preserve a new world order in which our country dominates. We have come to see that the former of these was an intolerable situation; we had to give up the principles of the racist tradition (and it is and was a tradition as defined in this book!) and accept an articulation of Christian principles that excludes racism. Some of us see that the same is true for the latter, but others would not find the principles underlying American citizenship and Christian citizenship incompatible.

The point is that many of us—probably all of us—do live in multiple traditions; the conflicts between them may not become evident until triggered by circumstances. And when that happens, we are in the same situation as described in chapter six: when the authority of multiple stories over us is at stake, we cannot simply appeal to one of them as authoritative. It is arbitrary to solve the problem of "multiple authorities" by an appeal to one of them. In short, although we can retrieve the biblical narrative in some ways, for example, by understanding the principles in it as Christian principles, we cannot make it authoritative when it is in conflict, as it is in many Christian hearts. We do not and cannot live "intratextually" but have our lives inscribed in many texts, many roles; we do not decide among them until we have to do so; and an intratextual account does not help us when we, as participants in a religious tradition, are *in extremis*.

Second, given the free-for-all regarding warrants and procedures among the practitioners of history, some have suggested that we can write history in ways more conformable to the work of Christians. We can write history that doesn't avoid warrants derived from faith (see Martin 1999; Baxter 1996; Wright in Borg and Wright 1999). Of course we can do that. Such work has important purposes. But it isn't history.

Our analysis of the historians' craft suggested that the audience for whom they wrote was important. Academic historians do their work to persuade other historians, their peers, of their claims. In doing so, they cannot appeal to warrants that their peers do not accept unless they either show their audience that those warrants ought be accepted because using them is revelatory of something previously hidden (Mason's appreciation of Abraham's work as discussed in chapter eight), or they construct arguments for the use of those warrants and convince their audience of the rightness of those warrants (Barzun and Himmelfarb reject psychohistory because they are not convinced of the acceptability of psychoanalytical warrants or, presumably, whatever backing argument Erikson or others supplied). Faith-based warrants are neither illuminating of what was hidden to historians nor supportable on historians' grounds.

In an essay supporting the traditional Christian claim that the resurrection should be accounted a historical fact (though one he does not accept) rather than a non-historical symbol, Rabbi Dan Cohn-Sherbok engages in an exercise in which he finds he can consent to about fifty percent of the Nicene Creed (1996, 184-85). Those parts he rejects, of course, are those creedal items distinctive to Christian faith: the Trinity, the incarnation, the Virgin Birth, the final judgment by Jesus, and the resurrection of the body. He simply doesn't accept the faith-based warrants for them. Cohn-Sherbok says he demands objective data as evidence that he would accept as warrant for the factual claim that the resurrection occurred. However, what he demands is, finally, the Second Coming, an objective proof not merely of the resurrection, but of the whole of the Christian Creed "televised on CNN and other forms of the world's media" (1996, 198). To get him to accept the warrants would be to convert him to Christianity. To convert him to Christianity, it would take a miracle. (And the disputes chronicled in chapter six have taught us about the evidentiary value of miracles!)

The use of faith-based warrants in academic history implies that other historians are not academic peers, but inferiors—not in a position to judge, because they do not accept those faith-based warrants as valid historical warrants. Arguments using acceptable evidence and warrants are not convincing. They involve special pleading using warrants that are as problematical as the warrants being backed and allegations of facts that are not clearly factual or evidential. Nor is it clear that using such warrants is illuminating to fellow historians, that it reveals operations in history that had been previously unseen. It is not that using faith-based warrants is wrong-headed. Rather, it is simply not history, but theology. So such an attempt to bypass the work of historians either demeans those who participate in the standard practices of the profession or is a confusion about the different practices of history and theology and the relationships between them as detailed in this book.

When Baxter (1996) finds fault with U.S. Catholic historians for not coming to hard judgments on the views of bishops, like Augustine Verot of Savannah, who supported the holding of slaves before the Civil War, he is finding fault with them for being practicing historians. While no modern and contemporary historians would condone slavery today or accept Verot's arguments, a judgment that he should not have made those arguments because they were not in line with the Catholic faith usually goes beyond the historians' competence. A theologian might point out that such arguments are inconsistent with the principle of the dignity of the human person, but it is not clear that such dignity was formulated in a way that made holding slaves (not buying or selling—that's a different issue) necessarily immoral. That is a question that is within the competency of historical work. Indeed, had it been formulated that way and accepted as a conviction in the Catholic community of that time, such a judgment might make sense as a historical judgment. But that claim is simply unwarranted.

That we can see more clearly the errors of our forebears goes without saying, just as our descendants will clearly see some of our sins more clearly than we do. That we need to avoid similar sorts of profound misjudgments now and in the future is an important point to be made in the tradition. But it is properly part of the practice of theologians, not of historians, to do so. That we should work against the structures of evil that linger today is a moral imperative that I would hope would be accepted by every person, including historians. But that is the personal, moral responsibility of each of us, not a role-specific responsibility—save for our roles as participants in both humanistic and religious traditions (for those of us who live in and live out such traditions).

In the end, then, I would argue that this was a necessary trip. Whether it has successfully plotted a way around the Troeltschian or other dualistic accounts of "faith and history" and has brought us to a resting point from which we can take new bearings and continue our journeys as historians, theologians, and believers is a judgment reserved to the reader.

Works Consulted

Anscombe, G. E. M.
  1957   *Intention.* Ithaca, N.Y.: Cornell University Press.
Austin, John L.
  1961   "A Plea for Excuses." In *Philosophical Papers,* edited by J. O. Urmson and G. J. Warnock, 123-52. Oxford: Clarendon Press.
Bagger, Matthew C.
  1999   *Religious Experience, Justification and History.* Cambridge: Cambridge University Press.
Baldovin, John, S.J.
  1997   "The Eucharist and Ministerial Leadership." In *Proceedings of the Fifty-second Annual Convention*, edited by Judith A. Dwyer, 63-81. N.p.: Catholic Theological Society of America.
Barzun, Jacques
  1974   *Clio and the Doctors: Psycho-History, Quanto-History, and History.* Chicago: University of Chicago Press.
Baxter, Michael J.
  1996   "Writing History in a World without Ends: An Evangelical Catholic Critique of United States Catholic History." *Pro Ecclesia* 5 (Fall): 440-69.
Borg, Marcus J.
  1994   *Meeting Jesus Again for the First Time: The Historical Jesus and the Heart of Contemporary Faith.* San Francisco: HarperSanFrancisco.
  1997a   *The God We Never Knew: Beyond Dogmatic Religion to a More Authentic Contemporary Faith.* San Francisco: HarperSanFrancisco.
  1997b   "From Galilean Jew to the Face of God: The Pre-Easter and Post-Easter Jesus." In *Jesus at 2000,* edited by Marcus J. Borg, 7-20. Boulder, Colo.: Westview Press.
  2001   *Reading the Bible Again for the First Time: Taking the Bible Seriously but Not Literally.* San Francisco: HarperSanFrancisco.
Borg, Marcus J., and N. T. Wright
  1999   *The Meaning of Jesus: Two Visions.* San Francisco: HarperSanFrancisco.
Braiterman, Zachary
  1998   *(God) After Auschwitz: Tradition and Change in Post-Holocaust Jewish Thought.* Princeton, N.J.: Princeton University Press.

Breisach, Ernst
1994   *Historiography: Ancient, Medieval, and Modern*. 2nd ed. Chicago: University of Chicago Press.

Brown, Peter
1971   "The Rise and the Function of the Holy Man in Late Antiquity." *Journal of Roman Studies* 61/1:80-101.

Buckley, Michael J., S.J.
1987   *At the Origins of Modern Atheism*. New Haven and London: Yale University Press.

Bultmann, Rudolf
1958   *Jesus Christ and Mythology*. New York: Charles Scribner's Sons.

Certeau, Michel de
1988   *The Writing of History*, translated by Tom Conley. New York: Columbia University Press.

Clark, Elizabeth A.
1992   *The Origenist Controversy: The Cultural Construction of an Early Christian Debate*. Princeton: Princeton University Press.
1999   "Rewriting Early Christian History." In *Theology and the New Histories*, 89-111. The 44th Annual Volume of the College Theology Society. Maryknoll, N.Y.: Orbis Books.
2004   *History–Theory–Text: Historians and the Linguistic Turn*. Cambridge, Mass.: Harvard University Press.

Clebsch, William A.
1979   *Christianity in European History*. New York: Oxford University Press.

Clifford, William K.
1877   "The Ethics of Belief." In *The Contemporary Review*. Citations to *The Ethics of Belief Debate*, edited by Gerald McCarthy, 19-36. AAR Studies in Religion 41. Atlanta, Ga.: Scholars Press.

Coday, Dennis, ed.
2003   "Sharia allowed as alternative." *National Catholic Reporter* 40/9 (December 26): 8.

Cohn-Sherbok, Dan
1996   "The Resurrection of Jesus: A Jewish View." In *Resurrection Reconsidered*, edited by Gavin D'Costa, 183-200. Oxford: Oneworld Publications.

Crossan, John Dominic
1991   *The Historical Jesus: The Life of a Mediterranean Jewish Peasant*. San Francisco: HarperSanFrancisco.

Cuneo, Michael
2001   *American Exorcism*. New York: Doubleday.

Datson, Lorraine
1994   "Marvelous Facts and Miraculous Evidence in Early Modern Europe." In *Questions of Evidence: Proof, Practice, and Persuasion across the Disciplines*, edited by James Chandler, Arnold I. David-

son, and Harry Harootunian, 243-89. Chicago: University of
Chicago Press.

Davidson, Arnold I.
1994   "Ginzburg and the Renewal of Historiography." In *Questions of
Evidence: Proof, Practice, and Persuasion across the Disciplines*,
edited by James Chandler, Arnold I. Davidson, and Harry
Harootunian, 304-20. Chicago: University of Chicago Press.

Dolan, Jay P.
1985   *The American Catholic Experience: A History from Colonial Times to
the Present*. Garden City, N.Y.: Doubleday.

Donner, Fred M.
1999   "Muhammad and the Caliphate: Political History of the Islamic
Empire up to the Mongol Conquest." In *The Oxford History of
Islam*, edited by John L. Esposito, 1-61. Oxford and New York:
Oxford University Press.

Donovan, Mary Ann, S.C.
1998   "Disputed Questions: How Catholic is the CTSA? Three Views."
Commonweal 125/6 (March 27): 14-16.

Dulles, Avery, S. J.
1982   *A Church to Believe In: Discipleship and the Dynamics of Freedom*.
New York: Crossroad.
1992   *Models of Revelation*. 2nd ed. Maryknoll, N.Y.: Orbis Books.
1996   "Historical Method and the Reality of Christ." In *The Craft of
Theology: From Symbol to System*, 211-24. New Expanded Edition.
New York: Crossroad.
1998   "Disputed Questions: How Catholic is the CTSA? Three Views."
Commonweal 125/6 (March 27): 13-14.

Dunn, James D. G.
1980   *Christology in the Making: A New Testament Inquiry into the Origins
of the Doctrine of the Incarnation*. Philadelphia: Westminster Press.
1985   *The Evidence for Jesus*. Philadelphia: Westminster Press.

Effross, Walter A.
2003   "Owning Enlightenment: Proprietary Spirituality in the 'New
Age' Marketplace." *Buffalo Law Review* 51/3:483-678.

Erikson, Erik H.
1958   *Young Man Luther: A Study in Psychoanalysis and History*. New
York: W. W. Norton.

Espín, Orlando O.
1997   *The Faith of the People: Theological Reflections on Popular Catholicism*. Maryknoll, N.Y.: Orbis Books.
2002   "Mexican Religious Practices, Popular Catholicism, and the
Development of Doctrine." In *Horizons of the Sacred: Mexican Traditions in U.S. Catholicism*, edited by Timothy Matovina and Gary
Riebe-Estrella, S.V.D., 139-52. Ithaca, N.Y., and London: Cornell
University Press.

Esposito, John L.
  1988   *Islam: The Straight Path.* New York and Oxford: Oxford University Press.
  1999   "Contemporary Islam: Reformation or Revolution." In *The Oxford History of Islam,* edited by John L. Esposito, 643-90. Oxford and New York: Oxford University Press.
Farley, Edward
  1990   *Good and Evil: Interpreting a Human Condition.* Minneapolis: Fortress Press.
Fiorenza, Francis Schüssler
  1984   *Foundational Theology: Jesus and the Church.* New York: Crossroad.
Flew, Antony G. N.
  1955   "Theology and Falsification." In *New Essays in Philosophical Theology,* edited by Antony Flew and Alasdair MacIntyre, 96-99. New York: Macmillan.
Frazier, E. Franklin
  1964   *The Negro Church in America.* 1st ed., 1963. New York: Schocken Books.
Fredriksen, Paula
  1988   *From Jesus to Christ: The Origins of the New Testament Images of Jesus.* New Haven and London: Yale University Press.
  1999   *Jesus of Nazareth, King of the Jews: A Jewish Life and the Emergence of Christianity.* New York: Alfred A. Knopf.
  2000   *From Jesus to Christ: The Origins of the New Testament Images of Jesus.* 2nd ed. A Yale Nota Bene Book. New Haven: Yale University Press.
  2003   "What Does Jesus Have to Do with Christ? What Does Knowledge Have to Do with Faith? What Does History Have to Do with Theology?" In *Christology: Memory, Inquiry, Practice.* The 48th Annual Volume of the College Theology Society, edited by Anne M. Clifford and Anthony J. Godzieba, 3-17. Maryknoll, N.Y.: Orbis Books.
Frei, Hans
  1974   *The Eclipse of the Biblical Narrative: A Study in Eighteenth and Nineteenth Century Hermeneutics.* New Haven: Yale University Press.
Ginzburg, Carlo
  1989   "Clues: Roots of an Evidential Paradigm." In *Clues, Myths, and the Historical Method,* translated by John and Anne C. Tedeschi, 96-125. Baltimore: Johns Hopkins University Press.
  1994   "The Judge and the Historian." In *Questions of Evidence: Proof, Practice, and Persuasion across the Disciplines,* edited by James Chandler, Arnold I. Davidson, and Harry Harootunian, 290-303. Chicago: University of Chicago Press.
  1999   *History, Rhetoric and Proof.* Hanover, N.H., and London: University Press of New England.

Goldberg, Michael
　1995　*Why Should Jews Survive? Looking Past the Holocaust toward a Jewish Future.* New York: Oxford University Press.

González, Justo L.
　2002　*The Changing Face of Church History.* St. Louis, Mo.: Chalice Press.

Gottwald, Norman
　1979　*The Tribes of Yahweh: A Sociology of the Religion of Liberated Israel, 1250-1050 B.C.E.* Maryknoll, N.Y.: Orbis Books.

Gould, Stephen Jay
　1989　*Wonderful Life: The Burgess Shale and the Nature of History.* New York: W. W. Norton.

Greeley, Andrew
　2000　*The Catholic Imagination.* Berkeley, Los Angeles, and London: University of California Press.

Gutiérrez, Gustavo
　1988　*A Theology of Liberation: History, Politics and Salvation.* 2nd ed. Translated by Sister Caridad Inda and John Eagleson. Maryknoll, N.Y.: Orbis Books.

Hacking, Ian
　1974　"Aristotle Meets Incest—and Innocence." In *Questions of Evidence: Proof, Practice, and Persuasion across the Disciplines*, edited by James Chandler, Arnold I. Davidson, and Harry Harootunian, 470-77. Chicago: University of Chicago Press.

Haddad, Yvonne Yazbeck
　1999　"The Globalization of Islam: The Return of Muslims to the West." In *The Oxford History of Islam*, edited by John L. Esposito, 601-41. Oxford and New York: Oxford University Press.

Haight, Roger, S.J.
　1999　*Jesus Symbol of God.* Maryknoll, N.Y.: Orbis Books.

Harvey, Van Austin
　1968　*The Historian and the Believer: The Morality of Historical Knowledge and Christian Belief.* New York: Macmillan, 1966. Reprint, New York: Macmillan, 1968. Page citations are to the reprint edition.

　1986　"The Ethics of Belief Reconsidered." *The Ethics of Belief Debate*, edited by Gerald McCarthy, 189-203. AAR Studies in Religion 41. Atlanta, Ga.: Scholars Press. Reprint from *The Journal of Religion* 59/4 (October, 1979): 406-20.

　2000　"Jesus and history, the believer and the historian." *Christian Century* 117/3 (January 26, 2000): 91-94.

Harvey, Anthony E.
　1982　*Jesus and the Constraints of History.* Philadelphia: Fortress Press.

Hauerwas, Stanley M.
　1988　*Christian Existence Today: Essays on Church, World and Living in Between.* Durham, N.C.: Labyrinth Press.

2001   *With the Grain of the Universe: The Church's Witness and Natural Theology: Being the Gifford Lectures Delivered at the University of St. Andrews in 2001.* Grand Rapids, Mich.: Brazos Press.

Herskovits, Melville J.
1958   *The Myth of the Negro Past.* 2nd ed. (1st ed., 1941). Boston: Beacon Press.

Hick, John
1993   *The Metaphor of God Incarnate.* London: SCM Press.

Hilberg, Raul
1961   *The Destruction of the European Jews.* Chicago: Quadrangle Books.
1996   *The Politics of Memory.* Chicago: Ivan R. Dee.
2003   *The Destruction of the European Jews.* 3rd ed. 3 vols. New Haven, Conn.: Yale University Press.

Himmelfarb, Gertrude
1987   *The New History and the Old.* Cambridge, Mass.: Harvard University Press.
1994   *On Looking into the Abyss.* New York: Alfred A. Knopf.

Howell, Martha, and Walter Prevenier
2001   *From Reliable Sources: An Introduction to Historical Methods.* Ithaca, N.Y., and London: Cornell University Press.

James, William
1956   "The Will to Believe." In *The Will to Believe and Other Essays in Popular Philosophy,* 1-31. New York: Longmans Green and Co., 1897. Reprint, New York: Dover Publications, 1956. Citations are to the reprint edition.

John Paul II and Mar Dinkha IV
1994   "Common Christological Declaration between the Catholic Church and the Assyrian Church of the East." Accessed 10 December 2003 at http://www.vatican.va/roman_curia/pontifical_councils/chrstuni/documents/rc_pc_chrstuni_doc_11111994_assyrian-church_en.html.

Johnson, Elizabeth
2003   *Truly Our Sister: A Theology of Mary in the Communion of Saints.* New York: Continuum.

Johnson, Luke Timothy
1996   *The Real Jesus: The Misguided Quest for the Historical Jesus and the Truth of the Traditional Gospels.* San Francisco: HarperSanFrancisco.

Kilmartin, Edward, S.J.
1998   *The Eucharist in the West: History and Theology,* edited by Robert J. Daly, S.J. A Pueblo Book. Collegeville, Minn.: Liturgical Press.

Knitter, Paul F.
2002   *Introducing Theologies of Religion.* Maryknoll, N.Y.: Orbis Books.

Kushner, Harold
1981   *When Bad Things Happen to Good People.* New York: Schocken Books.

Lindbeck, George
1984   *The Nature of Doctrine: Religion and Theology in a Postliberal Age.*
       Philadelphia: Westminster Press.
Livingston, James C.
1997   *Modern Christian Thought.* 2nd ed. Vol. 1, *The Enlightenment and
       the Nineteenth Century.* Upper Saddle River, N.J.: Prentice Hall.
2000   *Modern Christian Thought.* 2nd ed. Vol. 2, *The Twentieth Century*
       (with Francis Schüssler Fiorenza et al.) Upper Saddle River, N.J.:
       Prentice Hall.
Loisy, Alfred
1903   *The Gospel and the Church*, translated by Christopher Home. First
       published in French, 1902. London: Isbister and Company.
Mackey, James P.
2003   "The Social Role of the Theologian from the Dawn of Western
       Civilization to the Present Day." In *Between Poetry and Politics:
       Essays in Honour of Enda McDonagh*, edited by Linda Hogan and
       Barbara Fitzgerald, 32-50. Dublin: Columba Press.
Macy, Gary
1997   "The Eucharist and Popular Religiosity." In *Proceedings of the
       Fifty-second Annual Convention*, edited by Judith A. Dwyer, 39-58.
       N.p.: Catholic Theological Society of America.
1999   *Treasures from the Storeroom: Medieval Religion and the Eucharist.*
       Collegeville, Minn.: Liturgical Press.
Madigan, Daniel A.
2001   *The Qur'ân's Self-Image: Writing and Authority in Islam's Scripture.*
       Princeton, N.J.: Princeton University Press.
Mahony, Roger Cardinal
1998   "Correspondence." *Commonweal* 125/10 (May 22): 4.
Mannion, M. Francis
1998   "Correspondence." *Commonweal* 125/8 (April 24): 30.
Martin, Raymond
1999   *The Elusive Messiah: A Philosophical Overview of the Quest for the
       Historical Jesus.* Boulder, Colo.: Westview Press.
McClendon, James Wm., Jr.
1986   *Ethics.* Systematic Theology. Vol. 1. Nashville: Abingdon.
1994   *Doctrine.* Systematic Theology. Vol. 2. Nashville: Abingdon.
2000   *Witness.* Systematic Theology. Vol 3. Nashville: Abingdon.
McClendon, James Wm., Jr., and James Marvin Smith
1975   *Understanding Religious Convictions.* Notre Dame, Ind.: University
       of Notre Dame Press.
McDannell, Colleen
1995   *Material Christianity: Religion and Popular Culture in America.*
       New Haven, Conn.: Yale University Press.
McKenzie, John L.
1979   *The Old Testament Without Illusion.* Chicago: Thomas More Press.

Meier, John P.
   1991   *A Marginal Jew: Rethinking the Historical Jesus.* 4 vols. New York: Doubleday.
   1999   "The Present State of the 'Third Quest' for the Historical Jesus: Loss and Gain." *Biblica* 80:459-87.
Meltzer, Françoise
   1994   "For Your Eyes Only: Ghost Citing." In *Questions of Evidence: Proof, Practice, and Persuasion across the Disciplines,* edited by James Chandler, Arnold I. Davidson, and Harry Harootunian, 43-89. Chicago: University of Chicago Press.
Mendenhall, George
   1973   *The Tenth Generation: The Origins of the Biblical Tradition.* Baltimore: Johns Hopkins University Press.
Milbank, John
   1991   *Theology and Social Theory.* Oxford: Basil Blackwell.
Miller, Vincent J.
   2003   *Consuming Religion: Christian Faith and Practice in a Consumer Culture.* New York: Continuum.
Moltmann, Jürgen
   1996   "The Resurrection of Christ: Hope for the World." In *Resurrection Reconsidered,* edited by Gavin D'Costa, 73-86. Oxford: Oneworld Publications.
Montaigne, Michel de
   1958   *The Complete Essays of Montaigne,* translated by Donald M. Frame. Stanford, Calif.: Stanford University Press.
Morris, Thomas V.
   1986   *The Logic of God Incarnate.* Ithaca, N.Y.: Cornell University Press.
Mulira, Jessie Gaston
   1990   "The Case of Voodoo in New Orleans." In *Africanisms in American Culture,* edited by Joseph E. Holloway, 34-68. Bloomington and Indianapolis: Indiana University Press.
Murphy, Nancey C.
   1994   *Reasoning and Rhetoric in Religion.* Valley Forge, Pa.: Trinity Press International.
National Conference of Catholic Bishops
   1986   "Economic Justice for All: Pastoral Letter on Catholic Social Teaching and the U.S. Economy." Accessed 27 May 2003 at http://www.osjspm.org/cst/eja.htm.
Newman, John Henry
   1846   *An Essay on the Development of Christian Doctrine.* 2nd ed. London: James Toovey. Reprint of the first edition of 1845 with minor corrigenda.
Niebuhr, H. Richard
   1960   *The Meaning of Revelation.* New York: Macmillan Paperbacks. First ed., New York: Macmillan, 1946.

Novick, Peter
1988 *That Noble Dream: The "Objectivity Question" and the American His-torical Profession.* Cambridge: Cambridge University Press.

Orsi, Robert A.
1996 *Thank You, St. Jude: Women's Devotion to the Patron Saint of Hopeless Causes.* New Haven, Conn.: Yale University Press.

Padgett, Alan G.
1997 "Advice for Religious Historians: On the Myth of a Purely His-torical Jesus." In *The Resurrection: An Interdisciplinary Symposium on the Resurrection of Jesus*, edited by Stephen T. Davis, Daniel Kendall, S.J., and Gerald O'Collins, S.J., 287-307. New York: Oxford University Press.

Pannenberg, Wolfhart
1996 "History and the Reality of the Resurrection," In *Resurrrection Reconsidered*, edited by Gavin D'Costa, 62-72. Oxford: Oneworld Publications.

Patterson, Margot
2003 "Historian in Demand: Appleby takes low-key approach to explo-sive religious issues." *National Catholic Reporter* 40/9 (December 26): 11, 14.

Perrin, Norman
1974 *The New Testament: An Introduction.* New York: Harcourt, Brace, Jovanovich.

Plantinga, Alvin
1971 "The Free Will Defense." In *Philosophy of Religion*, edited by Basil Mitchell, 105-20. Oxford: Oxford University Press. First pub-lished in *Philosophy in America*, edited by Max Black. London: Allen and Unwin, 1965.

1974 *God, Freedom and Evil.* New York: Harper & Row.

1979 "The Probabilistic Argument from Evil." *Philosophical Studies* 26:1-53.

2000 *Warranted Christian Belief.* New York: Oxford University Press.

Pontifical Council for Promoting Christian Unity
2001 "Guidelines for Admission to the Eucharist between the Chal-dean Church and the Assyrian Church of the East." Rome: July 20. Accessed 16 September 2003 at http://www.vatican.va/roman_curia/pontifical_councils/chrstuni/documents/rc_pc_chrstuni_doc_20011025_chiesa-caldea-assira_en.html.

Power, Eileen
1924 *Medieval People.* London: Methuen and Company.

Quinn, John R.
1998 "The Exercise of the Primacy and the Costly Call to Unity." In *The Exercise of the Primacy: Continuing the Dialogue*, edited by Phyllis Zagano and Terrence W. Tilley, 1-28. New York: Cross-road/Herder.

Raboteau, Albert J.
1978   *Slave Religion: The "Invisible Institution" in the Antebellum South.* Oxford and New York: Oxford University Press.

Rubenstein, Richard L.
1966   *After Auschwitz: Radical Theology and Contemporary Judaism.* Indianapolis, Ind.: Bobbs-Merrill.
1974   *Power Struggle.* New York: Scribner.
1992a   *After Auschwitz: History, Theology and Contemporary Judaism.* 2nd ed. Baltimore: Johns Hopkins University Press.
1992b   "Religion and History: Power, History and the Covenant at Sinai." In *Take Judaism, For Example: Studies toward the Comparison of Religions,* edited by Jacob Neusner, 165-83. Atlanta: Scholars Press.
1993   "How My Mind Has Changed." In *What Have We learned? Telling the Story and Teaching the Lessons of the Holocaust.* Papers of the 20th Anniversary Scholars' Conference, edited by Franklin H. Littell, Alan L. Berger, Hubert G. Locke, 15-24. Lewiston, N.Y.: Edwin Mellen.
2001   "The Temple Mount and My Grandmother's Paper Bag: An Essay on Inter-Religious Relations." In *Jewish-Muslim Encounters: History, Philosophy and Culture,* edited by Charles Selengut, 141-64. St. Paul, Minn: Paragon House.

Rubenstein, Richard L., and John K. Roth
1987   *Approaches to Auschwitz: The Holocaust and Its Legacy.* Atlanta: John Knox Press.

Sanders, E. P.
1985   *Jesus and Judaism.* Philadelphia: Fortress Press.
1993   *The Historical Figure of Jesus.* London: Penguin Books.
2002   "Jesus, Ancient Judaism, and Modern Christianity: The Quest Continues." In *Jesus, Judaism and Christian Anti-Judaism: Reading the New Testament after the Holocaust,* edited by Paula Fredriksen and Adele Reinhartz, 31-55. Louisville, Ky.: Westminster John Knox Press.

Schatz, Klaus
1996   *Papal Primacy: From Its Origins to the Present,* translated by John A. Otto and Linda M. Maloney. Collegeville, Minn.: Liturgical Press.

Schillebeeckx, Edward
1979   *Jesus: An Experiment in Christology,* translated by Hubert Hoskins. A Crossroad Book. New York: Seabury Press.
1991   "The Role of History in What Is Called the New Paradigm." In *Paradigm Change in Theology,* edited by Hans Küng and David Tracy, 307-19. New York: Crossroad.
2002   "Prologue: Human God-Talk and God's Silence." In *The Praxis of the Reign of God: An Introduction to the Theology of Edward Schille-*

beeckx, edited by Mary Catherine Hilkert and Robert Schreiter, ix-xviii. New York: Fordham University Press.

Schleiermacher, Friedrich

1928   *The Christian Faith*. English translation of the second German edition, edited by H. R. MacKintosh and J. S. Stewart. Edinburgh: T & T Clark.

1958   *On Religion: Speeches to Its Cultured Despisers*, translated by John Oman. Harper Torchbooks. New York: Harper & Row.

Schüssler Fiorenza, Elisabeth

2000   *Jesus and the Politics of Interpretation*. New York: Continuum.

Schweitzer, Alfred

1910   *The Quest of the Historical Jesus: A Critical Study of Its Progress from Reimarus to Wrede*, translated by W. Montgomery. New York: Macmillan.

Shea, William

2004   *The Lion and the Lamb*. New York: Oxford University Press.

Shiflett, Dave

2003   "Uncertain Crusaders: Christians no longer worry much about converting 'heathens.'" *The Wall Street Journal Online*. Accessed 17 December 2003 at http://www.opinionjournal.com/taste/?id=110004301.

Smith, Theophus H.

1994   *Conjuring Culture: Biblical Formations of Black America*. New York: Oxford University Press.

Steinfels, Peter

1998   "Disputed Questions: How Catholic is the CTSA? Three Views." *Commonweal* 125/6 (March 27): 16-17.

Stout, Jeffrey

2004   *Democracy and Tradition*. Princeton, N.J.: Princeton University Press.

Sullivan, Francis A., S.J.

1992   *Salvation Outside the Church: Tracing the History of the Catholic Response*. New York/Mahwah, N.J.: Paulist Press.

Thiel, John

2000   *Senses of Tradition*. New York: Oxford University Press.

Tilley, Terrence W.

1985   *Story Theology*. Wilmington, Del.: Michael Glazier.

1995   *The Wisdom of Religious Commitment*. Washington, D.C.: Georgetown University Press.

1999   "Practicing History, Practicing Theology." *Horizons* 25/2:258-75.

2000   *Inventing Catholic Tradition*. Maryknoll, N.Y.: Orbis Books.

2001   "The Historical Fact of the Resurrection." In *Theology and the Social Sciences*. The 45th Annual Volume of the College Theology Society, edited by Michael Barnes, 88-110. Maryknoll: Orbis Books.

2003   "Teaching Christology: History and Horizons." In *Christology: Memory, Inquiry, Practice*. The 48th Annual Volume of the College Theology Society, edited by Anne M. Clifford and Anthony J. Godzieba, 265-76. Maryknoll, N.Y.: Orbis Books.

2004   "Experience and Narrative." *Journal of Hispanic/Latino Theology*, forthcoming.

Tilley, Terrence W., et al.

1995   *Postmodern Theologies: The Challenge of Religious Diversity*. Maryknoll, N.Y.: Orbis Books.

Tonnelli, Giorgio

1967   "Reimarus, Hermann Samuel." s.v. *The Encyclopedia of Philosophy*. New York: Macmillan and Free Press.

Torjesen, Karen Jo

1997   "'You Are the Christ': Five Portraits of Jesus from the Early Church." In *Jesus at 2000*, edited by Marcus J. Borg, 73-88. Boulder, Colo.: Westview Press.

Toulmin, Stephen

1958   *The Uses of Argument*. Cambridge: Cambridge University Press.

Tracy, David

1975   *Blessed Rage for Order: The New Pluralism in Theology*. New York: Seabury.

1981   *The Analogical Imagination: Christian Theology and the Culture of Pluralism*. New York: Crossroad.

Trevelyan, George Macaulay

1942   *English Social History: A Survey of Six Centuries, Chaucer to Queen Victoria*. London and New York: Longmans, Green and Co.

Troeltsch, Ernst

1898   "Über Historische und Dogmatische Methode in der Theologie." In *Gesammelte Schriften*. 2:729-53. Tubingen: Mohr-Siebeck, 1913. Eng. trans., "Historical and Dogmatic Method in Theology" translated by J. L. Adams and W. F. Bense. In *Religion and History*. Edinburgh: T & T Clark, 1991.

Trollinger, William Vance

1990   *God's Empire: William Bell Riley and Midwestern Fundamentalism*. Madison, Wis.: University of Wisconsin Press.

Tuchman, Barbara

1984   *The March of Folly: From Troy to Vietnam*. New York: Knopf.

Tyrrell, George

1963   *Christianity at the Crossroads*. London: George Allen and Unwin.

Urban, Linwood, and Douglas N. Walton

1978   *The Power of God: Readings on Omnipotence and Evil*. New York: Oxford University Press.

Veith, Gene Edward

2003   "Unbelieving 'born-agains.'" *World on the Web*. Accessed 17 December 2003 at http://www.worldmag.com/world/issue/12-06-03/cultural_4.asp.

Vidler, Alexander Roper
  1934   *The Modernist Movement in the Roman Church: Its Origins and Out-
          come.* Cambridge: Cambridge University Press.
Weber, Max
  1947   *The Theory of Social and Economic Organization*, translated by
          A. M. Henderson and Talcott Parsons. New York: Oxford Uni-
          versity Press.
Wink, Walter
  1997   "Response to Luke Timothy Johnson's *The Real Jesus.*" *Bulletin
          for Biblical Research* 7:1-16.
Wouk, Herman
  2002a   *The Winds of War.* Back Bay Books. Little, Brown and Co. (first
          published, 1971).
  2002b   *War and Remembrance.* Back Bay Books. Little, Brown and Co.
          (first published, 1978).
Wright, N.T.
  1996   *Jesus and the Victory of God.* Minneapolis: Fortress Press.
Zagzebski, Linda T.
  1996   *Virtues of the Mind: An Inquiry into the Nature of Virtue and the
          Ethical Foundations of Knowledge.* New York: Cambridge Univer-
          sity Press.

Index

Abraham, David, 153
  criticisms of, 123-24, 190
actions
  distinguished from events, 50-54,
    60
analogy
  axiom of, 39-40 (*see also* axiom)
  and correlation, 39-40, 46-47
  ontological foundation of, 41
Annales d'histoire économique et sociale,
  109-11
Annales school, 109-10, 123
Anscombe, G. E. M.
  on human action, 52
Appleby, Scott
  on question facing religious par-
    ticipants, 167-68
arguments
  grounds and warrants in, 116-17
assumptions
  and belief, 37-38
  distinguished from presumptions,
    37-38, 42
Austin, John L.
  on ordinary language, 50
authority
  of Bible, 1, 2, 73-74, 76-77
  centralization of, in Catholic
    church, 173-74
  institutional religious, 172-73
authorization
  problem of: and problem of his-
    tory, 73-74
axiom
  of analogy, 39-40
  of correlation, 39-40
  of probability, 39

Baldovin, John, S.J.
  on agency in eucharistic celebra-

  tion, 98, 100-101
Baxter, Michael J., 191
Beard, Charles A.
  on "noble dream," 107, 108
Becker, Carl L.
  on objectivity, 108
belief(s)
  and assumptions, 37-38
  history against, 10, 49-66
  religious: and historical evidence,
    86-105; immunized from history,
    67-85; morality of, 129, 186
believers
  and historians: dualism of, 6;
    responsibilities of, 28-36
  obligations of, 145-47
Bible
  authority of, 1, 2, 73-74, 76-77 (*see
    also* authority; biblical narrative)
  Frei on, 70-71
biblical narrative
  authority of, 76-77 (*see also* author-
    ity; Bible)
  eclipse of, 70-73, 80
  three principles of, 77
bishops, U.S. Catholic
  pastoral letter *Economic Justice for
    All,* 182-83
Borg, Marcus, 21, 88, 186-87
  on historical Jesus, 61-66, 131-41
  on historical methodology, 129
  on history and belief, 49-51
  on miracles, 93-94
  on problem of history, 50-51
Braiterman, Zachary
  on Rubenstein, 56
Breisach, Ernst
  on historical methodology, 126-27
Buckley, Michael
  on deism and atheism, 71-72